SEASON'S GREETINGS
FROM THE
WHITE HOUSE

SEASON'S GREETINGS FROM THE WHITE HOUSE

MARY EVANS SEELEY

A MASTERMEDIA BOOK
New York

*To my husband, Ron, who had the vision
and who unselfishly helped make the book a reality.
To our children, who were an encouragement—
may you carry on the dream.*

MASTERMEDIA and colophon are registered trademarks of MasterMedia Limited.

ISBN 1-57101-070-X

Designed by Antler & Baldwin, Inc.
Manufactured in the United States of America
10 9 8 7 6 5 4 3 2 1

Edward Lehman was commissioned to paint *The White House at Christmas* for the jacket of this book. Previously he had painted a series of White House State Rooms for President and Mrs. Kennedy. In 1962, his Red Room was reproduced as a gift print and given to the White House Staff; in 1963, his Green Room gift print was given to the staff following the President's death. The Blue Room painting that was prepared as the Kennedys' Christmas gift in 1964 was never used. The artist lives in Quakertown, Pennsylvania, where, at age 82, he continues to paint.

Frontispiece: **Creche in East Room, The White House** was selected by the President and Mrs. Kennedy for their official Christmas card in 1963 but was never sent. Less than 30 were personally signed by both the President and First Lady prior to their ill-fated trip to Dallas. This dual-signed Christmas card is among the rarest of Presidential Christmas memorabilia. HALLMARK CARDS

Contents

Foreword

This book began, as it should have, in Washington, D.C., many years ago. It was pushed into being, as it should have been, by an inveterate collector, my husband, Ron. It was written because it should have been written—but wasn't. If you can't understand how I ended up being the one to write it, you don't know what it's like to be married to an avid collector.

The first item he purchased on that medical convention trip to the nation's capital was a red velour presentation folder containing the portrait of George Washington. A gift from President and Mrs. Nixon to a White House employee, it eventually found its way into the political memorabilia shop where Ron found it. When he showed it to me that afternoon, he was excited; he was enthusiastic; his mood was contagious. Soon, I too, was learning everything I could about Presidential Christmas cards and gifts, and our quest began in earnest.

Along the way, we had the good fortune to meet Raleigh DeGeer Amyx of American Heritage Autographs and Collectibles. We were frankly overwhelmed by his careful preservation and beautiful presentation of American historical artifacts; his dedication to his work inspired us to continue our pursuit. Since then, we've acquired a Christmas gift book signed by William McKinley in 1900, Christmas cards and gift prints signed by many other later Presidents—including the rare Creche Card signed by President and Mrs. Kennedy just days before the assassination—and Presidential gift items made of wood, pewter, sterling silver, leather, glass and even yarn.

In time, the Seeley Collection gained us an invitation to the White House from its curator, Rex Scouten. He was especially interested in our early collection prior to President Eisenhower, and Ron and I were interested in learning from Mr. Scouten the history of many of our acquisitions. Our discussion of the facts and figures uncovered many discrepancies. Concerned about the accuracy of much of the information in circulation, Mr. Scouten stated: "Someone should write a book to set the record straight."

Ron was the one who knew I could write such a book; he already had me involved in this project when it still seemed like an impossible dream to me. It didn't take much persuasion, though, and with Mr. Scouten's endless assistance and Ron's enthusiasm, the book "to set the record straight" now exists—thousands of miles, hundreds of conversations and 3 1/2 years later.

Of invaluable research help were the greeting card companies that originally produced the Presidents' cards and gift prints; they also provided generous assistance in reproducing the art for this book. Jeannette Lee, consultant to Chairman Donald J. Hall at Hallmark, was a tremendous source of help after her 35 years of involvement in Presidential Christmas projects. She granted me the rare privilege of using the Hallmark Archives; Sharman Robertson, the Hallmark archivist, did the facts and figures work. At American Greetings, Barbara Hatala made the connections for me, including a memorable and informative luncheon with Harvey Levin, John Hernandis, Joe Cuffari, Chris Riddle, Paul Urban and the late Ed Pakish.

FOREWORD

For the human interest stories behind the creative compositions, I interviewed the artists and photographers whose work has adorned Presidential Christmas cards and gift prints. This list includes William Gemmell, Mark Hampton, Thomas W. Jones, Kamil Kubik, Robert Laessig, Edward Lehman, Thomas McKnight, James Steinmeyer, Cecil Stoughton and Jamie Wyeth. I hope I have succeeded in passing along my greater appreciation of their work and my new respect for them as artists.

For first-hand historical information, I went straight to the source, where possible, and the generous offerings of personal anecdotes and memories of former First Family members greatly enhance this work. The high point of this project, for me, was interviewing 87-year-old John Coolidge in the very village where his father had been sworn in as President of the United States in the middle of an August night back in 1923. The biggest surprise was picking up my telephone and hearing the voice on the other end say, "Hello, this is Barbara Bush...." Not that I'll ever forget the unique privilege that was mine when Ron and I met President Ronald Reagan in his office, only to be followed by an interview with Mrs. Nancy Reagan as she graciously reminisced about Christmas in the White House. I am also indebted to Mrs. Betty Ford and Mrs. Rosalynn Carter for taking the time to talk with me, and I appreciate the cooperation from First Ladies Mrs. Lady Bird Johnson and Mrs. Hillary Rodham Clinton and from the children of Presidents, namely John Eisenhower, Mrs. Lynda Bird Johnson Robb and Mrs. Julie Nixon Eisenhower.

Invaluable historic details were also supplied by Kay Holloway (Truman); Mary Jane McCaffree (Eisenhower); Bess Abell and Shirley James (Johnson); Helen Smith (Nixon); Maria Downs and Heidi Elzing (Ford); Madeline Edwards and Melissa Montgomery (Carter); Linda Faulkner, Lisa Cavelier, Cathy Busch and Joanne Drake (Reagan); Laurie Firestone, Patti Presock, Quincy Hicks (Bush), and Ann Stock and Anne McCoy (Clinton).

So many others have played major roles in making the book a reality. Jim and Carole Bowers helped Ron and me define the purpose of this project from its inception and offered encouragement all along the way. I'm also grateful for meaningful contributions from Terry Adams, Miller Alloway, Claudia Anderson, Russell Armentrout, Bill Bird, Cynthia Bittinger, the Blocker Family, Clement E. Conger, David Curfman, Susan Davis, Nelson Diaz, Ann Drexel, Claudia Dunne, George Elsey, Mary Finch, Bruce Foley, Sanford Fox, Kate Henderson, Janice Ingersoll, Luanne Knox, Carolyn Malenick, Bob and Liz McEwen, Kellie McQuire, Betty Monkman, Bob Munce, Lyn C. Probst, the late Joseph Riley, Chester Richardson, E. Ward Russell, Brooks Short, Jude Tolley, Nelson Whitman and Rebecca Zachritz. I am also deeply grateful for all the assistance so freely given by countless numbers of directors, archivists and audiovisual persons at all the Presidential libraries, the Library of Congress and the National Archives.

I don't know how I can ever adequately thank Susan Stautberg, president of MasterMedia Limited, who believed in my project and brought it to life; Virginia Koenke Hunt, my editor, who showed respect for my research and helped to make the words flow, and designer Bob Antler, whose creative talents are so evident in this work.

Above all, Ron and our children, Andrea, Michele, Todd and Mark, and their families, have been my support and strength. Each one encouraged me to be all I could be. When they needed me and I was elsewhere or preoccupied, they understood. Now, I have accomplished my impossible dream. I hope you will enjoy reading it as much as I have enjoyed writing it.

Mary Evans Seeley

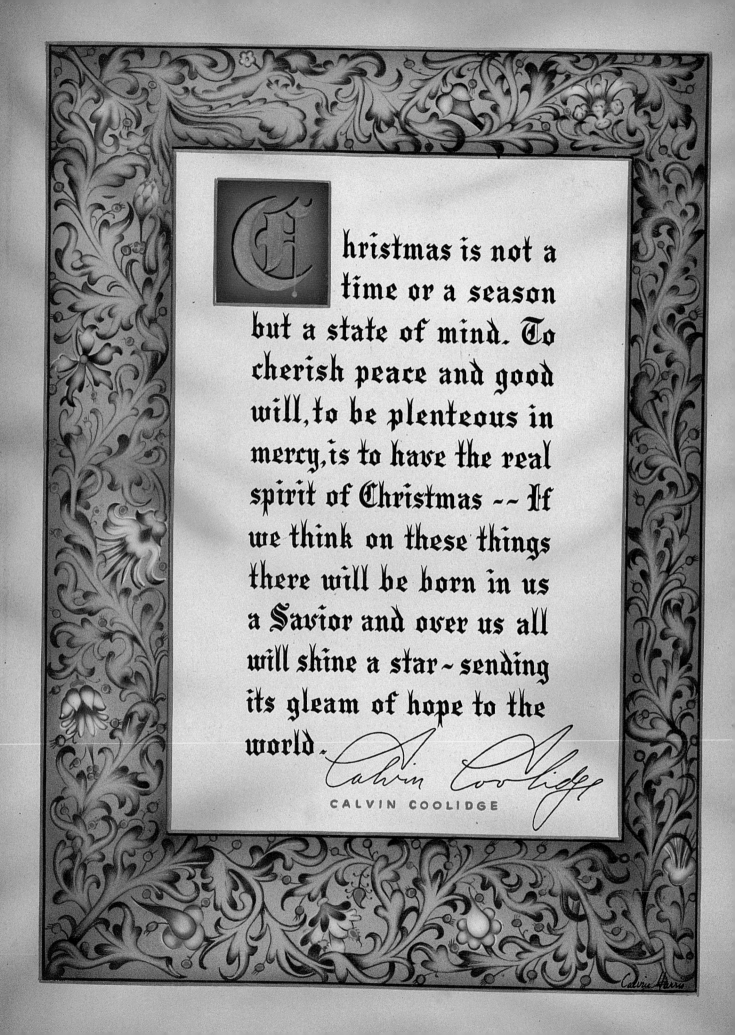

THE COOLIDGES
Beginning of a Tradition

*P*resident Calvin Coolidge issued the first official Christmas message to the American people in 1927. Written by his own hand on White House stationery, the statement appeared on Christmas Day in newspapers all across the country. The greeting came in response to numerous requests for the President to send a holiday greeting directly into the homes of America. While it took four years for Coolidge to honor these requests, every Chief Executive since, despite slightly differing ideologies, has delivered a Christmas message to the American people at a ceremony that is now a National Christmas Tree tradition.

1923: In the Beginning....

It all began in November 1923, when Lucretia Walker Hardy, the acting general director of the Community Center Department of the Public Schools of the District of Columbia, wrote to the President's secretary, C. Bascom Slemp, suggesting the erection of a Christmas tree on the south grounds of the White House. Such a location was to give the tree a national emphasis while the lighting of the tree by the President at a Christmas Eve ceremony would afford the local Washington community a holiday gathering in which all could participate. "The event which Christmas commemorates means more to the world as a whole than any other holiday that we observe," wrote Hardy. "The tree would be an outward evidence of the President's desire to give encouragement to the spirit of which it is symbolical."

Facing page: Artistic rendering of Calvin Coolidge's 1927 handwritten holiday message.

On December 4, Slemp denied Hardy the use of the White House grounds on Christmas Eve, because Mrs. Coolidge had already planned an event to which the public would be invited. Hardy finally agreed to erect the tree on the Ellipse and she invited the President to officially participate in the program. Thus was born the idea of the National Community Christmas Tree. To foster a national emphasis, Hardy suggested further that the tree be provided by the President's native state of Vermont; as to arranging the tree-lighting ceremony, Hardy offered the services of her department.

Shortly thereafter, the President received a letter from college president Paul D. Moody, who wrote: "Middlebury College counts it a privilege to send to you, from its forest preserve in the heart of the Green Mountains ... a National Community Christmas tree. It is our hope that this Vermont tree, when electrically illuminated in Washington will contribute toward a spread of the true Christmas spirit throughout the nation." The 60-foot fir was accepted on December 18, hauled to the Ellipse, south of the Treasury Building, and erected by the Potomac Electric Power Company.

The installation of an electric button to enable the President to light the Community Christmas Tree from the Executive Office, it was calculated, would cost about $500. Lucretia Hardy sincerely hoped, therefore, that the President would be able to walk to the Ellipse on December 24 for the lighting. In view of the expense, he agreed to do so if his schedule permitted; the question of his delivering a Christmas message was not discussed.

National Festivities

On Christmas Eve 1923, the Coolidges participated in a series of celebrations. At 5:05 in the afternoon, after walking to the Ellipse, the President pressed, with his foot, the button that illuminated the 3,000 light bulbs on the first National Community Christmas Tree. With a fanfare of trumpets, this symbol of the spirit of Christmas was converted into a national emblem signifying that the celebration of Christmas had begun.

While President Coolidge began the National Christmas Tree tradition on this, his first Christmas in office, he made no speech at the ceremony. The program for the event included a choir from the Epiphany Church, accompanied by a "quartette" from the Marine Band, which led the crowd of thousands in Christmas carols. At 7 o'clock, the full band put on a concert of holiday music.

At 9 o'clock, from the home of the President and First Lady, 65 members of the First Congregational Church filed out singing "O, Come, All Ye Faithful," the first of its many carols. A reporter for the *Washington Post* described the scene:

From the steps of the White house there went forth last night a message of "peace on earth, goodwill to men." It was the message echoing down through the ages from the days of the three shepherds, and as it passed from the throats of a choir on the portico of the White House, it was echoed by the President and his family and thousands of citizens, all in harmony with the reecho in the hearts of the people of the nation and the rest of the world. It was the reverence of a Christian people giving at the seat of their government the expression of their praise for the "King of Kings" on the eve of the anniversary of his birth.

The writer estimated that the caroling at the White House drew nearly 10,000 people "who sought with their official leader, to voice their feelings on Christmas Eve.... So the Capital, so the nation, and so the world welcomed the advent of the 1923 Christmas."

The inspiration for the caroling had come to Grace Coolidge while listening to hymns at her church. The Sunday *Evening Star* printed the verses of the carols in the order in which they appeared on the program. It was suggested that the music be clipped and carried to the White House, along with a personal light to facilitate one's participation. Arrangements were made with the Chesapeake and Potomac Telephone Company to have station WCAP broadcast the program; it is likely that more than a million Americans listened in on this significant national event in Washington via radio.

First Family Festivities

The spirit of Christmas permeated the White House. The historic mansion was dressed with holly and mistletoe and other greens. Even the President's office was draped with boughs of holly. Contrary to newspaper reports that the Coolidges had never had a Christmas tree and that they would not have one this year either, an eight-foot Norway spruce was purchased for the Blue Room and a smaller one for the family quarters. Both were decorated by Mrs. Coolidge and sons John and Calvin.

Once John and Calvin, Jr., had arrived home for the holidays from Mercersburg Academy, Mrs. Coolidge made it a practice to keep her schedule free to prepare for a real homey New England family Christmas. The boys accompanied their father on a window-shopping excursion, but they especially enjoyed the close companionship of their mother. She had made the arrangements for a Christmas dance in their honor in the Blue Room. Having invited 60 boys, she took a turn to dance with each one.

While their first Christmas in the White House was a happy one, the tragic death the following July of 16-year-old Calvin, from staphylococcus septicemia, cast a shadow on the observance of the holiday the following

The family poses at the lily pond on the White House grounds. Mrs. Coolidge reported that the President was never the same after the death of their younger son, Calvin, Jr. (center), who died in the summer of 1924. LIBRARY OF CONGRESS

year. The devastated President said in his autobiography: "When he went, the power and the glory of the Presidency went with him. The ways of Providence are often beyond our understanding. It seemed to me that the world had need of the work it was probable he could do. I do not know why such a price was exacted for occupying the White House." Mrs. Coolidge noted that her husband was never the same after young Calvin's death.

1924: One Member Missing

As Christmas drew near, Mrs. Coolidge prepared herself for an avalanche of emotions. According to Ishbel Ross in *Grace Coolidge and Her Era*, the First Lady wrote: "I shall not be sad at that happy time of year. I found a quotation the other day which seems to express Calvin and something of what he is to me, one 'whose yesterdays look backward with a smile.' Always he seemed to be just ahead of me and I can see his smile."

Christmas cards arrived at the White House in record numbers—about 12,000 in fact. The *New York Times* reported that while the Coolidges did send Christmas cards and gifts, it was mostly to relatives and close friends. The President left all of the shopping to his wife and did not enter any of the stores during the holidays, as he had with both of his sons the previous year.

The tradition of the National Community Christmas Tree almost vanished as quickly as it appeared when the President informed the American Forestry Association (AFA) that he was against the cutting down of Christmas trees. To preserve the tradition, Ovid Butler, the AFA's executive secretary, presented to the President a 40-year-old, 35-foot living Norway spruce to be planted in Sherman Plaza between the statues of General Sherman and Alexander Hamilton. Intended to be used every year as the National Community Christmas Tree, it survived five Christmases before succumbing to the abuse of ladders, the weight of heavy ornaments and the intense heat of the lights.

On Christmas Eve President and Mrs. Coolidge attended the dual celebrations as in the first year. Receiving the living Christmas tree from the AFA, the President said, "I accept this tree and I will now light it for this occasion." Shortly after 8 o'clock the President illuminated the tree with its thousand brilliant red, green and amber lights. With as much significance as any other formal national ceremony, the lighting of the National Community Christmas Tree ushered in the observance of Christmas.

From Sherman Park, the First Family moved to the picturesque but seldom used North Portico, now brightly lighted for the vested choir of the First Congregational Church. John Coolidge, home at the time from Amherst College, recalled in a 1994 interview, at age 87: "I was given a coonskin coat for Christmas that year and wore it on Christmas Eve. That was quite a nice event. Mother was very musical. My father didn't know one note from another. If he did, he didn't admit it. In church, he never sang a hymn. My mother and I did, of course. I sang a great deal."

1925: *The Mission of Mercy*

By the year 1925, the lighting ceremony for the National Community Christmas Tree achieved national significance as the spirit of the holiday extended from Washington to all parts of the country. Congressman Hamilton Fish, Jr., from New York, speaking for the radio networks, expressed their hope that "the President would speak for a couple of minutes, simply wishing the children of America a Merry Christmas and a Happy New Year." The President's secretary, Everett Sanders, responded that the Chief Executive would not be making any remarks on Christmas Eve.

As the chimes on the Church of the Epiphany announced the prelude to the Eve of Christmas, President and Mrs. Coolidge made their way from the White House to Sherman Park. At dusk, the Chief Executive humbly touched the switch that illuminated the living Norway spruce, a signal for community trees across the nation to be set aglow. Three hours after the ceremony at the tree, about 2,000 people were welcomed on the White House grounds by the First Family for the singing of carols, led, as in previous years, by

Mrs. Grace Coolidge gives out toys at the Central Union Mission's Christmas party. STOCK MONTAGE

Thousands wait in line to meet President and Mrs. Coolidge at the New Year's Day reception. The First Lady's "hand got so swollen, the glove would have to be cut off."
UNDERWOOD & UNDERWOOD/
THE BETTMANN ARCHIVE

the choir from the "President's Church." The message of Christmas sung from the front portico of the President's house was likewise broadcast by radio nationwide.

The spirit of Christmas that prevailed in the nation's capital that season was unprecedented. Enjoying the most prosperous Yuletide of the Coolidge Administration, Washingtonians appeared to be bent on a "mission of mercy." Never had the needs of the poor been met in so many ways. Mrs. Coolidge also participated in activities for them. She spent time holding and cuddling some of the 1,200 tots confined to the Children's Hospital. She assisted Santa Claus by giving out toys at Keith's Theater under the auspices of the Central Union Mission. At the Salvation Army hall, she joined in the religious service, made a brief speech and distributed baskets. Her compassionate caring for the needy would long be remembered in the hearts of Washington's poor.

While the country was geared to a lavish lifestyle, the President practiced and preached a message of thrift; to compensate for her husband's tight fist, the First Lady often gave little gifts to the staff. "What was austere and withdrawn in Calvin Coolidge was warm and gracious in his wife," wrote a reporter for the *New York Herald Tribune*. As husband and wife, they complemented each other.

For years the White House had held an official reception on New Year's Day for foreign dignitaries, national officials and ordinary citizens. "Silent Cal" had gained a reputation for the number of hands he could shake without suffering ill effects. Said John Coolidge: "My father had a pull-along handshake that didn't allow guests to linger and talk." On the first day of 1926, in the four and a half hours that the President and Mrs. Coolidge hosted the reception, between 3,000 and 4,000 people shook hands with them and received a smile and simple holiday greeting. "Mother would wear white gloves," her son remembered, "but still her hand got so swollen, the glove would have to be cut off."

1926: *Carols Across the Country*

Once again, on Christmas Eve, the President of a peaceful and prosperous nation set aglow the red, green and yellow lights of the National Community Christmas Tree. At that moment a flare illuminated the sky throughout Washington alerting Boy Scout buglers to sound the glad message of Christmas.

At 9 o'clock the choir of the First Congregational Church sang carols on the steps of the White House. A second celebration around the National Community Christmas Tree began at 10:30. An estimated 20 million people blended their voices with those of the 50-voice choir from the Central Congregational Church of Brooklyn, N. Y., in "seasonal fellowship and adoration." In Washington, the nationwide concert was carried by station WRC and sponsored by the *Evening Star*, which had issued a supplement containing all the words and music of the songs. President and Mrs. Coolidge, with John, gathered in front of the White House radio and joined the rest of the country in a reverent celebration that focused on the birth of Christ.

The generous outpouring of gifts and cards from all parts of the country reportedly touched the President in such a way that he gave a Christmas gift of a gold coin to each of the attachés and servants at the White House. Chief usher Ike Hoover, in *42 Years in the White House*, reported that despite "his reputation for being sphinx-like," the President went out of his way to know his employees personally. "It was one of his diversions to jest with them, and many is the time he saw fit to play jokes on them."

1927: *The Handwritten Holiday Message*

The following year, President Coolidge softened even more and finally replied to the many requests for a Christmas greeting from him. As usual, on Christmas Eve, he pressed the golden button that turned the stately spruce tree on the Ellipse into a conical pillar of 500 brilliant flashing lights and 2,000 reflecting jewels. The more elaborate lighting and decorations on the tree in 1927 were undertaken by the Electric League of Washington in cooperation with the General Electric Co. So as not to distract from the effectiveness of his Christmas Day message, the President addressed the crowd only as "Fellow Americans" and then lit the tree.

On Christmas morning, a short, simple, handwritten message from the Chief Executive appeared in every major newspaper. The *Evening Star* reported that the President was generally pleased with the wide circulation his message received and many favorable telegrams were sent in response.

THE WHITE HOUSE
WASHINGTON   December 25, 1927.

To the American People:—

Christmas is not a time or a season, but a state of mind. To cherish peace and good will, to be plenteous in mercy, is to have the real spirit of Christmas. If we think on these things, there will be born in us a Savior and over us will shine a star sending its gleam of hope to the world.

Calvin Coolidge

President Coolidge's handwritten holiday message to the nation. CALVIN COOLIDGE MEMORIAL FOUNDATION, INC.

Christmas Eve, 1927: the Coolidges at the National Community Christmas Tree.
UNDERWOOD & UNDERWOOD/THE BETTMANN ARCHIVE

On the fourth anniversary of his taking office, with his reelection virtually assured, Calvin Coolidge made the cryptic announcement, "I do not choose to run!" Never did he suggest that he would not accept the nomination, but his intentions were not publicly questioned. Haunted by his own words or lack of them, and humiliated by his party, Coolidge returned to Washington from the Republican National Convention a humbled man.

1928: *The President Speaks to the Nation*

Christmas of 1928 was Calvin Coolidge's last one in office. In a show of support, the largest Christmas Eve crowd, ever, gathered at Sherman Square. Praised for his Christmas tree spirit, the President then stepped to the front and spoke briefly. With the nation listening by radio, he said: "In token of the good-will and happiness of the holiday season and as an expression of the best wishes of the people of the United States toward a Community Christmas Tree, in behalf of the city of Washington, I now turn on the current which will illuminate this tree." At 8:05, under a full December moon, the President touched the button that transformed the tree

Calvin Coolidge is thought to have used this General Electric Co. switch plate at the lighting of the National Community Christmas Tree. LYN C. PROBST

from darkness into a burst of light.

This last Christmas at the White House was a happy one. Both President and Mrs. Coolidge appeared pleased about the prospects of returning to private life and regaining the freedom and privacy that had been denied them as the First Family. But it was also a poignant time. John, unable to leave his work in New Haven, Connecticut, was noticeably missing from the Yuletide celebration. To celebrate the Coolidges' first Christmas in the White House there had been two boys; this last year there were none. Death had claimed one and the world had prevented the other. The day after Christmas the President and Mrs. Coolidge left Washington for an extended vacation on Sapelo Island, off the coast of Georgia.

The Coolidge Christmas Legacy

The Coolidges' Christmas customs left an indelible mark on a White House Christmas. The tradition of lighting the National Community Christmas Tree initiated in 1923 has ushered in every Christmas since. A Christmas greeting by the President of the United States (or the Vice President on rare occasions) has been delivered to the American people every year since Coolidge's first handwritten message in 1927. Even the singing of carols had found its place in the White House at Christmas.

"Silent Cal" was not a sentimentalist, but in 1930, in his syndicated column *Calvin Coolidge Says*, he expressed these thoughts about the holiday: "Christmas represents love and mercy. It was ushered in by the star of hope and remains forever consecrated by the sacrifice of the cross. Christmas holds its place in the hearts of men because they know that love is the greatest thing in the world. Christmas is celebrated in its true spirit only by those who make some sacrifice for the benefit of their fellow men."

CHAPTER II

THE HOOVERS
Depression, Drought and a Natural Disaster

erbert Hoover tried to find a solution for the Great Depression throughout most of his ill-fated term in office; punctuating much of the Hoover Administration was a devastating drought that affected a large portion of the country. These economic and personal disasters resulted in a disillusioned public and an eventual political defeat for the President.

Upon taking office, Hoover wrote to a friend: "I have no dread of the ordinary work of the Presidency. What I do fear is the result of an exaggerated idea the people have conceived of me. They have a conviction that I am some sort of superman, that no problem is beyond my capacity.... If some unprecedented calamity should come upon the nation ... I would be sacrificed to the unreasoning disappointment of a people who expected too much...." Prophetic words! When Herbert Hoover failed to become "the savior of the Depression," he lost the Presidency and invariably became, himself, a victim of that crisis.

1929: Christmas During the Depression

The Great Depression started slowly with the October stock market crash. By the middle of November, the crisis had worsened; by Christmas, the nation was feeling the need to cut back its holiday spending. Taking time

Facing page: President Hoover astride his horse, Billy, at his camp in Virginia's Shenandoah Valley. This photograph was one of many given as a Christmas gift to his staff. STOCK MONTAGE

from the cares of the country to do some shopping, the President and First Lady, Lou Henry Hoover, visited various stores, including the most crowded "five and ten." The Chief Executive purchased dolls and toys to send to grandchildren Peggy Ann and Peter, who would be spending Christmas with their parents in California.

White House Prints

The First Lady was fond of old prints of Washington, particularly prints of the White House. Her secretary, Ruth Fesler, often shopped for her in secondhand book stores in Washington and New York. "I found in old books about Washington many lithographs and copies of etchings of the White House. It was an interesting project for me," she said, and it revealed a "sense of history that both President and Mrs. Hoover had about the White House." Their collection remained on display at the east end of the long corridor on the second floor of the White House.

One of the Hoover Christmas gifts in 1929 was this photograph of the White House West Wing and Rose Garden. HERBERT HOOVER LIBRARY

For Christmas, the President and Mrs. Hoover drew from this collection and gave their staff a reproduction of an etching of the South Portico; titled simply *The White House*, it was signed by the artist, M. Pierce. According to extensive lists compiled by Fesler, this etching was given to about 64 members of the Executive Office staff, the Medicine Ball Cabinet, White House aides, Secret Service agents and gardeners. A second etching of the North Portico of the White House by an unidentified artist was the gift selected for 75 employees detailed to the Executive Office. Engraved on the mat of this engraving was the greeting: "Best Wishes of Herbert Hoover and Lou Henry Hoover."

In addition to these gifts, 150 photographs of the South Lawn of the White House were ordered—some in gray, buff or green tones—and mounted on white stock. By Fesler's accounts, these photos, framed, cost $1.25 each and were presented to the White House police, clerks and horticultural employees. The President and First Lady gave two other photographs as staff gifts: one depicted the East Wing with the reflection pool in the foreground; the other showed the West Wing and its garden; each of these carried the message, "Best Wishes of Herbert Hoover and Lou Henry Hoover." To his personal staff the President also gave a photo of him on his horse, Billy, at Camp Hoover in the Shenandoah Valley. All in all, the First Family gave about 275 gift photographs to their staff for their first Christmas at the White House.

The Hoovers were certainly considerate of their employees, but there were times when the staff perceived that the President was less than cordial. Mrs. Hoover's maid, Lillian Rogers Parks, recalled how her coworkers viewed the First Family. In her book, *My Thirty Years Backstairs at the White House*, she said:

> *The servants couldn't get over the fact that the President, who had once been a great outdoor man, roughing it in the wilds, and a mining engineer, who was used to mixing with all classes of people, was completely aloof with the White House staff. He never spoke to them, and never paid the slightest bit of attention to anything they were doing. However, he was respected by everyone. They knew how busy he was. At Christmas, when the servants would have a party in the East Room, the President would simply walk in, say "Merry Christmas," and leave, and Mrs. Hoover would give us a little talk.*

Parks added that whenever an employee was ill, Mrs. Hoover would send a basket of food, flowers and a card. The First Lady was always there to step in for the President when he was reluctant to do so or preoccupied.

Tree Tradition Continues

Initiated during the Coolidge Administration, the tradition of lighting a National Community Christmas Tree was to be carried on by President Hoover. Preparations for the event had begun in March of 1929 with the planting of a new National Tree on Sherman Square to replace the previous one after it succumbed to the weight of heavy wiring and the heat of lighted bulbs. The new tree, a Norway spruce, was sent as a gift of the American Forestry Association from the Amawalk Nurseries in Amawalk, New York.

At the lighting ceremony on Christmas Eve, as the Marine Band struck up "Hail to the Chief," the President waved them to stop. Although he was not scheduled to speak, he delivered an impromptu greeting: "I want to have the privilege of wishing you all, and all the unseen audience, a merry Christmas and a prosperous New Year." Surrounded by a choir of junior high children, members of the President's Cabinet, Justices of the Supreme Court, members of Congress and District Commissioners, the President pushed the button to light the tree.

The Christmas Eve Fire

After the ceremony, President and Mrs. Hoover went back to the White House for Christmas Eve dinner with the families of their secretaries and aides. As the guests were finishing dessert, chief usher Ike Hoover discreetly notified the President that the White House was on fire! The blaze had been discovered by one of the White House police who had noticed smoke coming from the basement in the West Wing and had sounded the alarm at 8:09.

The President walked quickly to the scene of the fire—the Executive Office; in short order, though, he was forced to watch the fire from the roof of the Conservatory. Wearing a heavy blue topcoat and a black hat, he puffed nervously on a cigar. Secretary of War Pat Hurley ordered 150 soldiers from the Washington barracks to help the Metropolitan Police hold back the thousands of people who had gathered on the White House lawn and who were now trying to push forward for a closer look.

Meanwhile, the Christmas party inside continued. Although Mrs. Hoover was aware of the fire, she remained completely calm, never letting on that anything was amiss. The Marine Band continued playing Christmas carols at a volume calculated to drown out the sound of the arriving fire engines. Once the gifts were distributed, the party came to a quick close. Mrs. Hoover then escorted her guests out to the West Terrace, where in safety all could watch the fire fighters battle the third White House fire since 1814. The President's office finally succumbed to the fire and water, but not until the rescue of the most important documents, flags, rugs, and virtually all of the furnishings. His heavy desk could not be saved, but the secretarial

The President and Mrs. Hoover and numerous dignitaries at what was to be the last New Year's Day reception. With more than 6,300 guests filing through the White House, it was decided that the 129-year-old tradition was getting out of hand.

AP/WIDE WORLD PHOTOS

The President and Mrs. Hoover

cordially reciprocate

your holiday greetings

1929 - 1930

offices, the Cabinet Room, the Press Room and the Main Lobby suffered no more than water and smoke damage. It was a night before Christmas the Hoovers would not soon forget.

The fire did not cancel the New Year's Day reception at the White House. One of the largest crowds since the Theodore Roosevelt Administration came to meet the popular President and Mrs. Hoover. The three-hour party was divided into two shifts. At 11 o'clock, the First Family greeted the Justices of the Supreme Court, members of Congress, the diplomatic corps, government officials and military officers. After lunch, the public, 6,300 strong, filed past the Chief Executive and First Lady. For obvious reasons, Hoover was the last President to receive guests on New Year's Day.

In response to the hundreds of cards and gifts that poured in for their first White House Christmas, the Hoovers acknowledged many with one of the 3,100 cards from Brewood Engraving. While all 3,100 bore the Presidential Seal, four different messages were printed: 850 read, "The

President and Mrs. Hoover cordially reciprocate your holiday greetings, 1929-1930"; 1,500 read, "The President thanks you for your holiday greeting, 1929-1930"; 350 read, "The President and Mrs. Hoover thank you for your holiday greetings, 1929-1930"; and 400 read "Mrs. Hoover thanks you for your holiday greeting, 1929-1930."

1930: Gifts of Historic Wood

The old roof of the White House that had sheltered Presidents for 100 years was replaced during the latter part of the Coolidge Administration. Dumped on a trash pile, the discarded wood was reclaimed by the Hoovers to be fashioned into the First Family's gifts to its staff in 1930. The final output came to 13 sets of bookends; 35 ashtrays; 9 large boxes; 43 long pen trays; 61 square trays; 27 paper cutters; 28 small round trays and 13 small boxes; a cane was made for the chief usher, and, for the social secretary, candlesticks. Enclosed with each gift was an original poem by Mrs. Hoover describing the historic wood:

Wood discarded from the rebuilding of the White House roof was used to make candlesticks, wooden boxes and paper knives. HERBERT HOOVER LIBRARY

Recollections of a Piece of Wood 1930

A pine-tree on the hills of Maryland–through many summers'
  heats and winters' snows,
Felled, carted, quartered, sawn, a metamorphosis within a week.
And then a century buried deep within the White House walls,–
  unseen, unsung, but one of myriads holding firm together
  the storied structure.
Until,–a new age came and replaced steel for wood.
Then months upon the dump-heap,–the dump cart actually
  arrived for one last ride,–
And then a rescue. Now here I rest upon your desk for a short
  space; until,–the wastebasket and the fire.
Then once again I'll go,–free smoke before free wind,–to touch
  again the hills of Maryland.

With each gift also was an engraved card with the Presidential Seal and the words, "The White House, Washington." The greeting read, "The President and Mrs. Hoover take Christmas pleasure in presenting this historic bit of pinewood with their greetings." In addition to the gifts of wood, about $650 worth of framed prints were distributed to White House aides and other employees.

On Christmas Eve, several hundred people braved the bitter cold to witness the simple but impressive tree-lighting ceremony and to hear the President's brief, 37-word address. Following the lighting, the First Family hurried back to the White House to join a party planned for their grandchildren and the children of the White House secretariat. Among the surprises, President and Mrs. Hoover gave a bright red fire truck to the three sons of George Ackerson, secretary to the President, as a remembrance of the previous Christmas when fire had broken out in the Executive Offices.

1931: The Artists' Washington

By 1931, Mrs. Hoover's print collection had expanded even more; for Christmas she had her favorite etchings and photographs reproduced as gifts for family, friends and staff. Among the prints were etchings by J.C. Claghorn of the

A red fire truck was given to the sons of Presidential secretary George Ackerson as a memento of the White House fire on Christmas Eve of 1929. HERBERT HOOVER LIBRARY

A merry Christmas and a Happy New Year from Herbert Hoover

And from Lou Henry Hoover and Weegie and Pat.

1932-3

Dual photographs from the White House grounds: Herbert Hoover in the Rose Garden; Lou Henry Hoover, with pets Weegie and Pat, at the end of the Spanish reflection pool. HERBERT HOOVER LIBRARY

Washington Monument from South Portico, Arlington Memorial Amphitheater and *Mt. Vernon. The Capitol, March 4, 1929*, by Swann and the *Lincoln Memorial* by Cline were additional selections from which she chose her Christmas gifts. Some were framed, some were matted, and some were autographed. In addition, four photographs of the Washington Monument from different perspectives were matted, framed, signed and given as presents to the staff.

On Christmas Eve, President and Mrs. Hoover took their grandchildren, Peggy Ann and Peter, to the lighting ceremony in Sherman Square. At its conclusion, they all walked over to the tree for a closer look at the twinkling lights. Then they returned to the White House for a party with all the families of the White House secretariat and members of the President's personal and official household. The after-dinner program included the March of the Wooden Soldiers, in which the entire group of 50 participated. The women carried candles in brass holders and the men rang tiny brass bells as together they marched to the music of the Marine Band, upstairs and down and all through the house, in search of Santa. Invariably, he would be found in the East Room, waiting to hand out gifts. Devised by Mrs. Hoover, this march was led by the President himself, who, in all likelihood, participated with utmost reluctance.

1932: *Personal Photographs*

For their gift in 1932, the Hoovers gave a leather folder that included a photograph of the President walking through the White House Rose Garden on his way to the Executive Office. Mrs. Hoover was photographed separately at the end of the Spanish reflection pool with two White House police dogs. First maid Maggie Rogers had brought the overindulged First Pets to Mrs. Hoover, and then hid behind the bushes while the photograph was taken. The remembrances were personally inscribed and autographed: "A Merry Christmas and a Happy New Year from Herbert Hoover and from Lou Henry Hoover and Weegie and Pat 1932-33."

A failed election behind them, President and Mrs. Hoover chose to go on a 10-day cruise aboard the *USS Sequoia* over the Christmas holidays. For the first time since the inception of the tree-lighting ceremony, the Vice President presided. In the White House, the 1929 total of 16 decorated trees had been reduced in 1932 to only one tall Norway spruce. Decorated under the supervision of Mrs. Hoover, the lone tree was placed in the East Room for visitors. With the Hoovers cruising the semitropical waters off Florida and Georgia, their domicile was dark and quiet.

Herbert Hoover, during his single term in office, had tried to bring the economy around with every progressive, corrective measure in his power, but his best efforts were just not enough. Now he was ready to lay aside the cares of his office and let it be known that for a time the President, an enthusiastic angler, had gone fishing.

Season's Greetings

AMERICA PAUSES AT THIS CHRISTMAS SEASON

TO EXTEND TO HER FRIENDS A GREETING OF GOOD WILL

AND GOOD CHEER. IT IS OUR PRIVILEGE TO JOIN

OUR VOICES IN THIS SINCERE GREETING TO ALL OUR

FRIENDS. MAY YOU HAVE A MERRY CHRISTMAS

AND MANY HAPPY YEARS IN WHICH TO ENJOY

PEACE ON EARTH GOOD WILL TOWARD MEN.

CHAPTER III

THE ROOSEVELTS
The Twelve Years of Christmases

ranklin and Eleanor Roosevelt loved Christmas: the scent of a fresh evergreen tree warmed by the fire of candles; the President's Christmas Eve ritual of reading and reciting from memory the Dickens classic *Christmas Carol*; the First Lady's gift buying for family, friends and the hundreds of people who made their life at the White House more enjoyable. Though half of the Christmases of the Roosevelts' 12-year tenure were seasoned by war, "There never was a Christmas in the White House while they were there that wasn't joyous," said their longtime housekeeper Henrietta Nesbitt in her *White House Diary*. "I never saw so much excitement and so much affection shown. I never knew people that loved Christmas the way the Roosevelts did."

"When Christmas is spent outside one's own home, particularly in government surroundings such as the White House," Mrs. Roosevelt explained in her *Christmas Book*, "you divide your Christmas in two parts. One covers your official obligations; the other, as far as possible, is the preservation of the home atmosphere and the home routine." Added Nesbitt, "Everyone in America knew what went on in the White House at Christmastime, because the Roosevelts wanted everyone to know and share in it, but only those inside knew the work that led up to it."

"It Is Better to Give...."

Eleanor Roosevelt enjoyed giving and believed she had "the right to give." In the December 1934 issue of *Home Companion* she wrote: "The real

Facing page: A patriotic card sent to card collector Franklin Delano Roosevelt during the war years. FRANKLIN D. ROOSEVELT LIBRARY

The East Room is decked out for the annual party for the staff and their children. AP/WIDE WORLD PHOTOS

spirit of Christmas is the joy of giving. We all of us enjoy what we receive, primarily because of the fact that behind each gift lies the loving thought of some individual. But for everyone the real thrill is the thrill of being able to give something no matter how small."

After one Christmas had passed, the First Lady was on to the next. Every January, with great foresight—and armed with the latest list of the White House employees and the names and ages of their children—she began shopping, collecting gifts as she went. Whenever she saw something on her travels, she would buy it. "That's for Christmas" she would say. "Just put it away," and into her "Christmas Closet" it would go. Her purchases: exquisitely fine needlework in Puerto Rico; furniture from a handicraft shop in West Virginia; pottery from a roadside stand in New England; baskets from a New York school for the blind; dollies from Tennessee mountaineers; woven rugs from Berea College, Kentucky, and pewter from her own Val-Kill shop at Hyde Park. Mrs. Roosevelt liked handmade objects and was attracted to anything that people enjoyed making. Wanting to share her travels with others, she did so by buying and giving gifts.

As Santa for the children of her staff, the First Lady purchased toys by the dozens from various manufacturers. As early as autumn, the gifts for the children were wrapped and staff Christmas cards containing cash were addressed. Mrs. Roosevelt was very careful to see that no one was overlooked and, to that end, relied heavily on the organization and planning of her staff. At first they were appalled at the amount of paper and ribbon it took to wrap the gifts; eventually they got used to buying in bulk. Final wrapping of the gifts would sometimes continue late into the night, but everything would invariably be ready for the White House staff party on the afternoon of Christmas Eve.

Mrs. Roosevelt started her first Christmas book in 1922; in this journal she had recorded the gifts she had given over the years to family, friends and those who had worked for the family. In 1935 the First Lady started on her second Christmas book. It contained hundreds of names and grew eventually to be two inches thick. To Presidential secretary Grace Tully, for instance, she gave $10 and stockings in 1935. In other years, the First Lady gave the secretary copies of her books, stamps, checks, and grapefruit and oranges. The 4 x 7-inch Christmas book sheets were alphabetized and kept systematically until Mrs. Roosevelt's death in 1962.

Holiday festivities for the White House staff and their families were usually held in the East Room on the afternoon of Christmas Eve. A 20-foot spruce from the New York State Conservation Commission was set up in the east window, between the portraits of George and Martha Washington. With the lighted tree decorated completely in white and silver, the toys for the children scattered under it, and "the tables fanning out on either side laden with the older people's gifts, the scene was festive and beautiful," recalled the First Lady. Each member of the staff was presented a gift of money and a cornucopia of candy. The police guards usually received a tie or a handkerchief, a fruitcake and candy. Children under 12 were given candy and a doll, a car or a stuffed animal from among the dozens that the First Lady had selected well in advance of the occasion.

The Family Celebration

Christmas was a three-day festival for the Roosevelt family, with four generations gathering at the Executive Mansion. The President's mother and half-sister-in-law joined them along with as many of the children and grandchildren as could make it for the activities stretching from Christmas Eve until the children's party the day after Christmas.

"Our Christmas tree was usually ready Christmas Eve, the older children helping to trim it," said Mrs. Roosevelt. "Franklin always directed the placing of every ornament or string of tinsel, even after he had polio, and never, as long as he lived, would he hear of our using anything but real candles." The fragrance of burning wax candles on a fresh evergreen was so reminiscent of the President's childhood at the family's home in Hyde Park, New York, that he insisted on real candles for the tree in the family quarters. "For all his advanced political theories," said the First Lady, "he clung to the old-fashioned traditions in many curious little ways." Eventually the *Washington Herald* reported that real wax candles were being used on the family tree because "the President will have none of these newfangled electric contraptions for lighting his family tree." That prompted a rise from an insurance company president who thought that the Chief Executive's proclamation during Fire Prevention Week was inconsistent with his tradition at Christmas.

A family Christmas gathering before the war: four generations of Roosevelts convene for a three-day Christmas festival. FRANKLIN D. ROOSEVELT LIBRARY

Marguerite (Missy) LeHand, the President's private secretary, tried to clarify the fact that there were *two* trees in the White House. The large one in the East Room where many people gathered was lighted with electric bulbs; wax candles were used only on the family's tree. She indicated that this had always been the family custom and that no one but the family gathered around it. Therefore, the Roosevelts believed they were entitled to carry on their family tradition. Furthermore, LeHand assured the insurance executive, no one would be "more careful in regard to fire prevention than the President."

On Christmas Eve, the President reveled in his annual rendering of the Charles Dickens holiday tale. Mrs. Roosevelt recalled the annual tradition: "I think the part he enjoyed most was the story of Fezziwig and the Christmas party. He always read that with relish," she wrote in *This I Remember*. "And of course having a great sense of the dramatic, he always put a great deal of drama into his reading of the parts about the ghosts. In fact, whenever he read anything aloud like this, he acted it out straight through, which was why he held the attention of the little children so well, even before they could understand the meaning of the words." After the reading, each member would file up to the President's bedroom to hang his or her stocking on the mantel. No ordinary stockings, each one was custom-stitched by Mrs. Roosevelt's maid, Lillian Rogers Parks. The First Lady would fill them late that night and be the first one up Christmas morning to put down the windows and light the fires before the pandemonium started. As soon as the grandchildren woke up, they woke everyone else up with their shouts of joy as they descended upon "Papa" at dawn. FDR was not ordinarily an early riser, but there was no escaping Christmas morning.

Gifts Galore From Val-Kill

The Forge was a part of the Val-Kill Industries that Eleanor Roosevelt and her partners established in 1934 with the idea of providing jobs for young men willing to learn the art of metal craft. The first of these, the Norwegian Arnold Berge, was trained in pewter-making by a Danish metal craftsman brought in for just that purpose. The products of this enterprise made their first appearance in April 1935 and were stamped with the Val-Kill trademark.

Over the years, The Forge continued to produce beautiful articles of pewter, brass, copper and iron. Although Mrs. Roosevelt purchased gifts of all kinds all through the year, she continued to rely heavily on The Forge for a variety of Christmas items, including matchboxes, bud vases, cheese knives, card cases, salad sets, salt containers, spoons and five-inch plates. She appreciated the craftsmanship of articles made at The Forge, visited the shop herself and paid retail prices for all her purchases. The First Lady, having established The Forge to provide jobs for others, was also one of its best customers.

1933: *The First Christmas*

On December 22, the Chief Executive invited his secretariat and all the members of his executive and social staffs into his office for a party. He presented each one a personally autographed copy of his book *Looking Forward*. The following day, President and Mrs. Roosevelt entertained the White House police force and their families in the East Room. At another reception later the same day they received the household servants, chauffeurs, maintenance men and their families.

The Chief Executive was deeply touched by the number of people who remembered him and his family with gifts and greetings during his first White House Christmas. The *New York Times* reported that on December 23 alone, 40,000 cards and letters were received, breaking all previous Christmas records. A special staff was assigned to handle the Christmas mail that amounted to approximately 300,000 greetings. According to Stephen Early, assistant secretary to the President, FDR did not send out Christmas

cards on a large scale, but the First Family did give cards with gifts to their personal friends and members of their family.

The Roosevelts' personal Christmas card was a 5 x 7-inch single-sided card with an attractive etching of the South Portico and reflection pool. Henrietta Nesbitt wrote in her diary that White House engraver A.B. Tolly prepared the lithograph by hand, lettered the words and had it reproduced by a Washington printer, Brewood Engraving.

A Tree-Lighting Speech

The official celebration of Christmas began on December 24, when the Chief Executive lit the National Community Christmas Tree in Sherman Square. More than 5,000 people formed a semicircle around the tall fir, which burst into a rainbow of colors and signaled the simultaneous lighting of thousands of other Christmas trees across the country. On the tenth anniversary of the lighting ceremony for the National Christmas Tree, President Roosevelt's greeting was broadcast to the nation. He delivered the longest tree ceremony speech to date and firmly established the practice as a holiday tradition, speaking directly and openly to his national audience.

For me and my family it is, I am sure, the happiest of Christmases. To the many thousands of you who have thought of me and have sent me greetings (and I hope all of you are hearing my voice) I want to tell you how profoundly grateful I am. If it were within my power so to do I would personally thank each and every one of you in every part of the land for your remembrances of me, but there are so many thousands of you that that happy task is impossible....

1934: *Tree Lighting Ceremony Grows*

The President gave more than 100 of his executive staff an appropriately autographed, dated copy of his book *On Our Way*. Mrs. Roosevelt ordered 400 Christmas cards and envelopes from Brewood Engraving to be enclosed with their gifts. A 2 3/8 x 3-inch photograph of the President and Mrs. Roosevelt seated on a leather sofa in front of the fireplace was inserted in a panel at the top of the single-sided card. The White House crest was stamped on the flap of the envelope.

Two New Trees and a New Location

To accommodate the ever increasing crowds attending the tree lighting, the ceremony was moved to Lafayette Park. A few weeks prior to Christmas, two Fraser firs from North Carolina were planted in the park. To minimize the effects of the intense heat of the bulbs, the 23-foot tree was to be alternated with the 30-foot tree as the National Community Christmas Tree. President Roosevelt always preferred the one located west of the monument of General Andrew Jackson because it was more visible from the North Portico of the White House.

About 10,000 people were on hand as the President officially opened the Christmas season by lighting the tree. As he pushed the button to transform the living tree into a blaze of color, there was a malfunction for a few seconds while he looked on, puzzled. Suddenly the light burst forth as the combined glee clubs of the Potomac Electric Power Company and the Chesapeake & Potomac Telephone Company launched into a program of Christmas carols. In his address, the President spoke of the courage and patriotism of Andrew Jackson.

1935: Val-Kill Productions

Products from The Forge first made their appearance in April 1935 and were stamped with the Val-Kill trademark. The Roosevelts gave a pewter matchbox cover crafted at The Forge to the 170 members of the executive staff. The cover had a small seal of the President's profile soldered on it and the words, "President Franklin D. Roosevelt, Hyde Park, N.Y." printed around it. FDR's initials were also engraved on the keepsake gift. The single-sided 3 1/2 x 5 1/2-inch card bore a black

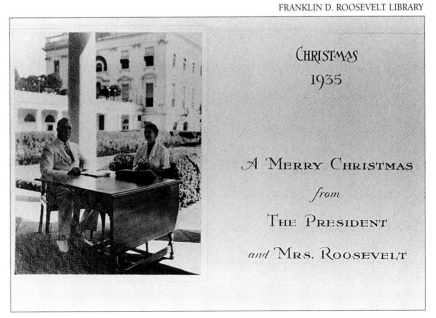

CHRISTMAS
1935

A MERRY CHRISTMAS
from
THE PRESIDENT
and MRS. ROOSEVELT

FDR's gift to his staff in 1935 was a handcrafted pewter matchbox cover.

and white photograph of the President and Mrs. Roosevelt seated at a drop leaf table before the Executive Office. From Brewood Engravers, the First Lady ordered 400 cards with the White House crest on the envelopes. The President and Mrs. Roosevelt received more than 6,000 Christmas cards themselves that year.

1936: Scrooge at the Tree Lighting

From The Forge, the First Lady ordered 200 pewter paper knives for the President to give his staff. The rounded edge of the utensil bore a facsimile of the Presidential Seal and below it, the initials of the President, all for a cost of $3 each. The card printed for the First Family by Brewood Engravers was marked with simplicity. In place of the photograph of previous years was a small lithograph of a snowbound farm. The two red barns and two green trees provided a touch of color to the 3 x 4 card. The 600 cards carried an engraved greeting.

At the tree-lighting ceremony, the President told the 3,000 spectators and the untold numbers in his radio audience to keep the spirit of Christmas alive all through the year like the reformed Scrooge in Charles Dickens' classic. He said: "I have been reading the *Christmas Carol* to my family, in accordance with our old custom. On this eve of Christmas I want to quote to you the pledge of old Scrooge when, after many vicissitudes, he had come to understand in his heart the great lesson and the great opportunity of Christmastide. 'I will honor Christmas in my heart and try to keep it all the year. I will live in the Past, the Present and the Future. The Spirits of all Three shall strive within me. I will not shut out the lessons that they teach.'"

Staff gifts from The Forge: in 1936, a pewter paper knife; in 1937, a pewter desk pad.

The spirit of Christmas was reflected in the hearts and on the smiling faces of the throngs of people who flooded downtown Washington. Gone was the gloominess of the depression years. The *Evening Star* reported that never had "the Capital's stores been so busy as during the past week. All-time postal records have been shattered, attesting to an all-time volume of Christmas packages, letters and cards. The poor, the homeless and the needy have been remembered, fed and warmed."

1937: Disintegration of Peace

With many people now aware of the Roosevelt family *Christmas Carol* tradition, Columbia Broadcasting System originated the idea of inviting the President to broadcast his family reading of the holiday classic. In October Sterling Fisher of CBS wrote a letter to the President's son James. "It seems to me," it read, "that this would have a very happy psychological effect in this country.... In a moment of wars and dread of wars, it would, throughout the world, emphasize kindliness, humanity and peace."

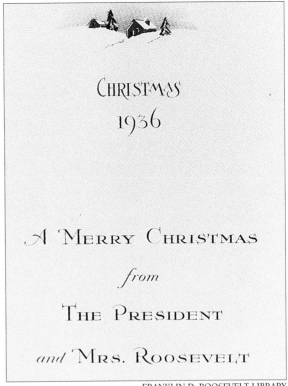

CHRISTMAS 1936

A Merry Christmas from The President and Mrs. Roosevelt

FRANKLIN D. ROOSEVELT LIBRARY

A prompt but negative answer came within two days from Stephen Early, secretary to the President. President Roosevelt's quotations from Dickens in his 1936 Christmas message would be the closest recitation of the story the public would ever hear.

President and Mrs. Roosevelt purchased 475 pewter articles from the Val-Kill shop for Christmas gifts. For the President, The Forge crafted 175 small pewter desk pads with the President's profile on the top for a special price of $1.25. The item also came in a larger size at $2.25 apiece. Only the year, 1937, distinguished the First Family's Christmas card from the previous year's card. The order came to 600 cards with the White House crest on the envelope.

"Many Are Weeping"

Peace in the world had begun to disintegrate. The situation in Europe and Asia was deteriorating rapidly.

On Christmas Eve, the President illuminated the living Christmas tree in Lafayette Square. In his greeting to the nation and to the 2,000 rain-soaked people in attendance, he called upon all Americans to forget all enmities and, in the Christian spirit of goodwill, to forgive everybody, as Christ had bestowed forgiveness upon Judas Iscariot. His message was taken almost in its entirety from New York newspaper columnist Heywood Broun's piece of the previous day.

On Christmas morning, a 35-year-old Rev. Peter Marshall, preaching his first sermon to a President, chose for his theme the same angel's song, "Peace on Earth, Goodwill Toward Men," that President Roosevelt had referred to in his Christmas greeting to the nation. The President heard Rev. Marshall call the song "the lost refrain." *The Washington Star* reported that Rev. Marshall went on to say that: "Christmas comes to mock us for our infidelity. It is Christmas Day in Spain—and machine guns rattle in the hills.... It is Christmas Day in China—and shrapnel is falling in the rice fields.... It is Christmas Day all over the world—and little children are being taught how to wear gas masks.... It is Christmas Day in Washington—and many are shivering, many are weeping. Peace on earth, goodwill toward men! Say the words over and over and you will be shocked at the hypocrisy of a world celebrating in solemn manner something it had not taken to heart."

1938: Lifting up Swords

From The Forge the President ordered 200 pewter paperweights for his office staff at a price of $1.25 each. For the third year, the Roosevelts' Christmas card remained the same except for the year, 1938. The small card met their needs and there appeared to be no reason to change.

On the day before Christmas Mrs. Roosevelt herself, accompanied by the press, went about the city giving the message of Christmas to 3,000 poor and needy people at five different charity programs. She told them, according to a *New York Times* account of the event, that "she realized as they did that 'love does not yet rule the world.'" To a group of 500 she said, "Many people thought Jesus of Nazareth a failure, but the mere fact that we still celebrate his birthday once a year and recall the ideas he lived for should give us courage."

All of 8,000 chilled souls braved an inclement Christmas Eve to see the Chief Executive push the button that illuminated the 20-foot fir into a rainbow of colors. In his mes-

The gift to the staff in 1938 was a pewter paperweight.

The First Lady helps Santa distribute gifts to underprivileged children at the Central Union Mission's annual party. UPI/THE BETTMANN ARCHIVE

sage, the President pledged to do whatever was in his power to bring about the day spoken of by the prophet Isaiah, when men "shall beat their swords into ploughshares and their spears into pruning hooks; when nation shall not lift up sword against nation, neither shall they learn war any more."

1939: A Shattered Hope for Peace

It was the year when Germany occupied Czechoslovakia and bombed Poland; Russia invaded Finland; Italy occupied Albania; France and Great Britain declared war on Germany. Hope for peace was shattered. On the eve of Christmas, Americans wondered if they would stay out of the conflict or if their Christmas too would be seasoned by war. Nevertheless, the Christmas of 1939 was celebrated as usual. The President made one more trip to The Forge and ordered 200 pewter letter holders at $1.25 each. On the front was the President's profile and beneath it, his initials. He also ordered ashtrays for his cabinet and close associates and had their initials put on them. With the outbreak of war and the resulting lack of raw materials, Arnold Berge was soon to close his pewter business. Consequently, the gifts FDR purchased from The Forge in 1939 were the last ones of this type he would give.

The ceremony for the lighting of the National Community Christmas

A Christmas 1939 staff gift from The Forge: a pewter letter holder.

Tree was returned to the Ellipse, where the annual tradition had begun in 1923. Concerned for the safety of the President, the Secret Service pushed for this move from Lafayette Park. The new location gave the nation's Christmas tree, a 36-foot red cedar from George Washington's estate in Virginia, greater visibility from all directions as well as affording the Chief Executive greater protection by its openness.

Joined by 17 members of his family and White House guests, President Franklin D. Roosevelt thanked God for "the interlude of Christmas" in a world "bowed down under the burden of suffering laid upon it by man's inhumanity to man." Speaking to the 8,000 shivering people who had come to the Ellipse to hear his Christmas message, the President called upon the warlike nations to read the Sermon on the Mount. "In these days of strife and sadness in many other lands," he said, "let us in this nation and in the other nations which still live at peace, forbear to give thanks not only for our good fortune in our peace. Let us rather pray that we may be given strength to live for others, to live more closely to the words of the Sermon on the Mount, and to pray that peoples in the nations which are at war may also read, learn and inwardly digest these deathless words."

1940: Europe at War

By Christmas, Nazi Germany had overrun most of Europe, Russia was still Hitler's partner in aggression, Japan occupied much of China, Great Britain suffered from constant air attacks, and the President of the United States felt the responsibility for preventing the enslavement of mankind as he entered his third term of office. Like many, the First Lady feared not only for humanity but also for the safety of her sons as they went off to war. In his foreword to Eleanor Roosevelt's *Christmas 1940*, Elliott Roosevelt wrote that his mother "believed that it was God's purpose that we should love and help our neighbors—an element of her faith that her own life exemplified with rare beauty.... I have known almost no one who could draw strength the way she did from her confident belief that some truths cannot be overcome by lies, that mankind will ultimately fight off every oppression, and that somehow we will achieve our Creator's purpose for us."

For Christmas 1940, FDR's Scotch terrier, Fala, was featured on this key chain.

Despite the gloom of the war and the uncertainty for the future, indicators revealed that holiday giving was greater than in any year in the past decade. As always, the First Lady bolstered the economy by ordering carton after carton of toys from Louis Marx & Company for the 200 children of the guards and servants who would be attending the White House Christmas party. The most popular toys ordered were the airplanes from the toy factory in Glendale, West Virginia.

The President was also most generous when it came to gift giving. His private secretary, Missy LeHand, ordered 212 Scottie key chains from Hammacher Schlemmer in New York for $1 each, including gift wrapping. Arrangements were made for any extras to be returned. In January, 15 of the sterling silver key chains were sent back for credit. The dog on the gift was a remembrance of Roosevelt's Scotch terrier, Fala. Devoted to his master, Fala soon became a prominent subject in photographs, cartoons and anecdotes. LeHand also ordered for the President silver money clips and silver key chains with a 25-cent coin from Cartier in New York. Costing $1.75 and $2.50, respectively, the gifts were personalized with the initials of each recipient. The President gave 42 initialed desk pads to members of his Cabinet and other close associates. The Christmas greeting card from The President and Mrs. Roosevelt remained the same as it had been in previous years and was titled "Christmas 1940."

Speaking informally to the crowd prior to the radio broadcast, the President stated that he and Mrs. Roosevelt would like to make the following year's ceremony "more homey" with a tree planted on the South Lawn; then he invited all the "good people in the District who come to this ceremony" to go to the White House in 1941 and he would deliver his Christmas greeting from the porch of the Executive Mansion. To the nation at large he said that we must "keep on striving for a better and happier world.... For most of us it can be a happy Christmas if by happiness we mean that we have done with doubts," the President concluded, "that we have set our hearts against fear, that we still believe in the golden rule for all mankind, that we intend to live more purely in the spirit of Christ, and that by our works, as well as our words, we will strive forward in faith and in hope and in love."

Describing the ceremony in the Christmas edition of the *Washington Post*, staff writer George Bookman wrote:

There is nothing in the Constitution of the United States, nothing in the Declaration of Independence, nothing in the Oath of Office of the President of the United States, about what took place last night on the browned turf of Washington's Ellipse, where President Roosevelt lit a Christmas tree and stood bareheaded listening to Christmas carols. Yet to 8,000 people who witnessed the ceremony and to millions more who heard it by radio, the brief, informal celebration gave new meaning to the democratic words, 'life, liberty and the pursuit of happiness.'

1941: War and a British Prime Minister

World events had cast their shadow over the holiday season, and Japan's December 7 attack on Pearl Harbor created an immediate state of emergency. For the next month, the United States was more preoccupied with mobilizing for war than preparing for Christmas. Nevertheless, the holiday was celebrated and the spirit of the season touched people like never before. There were indications that this may have been Washington's biggest Christmas. Department stores were filled with last-minute shoppers in search of gay and frivolous gifts. Train, bus and airport terminals were jammed with travelers, and post office receipts broke a 10-year record. Christmas lights twinkled in homes across the land and Christmas carols were sung wherever people gathered. Yet, in spite of it all, no one would be able to forget that America was at war.

For Christmas, 404 employees each received a 10 x 14-inch autographed photo of President and Mrs. Roosevelt. Taken on July 4 by George Skaddings of the Associated Press, the photograph was reproduced by Harris and Ewing for $50 a hundred. Bound copies of the President's campaign addresses were presented to members and ex-members of his Cabinet, administrative heads in the Executive Office, his immediate official family and a few friends, including Prime Minister Winston Churchill, the Crown Princess of Norway and Madame Chiang Kai-shek.

Tree Lighting Comes Home to the White House

Prime Minister Winston Churchill was the Roosevelts' houseguest in December of 1941. He had arrived secretly to discuss with the President the joint Allied operations in various theaters of the world. Together with American and British experts in strategy, the leaders of the world were working out a master plan for the war against the Axis.

Prior to the occasion, the President had selected two living Oriental spruce trees, each about 35 feet in height, to be planted just inside the grounds of the South Lawn. These were used alternatively as the National Tree for the next 13 years. On Christmas Eve, between 15,000 and 20,000

This photo of President and Mrs. Roosevelt on the south porch of the President's Hyde Park home was a Christmas gift to their staff in 1941. AP/WIDE WORLD PHOTO

people accepted the President's invitation of the previous year to come to the White House grounds for the ceremony.

As it turned out, just 17 days after Pearl Harbor, the two leaders of democracy delivered their Christmas messages from the South Portico of the White House. Their words were broadcast coast to coast to the American people and were transmitted to the rest of the world by short-wave radio. The realization that America was at war was unmistakable as both President Roosevelt and Prime Minister Churchill delivered messages plain in words and deep in conviction. From the President came an appeal for a preparation of American hearts and the proclamation of a day of prayer.

Winston Churchill expressed his pleasure at the privilege of being able to speak to the American people on Christmas Eve. He addressed them as

"Fellow workers in the cause of freedom." He continued:

Therefore we may cast aside, for this night at least, the cares and dangers which beset us, and make for the children an evening of happiness in a world of storm. Here then for one night only, each home throughout the English-speaking world should be a brightly lighted island of happiness and peace. Let the children have their night of fun and laughter—let the gifts of Father Christmas delight their play. Let us grownups share to the full in their unstained pleasures before we turn again to the stern tasks and formidable years that lie before us, resolved that by our sacrifice and daring these same children shall not be robbed of their inheritance or denied their right to live in a free and peaceful world....

On Christmas Day, the President and Mrs. Roosevelt and their distinguished guest attended interdenominational services at the Foundry Methodist Church. On New Year's Day, Roosevelt and Churchill visited the tomb of George Washington at Mount Vernon, after worshipping at the same Christ Church in Alexandria, Virginia, that Washington had helped establish in 1773. The two leaders sat in the same white pew that the first President had used; together they prayed for the success of the Allied forces as soldiers marched past the windows, protecting their freedom to worship.

In her *Christmas Book*, Eleanor Roosevelt wrote, "I remember especially the Christmas that Mr. Churchill was with us after we were involved in World War II. After that year, the Christmases weren't so cheerful. My mother-in-law died in the autumn before that first war Christmas. The boys all went off to different war theaters. Their absence meant that we did what we could to cheer their families if they were with us, or we tried to get in touch with them by telephone if they were far away. We did more in those years for foreign people cut off from their homelands by war, but it was no longer the old-time Christmas and never was to be again." Unbeknown to Mrs. Roosevelt at the time was the fact that 1941 would also be the last time President Roosevelt pushed the button to light the National Christmas Tree. Over the next four years, due to the demands of war, the electric lights on the tree were to be eliminated.

1942: "Only Prayer Was Not Rationed"

By a joint resolution of Congress on December 26, 1941, the fourth Thursday of November became the legal holiday of Thanksgiving. On that first Thanksgiving, President Roosevelt joined with 250 government leaders, heads of the armed forces and friends in the East Room of the White House to participate in an unprecedented ceremony of song, scripture and prayer.

The 1942 gift to the staff was a black leather savings stamp album and a 25¢ war stamp with which to begin a collection that could be redeemed for a savings bond.

Broadcast to the nation, the 30-minute service began with the President reading a Thanksgiving proclamation and the 23rd Psalm. It was said that, at this critical time in history, "only prayer was not rationed." There was prayer for victory and peace, prayer for the President, prayer for the nation, prayer for all those in the service of the country and for the nation's Allies, prayer for those in mourning and a prayer of thanksgiving.

All during the year, the Treasury Department had been distributing United States savings stamps through retail stores to encourage the purchase of defense bonds and stamps. Supporting the defense drive, President and Mrs. Roosevelt's 1942 personal gift to their White House staff was a black leather savings stamp album. The Executive

FDR, an avid collector of Christmas cards, entered these patriotic greetings into his collection in 1942. FRANKLIN D. ROOSEVELT LIBRARY

Office administrative staff, the Cabinet, family and close friends received a copy of the 1941 Christmas messages of Prime Minister Churchill and President Roosevelt. One hundred copies were made at a cost of $2.50 each. The President's Christmas card was a departure from the design of the previous six years. The 1942 card included a photograph of the President and Mrs. Roosevelt seated at a drop leaf table with the Executive Office in the background.

President Roosevelt enjoyed sending Christmas cards as much as he enjoyed receiving them. For years he collected cards, not only the ones he considered interesting but also those that expressed the spirit of the times. His collection was kept in huge boxes and classified according to their historic value, with Missy LeHand in charge of its maintenance. *Life* magazine of January 1940 indicated that the collection numbered in excess of 3,000 pieces, including a series of patriotic cards that depicted Christmas in war.

A Tree Without Lights

In the Capital's second Christmas at war, even the lighting of the National Community Christmas Tree was affected by it. For the first time in the 19-year ceremony, the President did not pull the switch to illuminate the giant tree, but rather sounded chimes that were broadcast over nationwide radio. Because of wartime rationing, there were no electric lights on the tree; it was instead decorated with hundreds of ornaments donated by Washington schoolchildren. For the second year, Franklin Roosevelt delivered his Christmas message from the South Portico of the White House. A sparse crowd of 1,500 people gathered around the darkened tree to hear his solemn address.

This year, my friends, I am speaking on Christmas Eve not to this gathering at the White House only but to all of the citizens of our nation, to the men and women serving in our American armed forces and also to those who wear the uniforms of the other United Nations. I give you a message of cheer. I cannot say "Merry Christmas,"—for I think constantly of those thousands of soldiers and sailors who are in actual combat throughout the world—but I can express to you my thought that this is a happier Christmas than last year in the sense that the forces of darkness stand against us with less confidence in the success of their evil ways.

To you who toil in industry and in offices, toil for the common cause of helping to win the war, I send a message of cheer, that you can well continue to sacrifice without recrimination and with a look of Christmas cheer, a kindly spirit toward your fellow men. To you who serve in uniform I also send a message of cheer, that you are in the thoughts of your families, your friends at home, and that Christmas prayers follow you wherever you may be. To all Americans I say that loving your neighbor as we love ourselves is not enough, that we as a nation and as individuals will please God best by showing regard for the laws of God....

It is significant that tomorrow–Christmas Day–our plants and factories will be stilled. That is not true now of the other holidays we have long been accustomed to celebrate. On all other holidays work goes on, gladly, for the winning of the war.

So Christmas Day becomes the only holiday in all the year. I like to think that this is so because Christmas is a holy day. May all that it stands for live and grow through all the years.

The President's speech was followed by the singing of carols, during which a baby's cries could be heard from within the White House. One-year-old Christopher, the son of Lt. Franklin Roosevelt, Jr., was visiting without his father. Again this Christmas, none of the four Roosevelt sons would be home. Only three small stockings hung on the President's mantel.

1943: The First Lady Saves the Tree

In early December, while President Roosevelt was attending the Cairo and Teheran Conferences with Winston Churchill and Josef Stalin, the Board of Commissioners of the District of Columbia recommended that the National Community Christmas Tree be abandoned in an effort to conserve electricity and the resources of transportation. Commercial establishments had been asked to cut down on electric Christmas displays, and citizens were encouraged to curtail any unnecessary use of street cars, which were operated by electricity. Christmas shopping and the National Tree ceremony brought out the crowds and constituted a tremendous burden on the street car system. In the absence of the President, his secretary, William D. Hassett, accepted the recommendation of the Board of Commissioners.

It was Eleanor Roosevelt who interceded to save the 20-year tradition. She appealed to the board to spare the tree unless it was *absolutely* necessary to abolish the custom. Americans had sacrificed much, and the ceremony at the National Community Christmas Tree would usher in the only real holiday the country had left. Commissioner Guy Mason granted the First Lady's request. Conforming to war restrictions, however, electric lights would not be placed on the tree; instead schoolchildren were asked to make ornaments dedicated to a loved one serving in the armed forces.

Mrs. Roosevelt also informed the Commissioner that the President would not be attending the ceremony on the Ellipse, but would broadcast a

The domed magnifying glass paperweight.

1943

WITH CHRISTMAS GREETINGS

AND OUR BEST WISHES

FOR A

HAPPIER NEW YEAR

THE PRESIDENT

AND

MRS. ROOSEVELT

FRANKLIN D. ROOSEVELT LIBRARY

holiday message to the troops. After spending 10 Christmases at the White House, the Roosevelts had decided to return to their family home, Springwood, in Hyde Park.

In anticipation of going home, the Roosevelts' Christmas card included a photograph of them seated at a square, cloth-covered table in the yard at Val-Kill. With its photograph by Ralph Short of the *Poughkeepsie New Yorker*, the greeting card was made in two sizes; approximately 3 x 4 and 5 x 7.

On December 11, a Christmas tree from the President was shipped to Winston Churchill in Chequers, England. Back in October, FDR had decided he wanted to send the British Prime Minister such a gift from his tree farm. He then enlisted Grace Tully's services to be certain that the tree would arrive before Christmas, even if it had to be delivered by a bomber.

The President also instructed the Government Printing Office to put together a book of his three Inaugural Addresses. Costing $2.50 each, 100 copies of the gift book were given to members of his family, Cabinet, administrative assistants and foreign dignitaries.

On Thursday, December 23, the President received the White House executive staff in his office and gave each member a desk magnifying glass paperweight. The 300 gift paperweights had been purchased by Grace Tully from Belmont Advertising Specialties, in Bronx, New York, for 65 cents each. Recipient George Elsey remembered shaking hands with the President, being handed a gift by an aide and moving on through the line. "There were no extras such as food or entertainment," he said. "It was wartime." The President stated that, in the interest of war conservation, his gifts would not be wrapped; he preferred that gifts to him from his friends and family would follow his example.

The Tree: No Lights, No President

The 21st annual National Community Christmas Tree ceremony was held on the South Lawn of the White House. Because of the President's absence, the crowd of 15,000 was able to get closer to the gaily decorated giant cedar and consequently found it to be more "homey" than in previous years. Among the 1,800 personalized children's decorations was a red ball with a white tag bearing the inscription, "William Hawk, killed in action." Another tag penned by a child simply read, "Dedicated to my daddy, Russell H. Brown, Lt. U.S.N.R." A green ball remembered "Charles Harris, Medical Corps, prisoner in Philippines." The inscriptions told a story of happier Christmases and the children's prayers for their loved ones at war. Despite wartime restrictions that prevented the lighting of the tree for the second year in a row, Harold Snyder of the District Recreation Department, who supervised the trimming of the tree, was quoted in the *Washington Star* as saying, "This is the most beautiful tree we have ever had."

The President delivered his Christmas message from his library in Hyde Park and it was extended to 30 minutes to enable him to report on the Cairo and Teheran Conferences. His remarks were carried by four radio networks, broadcast to the armed forces abroad and piped to the audience on the White House lawn by means of a special cable running out to the National Tree. The Chief Executive promised the nation and the world that they could expect peace with "certainty" even though "the cost may be high and the time long." He said that the United States, Great Britain, Soviet Russia and China all agreed to use force to maintain that peace "for as long as it may be necessary." He concluded with words of resolve, comfort and hope:

> *The massive offensives which are in the making—both in Europe and the Far East—will require every ounce of energy and fortitude that we and our allies can summon on the fighting fronts and in all the workshops at home. As I have said before, you cannot order up a great attack on a Monday and demand that it be delivered on Saturday.*
>
> *Less than a month ago I flew in a big Army transport plane over the little town of Bethlehem, in Palestine. Tonight, on Christmas Eve, all men and*

women everywhere who love Christmas are thinking of that ancient town and of the star of faith that shone there more than nineteen centuries ago.

American boys are fighting today in snow-covered mountains, in malarial jungles, and on blazing deserts. They are fighting on the far stretches of the sea and above the clouds, and the thing for which they struggle is best symbolized by the message that came out of Bethlehem. On behalf of the American people—your own people—I send this Christmas message to you who are in our armed forces: In our hearts are prayers for you and for all your comrades in arms who fight to rid the world of evil. We ask God's blessing upon you—upon your fathers and mothers, wives and children—all your loved ones at home. We ask that the comfort of God's grace shall be granted to those who are sick and wounded, and to those who are prisoners of war in the hands of the enemy, waiting for the day when they will again be free. And we ask that God receive and cherish those who have given their lives, and that He keep them in honor and in the grateful memory of their countrymen forever.

God bless all of you who fight battles on this Christmas Eve. God bless us all. Keep us strong in our faith that we fight for a better day for human kind— here and everywhere.

In his speech the President announced that General Dwight D. Eisenhower would command the Anglo-American army. The Chief Executive and Prime Minister Churchill had put control in the hands of "the soldier who, in all history, has had the most experience in directing vast combined land, sea and air operations." Fellow officers described the general as one who worked long hours, expected the same of his associates and had the capacity to grasp every detail of a campaign. Sharing his philosophy of war, General Eisenhower once said: "You can't hit a home run by bunting. You have to step up there and take your cut at the ball."

1944: Franklin Roosevelt's Last Christmas

Throughout 1944, there was never any question that ultimately victory would come to the Allies. Rome, Paris and the Philippines, under General Douglas MacArthur, had been liberated and victories were commonplace throughout Europe and in the Pacific. In June, after the D-Day invasion of Normandy, and as the landing craft began unloading American soldiers on Omaha Beach, President Roosevelt read to the nation over the radio a prayer that he had composed. By way of introduction, he said: "Last night, when I spoke with you about the fall of Rome, I knew at that moment that troops of the United States and our Allies were crossing the Channel in another and greater operation. It has come to pass with success thus far. And so, in this

D-Day Prayer

by President Franklin D. Roosevelt from the White House · June 6, 1944

Last night, when I spoke with you about the fall of Rome, I knew at that moment that troops of the United States and our Allies were crossing the Channel in another and greater operation. It has come to pass with success thus far.

And so, in this poignant hour, I ask you to join with me in prayer:

Almighty God: our sons, pride of our Nation, this day have set upon a mighty endeavor, a struggle to preserve our Republic, our religion, and our civilization, and to set free a suffering humanity.

Lead them straight and true; give strength to their arms, stoutness to their hearts, steadfastness in their faith.

They will need Thy blessings. Their road will be long and hard. For the enemy is strong. He may hurl back our forces. Success may not come with rushing speed, but we shall return again and again; and we know that by Thy grace, and by the righteousness of our cause, our sons will triumph.

They will be sore tried, by night and by day, without rest—until the victory is won. The darkness will be rent by noise and flame. Men's souls will be shaken with the violences of war.

For these men are lately drawn from the ways of peace. They fight not for the lust of conquest. They fight to end conquest. They fight to liberate. They fight to let justice arise, and tolerance and good will among all Thy people. They yearn but for the end of battle, for their return to the haven of home.

Some will never return. Embrace these, Father, and receive them, thy heroic servants, into Thy kingdom.

And for us at home—fathers, mothers, children, wives, sisters and brothers of brave men overseas—whose thoughts and prayers are ever with them—help us, Almighty God, to rededicate ourselves in renewed faith in Thee in this hour of great sacrifice.

Many people have urged that I call the Nation into a single day of special prayer. But because the road is long and the desire is great, I ask that our people devote themselves in a continuance of prayer. As we rise to each new day, and again when each day is spent, let words of prayer be on our lips, invoking Thy help to our efforts.

Give us strength, too—strength in our daily tasks, to redouble the contributions we make in the physical and the material support of our armed forces.

And let our hearts be stout, to wait out the long travail, to bear sorrows that may come, to impart our courage unto our sons wheresoever they may be.

And, O Lord, give us faith. Give us faith in Thee; faith in our sons; faith in each other; faith in our united crusade. Let not the keenness of our spirit ever be dulled. Let not the impacts of temporary events, of temporal matters of but fleeting moment—let not these deter us in our unconquerable purpose.

With Thy blessing, we shall prevail over the unholy forces of our enemy. Help us to conquer the apostles of greed and racial arrogancies. Lead us to the saving of our country, and with our sister nations into a world unity that will spell a sure peace—a peace invulnerable to the schemings of unworthy men. And a peace that will let all men live in freedom, reaping the just rewards of their honest toil. Thy will be done, Almighty God. AMEN

Christmas · 1944 · from
F·D·R

A reproduction of the D-Day Prayer was the President's gift to his staff in 1944.

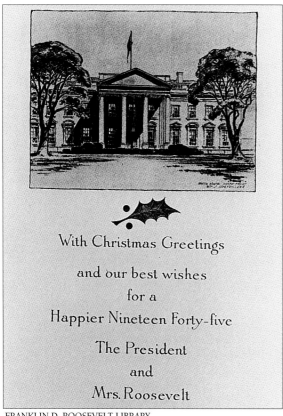

With Christmas Greetings

and our best wishes

for a

Happier Nineteen Forty-five

The President

and

Mrs. Roosevelt

poignant hour, I ask you to join with me in prayer."

The text of the prayer had been read to Congress and printed in newspapers so that millions of Americans could read the words as the President prayed. House Minority Leader Joseph W. Martin of Massachusetts warned that "many heartbreaking days lie ahead." The Majority Leader, Senator Alben W. Barkley of Kentucky, said, "All we need or ought to do or can do is pray fervently and devoutly for the success of our troops and those of our allies."

For Christmas, the large D-Day Prayer scroll was presented to each member of the Executive Office staff along with the Roosevelts' personal card on Thursday, December 21. The prayer was also printed and bound into a book. The 100 copies were given to members of his family, Cabinet, Congress, administrative staff and close friends. The Christmas card of the First Family featured a front view etching of the North Portico of the White House, flanked by two large trees. While each of the staff received a card with his or her gift, it was noted this year that President Roosevelt also sent his greeting card to a number of heads of state.

The year 1944 had been a grueling one for the President, and his election to a fourth term came only after an exhausting campaign. His health had been failing ever since the Cairo-Teheran conferences of a year earlier. Adolf Hitler's last-ditch attempt in mid-December to thwart the Allied armies in the Battle of the Bulge proved costly in human lives and ushered in a Christmas that was truly seasoned by war. For the second year in a row, the Roosevelts decided to spend Christmas at Hyde Park; hoping to get some much needed rest, their plans were not announced to the press. Leaving on the evening of the 23rd, they arrived home early Christmas Eve day.

From his library, the President delivered one of his most eloquent Christmas messages to the families and the fighting men and women around the world.

It is not easy to say "Merry Christmas" to you, my fellow Americans, in this time of destructive war. Nor can I say "Merry Christmas" lightly tonight to our armed forces at their battle stations all over the world—or to our Allies who fight by their side.... Our own thoughts go out to them, tonight and every night, in their distant places....

On this Christmas Day, we cannot yet say when our victory will come. Our enemies still fight fanatically. They still have reserves of men and military power. But, they themselves know that they and their evil works are doomed. We may hasten the day of their doom if we here at home continue to do our full share. And we pray that that day may come soon. We pray that until then God will protect our gallant men and women in the uniforms of the United Nations–that He will receive into His infinite grace those who make their supreme sacrifice in the cause of righteousness and the cause of love of Him and His teachings.

We pray that with victory will come a new day of peace on earth in which all the nations of the earth will join together for all time. That is the spirit of Christmas, the holy day. May that spirit live and grow throughout the world in all the years to come.

The war had taken its toll on Franklin Delano Roosevelt. He had longed for an early and lasting peace and for the rebuilding of the world after the war. In February, he agreed to go to Yalta in the Russian Ukraine with the hope that it might strengthen his relationship with Marshal Stalin. The President felt the conference was successful but exhausting.

Still weary from the negotiations, FDR uncharacteristically chose to be seated as he delivered his Yalta report to both houses of Congress on March 1. After a weekend in Hyde Park, the President left on March 29 for Warm Springs, Georgia, and a longer rest. Confident that peace was at hand, the Chief Executive penned an addendum to an address he was about to give for the Jefferson Day dinners throughout the land. His final sentence was: "The only limit to our realization of tomorrow will be our doubts of today. Let us move forward with strong and active faith."

On April 11, 1945, President Roosevelt passed away in his sleep, never knowing how close the nation was to peace.

A Proclamation

THE ALLIED ARMIES, THROUGH SACRIFICE AND DEVOTION AND WITH GOD'S HELP, HAVE WRUNG FROM GERMANY A FINAL AND UNCONDITIONAL SURRENDER.

The western world has been freed of the evil forces which for five years and longer have imprisoned the bodies and broken the lives of millions upon millions of free-born men. They have violated their churches, destroyed their homes, corrupted their children, and murdered their loved ones. Our Armies of Liberation have restored freedom to these suffering peoples, whose spirit and will the oppressors could never enslave.

Much remains to be done. The victory won in the West must now be won in the East. The whole world must be cleansed of the evil from which half the world has been freed. United, the peace-loving nations have demonstrated in the West that their arms are stronger by far than the might of the dictators or the tyranny of military cliques that once called us soft and weak.

The power of our peoples to defend themselves against all enemies will be proved in the Pacific war as it has been proved in Europe.

For the triumph of spirit and of arms which we have won, and for its promise to the peoples everywhere who join us in the love of freedom, it is fitting that we, as a nation, give thanks to Almighty God, Who has strengthened us and given us the victory.

Now, therefore, I, Harry S. Truman, President of the United States of America, do hereby appoint Sunday, May 13, 1945, to be a day of prayer.

I call upon the people of the United States, whatever their faith, to unite in offering joyful thanks to God for the victory we have won and to pray that He will support us to the end of our present struggle and guide us into the ways of peace.

I also call upon my countrymen to dedicate this day of prayer to the memory of those who have given their lives to make possible our victory.

In witness whereof, I have hereunto set my hand and caused the seal of the United States of America to be affixed.

Washington, D.C., May 8, 1945

Harry Truman

CHAPTER IV

THE TRUMANS
Home for the Holidays

arry S. Truman had been Vice President for only 83 days when news of FDR's death hit Washington; the man from Missouri was elevated to the Presidency suddenly and at a crucial time in history. The Trumans moved into the White House on May 7, 1945. The following day was both historic and memorable. Germany surrendered unconditionally to bring the war in Europe to an end, and the President celebrated his 61st birthday.

The jubilant Chief Executive announced the long-awaited surrender in a proclamation to the American people on May 8, which became known as V-E Day. Writing to his mother, he remarked, "Isn't that some birthday present?" The war in the Pacific ended three months later after the atomic bombing of Hiroshima on August 6 and of Nagasaki three days later. Japan surrendered, and peace was at last won after four wartime Christmases.

1945: A Christmas to Celebrate

The White House was adequately decorated in a festive and colorful manner. Evergreens and poinsettias added gaiety to the State Rooms and Great Hall. Cedar wreaths hung in the north windows complementing the two decorated Norway spruces that flanked the front door. Noticeably missing was the tinseled tree in the East Room, because the Trumans went home for the holidays to Independence, Missouri.

While it became a tradition for the First Family to go home for Christmas, the President always remained in Washington until after the staff

Facing page: V-E Day Proclamation, the Trumans' first Christmas gift to their staff.

Christmas party. Lillian Rogers Parks, a White House maid, said that the whole staff looked up to the President and Mrs. Truman. The genuine appreciation the Trumans felt toward their help seemed to come naturally. "You were just as important as anyone else, and you were treated with the respect of an equal," remarked the maid. She went on to say that the First Family never did anything for show. In fact, Mrs. Truman gave many gifts anonymously. The President also requested that each Christmas a needy white and a needy black family be singled out and supplied with cooked turkeys and gifts. Head butler Alonzo Fields was assigned to the detail of secretly helping the needy on behalf of the President.

Victory in Gifts and Tree Lights

For their first Christmas at the White House, President and Mrs. Truman gave the staff an embellished scroll of the V-E Day Proclamation bearing the signature of the new President. On December 22, the Commander-in-Chief sent season's greetings to the members of the armed forces. Thousands of them were awaiting discharge or furlough papers; others jammed transportation lines trying to get home for Christmas. To them all, he said: "On this Christmas Day I send a sincere and heartfelt greeting to you men and women of the United States Armed Forces who have brought us victory. I speak in behalf of a nation grateful for your service, your devotion and your sacrifice. We shall not forget the price you have paid...."

President Truman led the nation in celebrating its first peacetime Christmas in four years by lighting the hundreds of bulbs on the National Community Christmas Tree. Speaking in his gentle Missouri drawl, the President looked ahead with hope to a "long peace."

This is the Christmas that a war-weary world has prayed for through long and awful years. With peace come joy and gladness. The gloom of the war years fades as once more we light the National Community Christmas Tree.... Peace has its victories no less hard won than success at arms. We must not fail or falter. We must strive without ceasing to make real the prophecy of Isaiah: "They shall beat their swords into ploughshares and their spears into pruning hooks: nation shall not lift up sword against nation, neither shall they learn war any more."

Nearly 10,000 spectators had filed onto the White House grounds to watch the lighting ceremony—the first in four years. At the head of the line, Sgt. Eldwin Bell explained, "I have waited outside the gate since 2 p.m.—an hour and a half before opening time. We can't get home to Texas for our family Christmas tree so we thought we ought to attend Harry's party."

Two women fainted during the long, cold wait; after being revived and wrapped in blankets, they stayed through the whole event. Many shoppers arrived laden with packages that were forbidden on the grounds for security reasons. So anxious were they to see the whole ceremony, they simply parked their unmarked packages with a hasty plea, "Watch these for me, will you?" Needless to say, bedlam broke loose at the guardhouse as homebound shoppers sought to retrieve their holiday purchases.

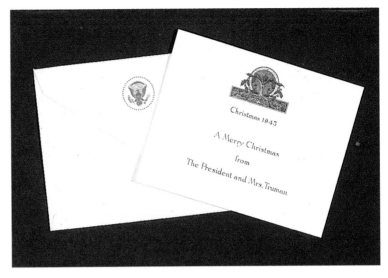

Though snow, sleet and freezing rain were predicted on Christmas Eve, the President refused to take that night's train to join the First Lady, her mother, and the Trumans' daughter, Margaret, all of whom were already back in Missouri. He instead decided to fly back to Independence Christmas morning on his Presidential plane, the *Sacred Cow*, only to have bad weather ground all commercial planes in the area. The President, with every intention of being home for Christmas, waited until noon before he and his veteran pilot took off.

Daughter Margaret, in her *Bess W. Truman*, recalled: "It was one of the wildest flights of his life. The *New York Times*, the *Washington Post* and other guardians of the republic castigated the President for 'taking chances with his personal safety.' Bess' comments when he got to 219 North Delaware Street were not much more cordial.... 'So you have finally arrived,' Bess said. 'I guess you couldn't think of any more reasons to stay away. As far as I am concerned, you might as well have stayed in Washington.'"

To make matters worse, two days later the President was called back to Washington to deal with a crisis concerning the Moscow conference. Still upset with his wife over her cutting remarks, Truman sent her a curt letter via special delivery. The next day, after a change of heart, he called Margaret and asked her to intercept the letter and "burn it." He then composed a second letter in which he was more understanding; he apologized for exasperating her and asked for her continued support.

1946: Enter the TV Cameras

The *Sacred Cow* played a safer yet significant role in the Trumans' 1946 Christmas, as the backdrop for their Christmas gift to their White House staff. Waving and smiling broadly, the First Couple posed for a photograph

Christmas 1946

The 1946 gift print features Harry and Bess Truman boarding the President's private plane, the *Sacred Cow.* AP/WIDE WORLD PHOTOS
Below: Brewood Engravers designed 800 small enclosure cards for the First Family in 1946.

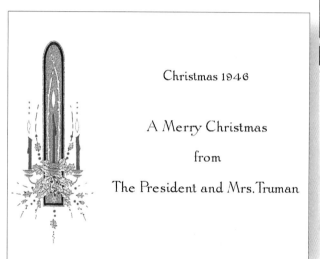

Christmas 1946

A Merry Christmas

from

The President and Mrs. Truman

before entering the plane. The White House ordered 1,000 copies of the black and white photograph at a cost of $402. On December 23, the President greeted 575 of his White House employees at an informal ceremony in his office and presented each an autographed photograph of himself and Mrs. Truman.

Before heading home to join the First Lady and Margaret, President Truman greeted the nation and a crowd of 10,000 at the lighting of the National Christmas Tree. For the first time in history, the ceremony was televised, though with both transmission and reception limited. He began with the message of Bethlehem:

If we as a nation, and the other nations of the world, will accept it, the star of faith will guide us into the place of peace as it did the shepherds on that day of Christ's birth long ago. I am sorry to say all is not harmony in the world today. We have found that it is easier for men to die together on the field of battle than it is for them to live together at home in peace. But those who died have died in vain if, in some measure, at least we shall not preserve for the peace that spiritual unity in which we won the war.

The problems facing the United Nations—the world's hope for peace—would overwhelm faint hearts. But as we continue to labor for an enduring peace through that great organization, we must remember that the world was not created in a day. We shall find strength and courage at this Christmas time because so brave a beginning had been made. So with faith and courage we shall work to hasten the day when the sword is replaced by the plowshare and nations do not "learn war any more".... We have made a good start toward peace in the world. Ahead of us lies the larger task of making the peace secure....

The illusion of peace weighed heavily on the President. In a letter to the Pope earlier in the year, Truman had also expressed his deep concern. "Although hostilities have ceased, peace has not yet been achieved.... We must employ every resource at our command to bring to this sadly troubled world an enduring peace and no peace can be permanent which is not based upon Christian principles."

1947: First Christmas in Washington

For their Christmas gift to the staff, the Trumans gave a maroon leatherette wallet bearing a gold-stamped Presidential Seal. Designed to hold identification cards, the 760 wallets were produced by Brown and Bigelow of St. Paul, Minnesota, at eight cents each. Because the gift itself carried the President's Christmas greeting, it was concluded that a separate Christmas card would be an unnecessary expense. For his Cabinet, President Truman ordered 40 black genuine leather identification billfolds, each with the White House pass in it, at a

The President's 1947 gift to his employees was a leatherette wallet designed to hold identification cards.

cost of 33 cents each. Each of 11 billfolds was stamped with the recipient's title and the Presidential Seal in gilt. The remaining cases were printed with only the seal and were distributed as gifts throughout the year. A Christmas card from the President and Mrs. Truman was enclosed with their gift to the Cabinet. A.B. Tolley reportedly ordered only 100 Christmas cards from Brewood Engravers in 1947. It is uncertain who received the rest of the cards.

The Trumans had invited their whole family to the White House for the holidays and to attend Margaret's voice recital on December 22. In preparation, the President supervised the trimming of the tree, although he never participated in the work. Margaret recalled him just sitting there giving instructions: "You need more lights over here; you need more ornaments over there."

The Chief Executive continued in his gift-giving mood on Christmas Eve as he pledged U.S. aid abroad. Speaking on the 25th anniversary of the first National Community Christmas Tree, the President offered hope to those left desolate by war.

The great heart of the American people has been moved to compassion by the needs of those in other lands who are cold and hungry.... In extending aid to our less fortunate brothers we are developing in their hearts the return of "hope." Because of our efforts, the people of other lands see the advent of a new day in which they can lead lives free from the harrowing fear of starvation and want. With the return of hope to these peoples will come renewed faith–faith in the dignity of the individual and the brotherhood of man.

Chrismas dinner was at two o'clock in the family dining room. Margaret explained, in an article for *Family Weekly*, that her "Father wouldn't carve anything, and so we all had a good time when they set the turkey down in front of him. It turned out that the butler had carved the turkey and then put the skin back on. As soon as I realized what they had done, I looked at my father and said, 'I want some skin.' He said, 'You'll get what you are given.' He wasn't about to have that little ploy revealed."

The staff was dismissed after dinner. Before going, they readied the makings for sandwiches so the First Family could take care of themselves. In *Upstairs at the White House*, chief usher J.B. West added, "That's the way the entire Truman family was. They didn't want to be a bother to anybody on the staff, they asked for very little. They treated the staff with respect—respect for us personally, and respect for the work that we did."

1948: The President Beats the Odds

The election of 1948 marked one of the biggest upsets in political his-

This brown leather bookmark was the President's gift to his staff in 1948.

tory. The Republicans had gained control of the Congress in 1946. Odds were 20 to 1 that Republican Thomas E. Dewey would take the Presidency in a landslide vote, but Harry Truman rose to the challenge. Traveling 21,928 miles in his railroad car, the *Ferdinand Magellan*, the President took his family on a "whistle-stop campaign" across the heartland, where he attacked what he labeled "the do-nothing 80th Congress," calling it "the worst in my memory." When the American people went to the polls in November, they elected Truman to a full term.

Prior to Thanksgiving, severe structural problems in the White House necessitated renovation, forcing the victorious Trumans to move into Blair House across the street until its completion. "Doesn't that beat all!" joshed the President. "Here we've worked ourselves to death trying to stay in this jailhouse and they kick us out anyway!" It was well into December before the mansion was completely cleared out. Mrs. Truman placed on tables several odds and ends that would not be returning to the new White House, allowing the staff to select wonderful souvenirs from the move.

The Chief Executive's Christmas gift to his staff was a brown leather bookmark embossed with the Presidential Seal and his motto: "I would rather have peace in the world than be President." No separate gift card was given with the bookmark to the 740 employees at the White House. For his Cabinet, the President gave a paperweight with a bronze casting of the Presidential Seal on a wooden base. On the front of the plaque were the words: "Christmas Greetings From the President 1948." The back read: "This wood was part of the White House used in its reconstruction about 1817 and removed in 1948." Of the 45 paperweights made, only 16 were used as Christmas gifts in 1948.

Long-Distance Tree Lighting

President Truman offered season's greetings on Christmas Eve from his home in Independence. Despite his absence, some 2,100 Washingtonians gathered on the South Lawn of the White House to hear his broadcast speech and to be on hand when the switch thrown in Missouri lit up the National Community Christmas Tree in Washington. Celebrating "the great home festival" in the midst of his kinfolk, the President tried to reassure Americans that he was continuing to work for the cause of peace. He said:

The Christmas tree which we have just lighted in the South Grounds of the White House back in Washington symbolizes the family life of the Nation.

The 1949 staff gift was a leather key holder.

There are no ties like family ties. That is why I have made the journey back to Independence to celebrate this Christmas Day among the familiar scenes and associations of my old hometown.... I have been thinking of all these things here in my home on North Delaware Street in Independence. I am speaking to you from our living room. As I came up the street in the gathering dusk, I saw a hundred commonplace things that are hallowed to me on this Christmas Eve–hallowed because of their associations with the sanctuary of home....

We have had difficult problems, and that is why we can understand the problems of other peoples. Our own struggle fostered this feeling of goodwill. And goodwill, after all, is the very essence of Christmas; peace and friendship to men of goodwill.... I want to say once more, with all the emphasis that I can command, that I am working for peace. I shall continue to work for peace. What could be more appropriate than for all of us to dedicate ourselves to the cause of peace on this Holy Night?

1949: "Man From Independence"

The Trumans gave their staff a leather key holder. About 20 of the President's closest aides, secretaries and administrative assistants also received the wooden paperweight made the previous year, but the date was changed to 1949. The President's Christmas gift to his Cabinet was a bound book, *Selected Speeches and Statements on Foreign Affairs by Harry S. Truman.*

Once again the President left Washington before the lighting of the National Community Christmas Tree ceremony to go home for Christmas. Known as "the man from Independence," he enjoyed the informality of America's heartland and walking with and talking to family and friends. From his music room, the Chief Executive called upon the American people to "dedicate ourselves anew to the love of their fellowmen."

1950: Troops Back in Asia

In April 1949, the United States and 11 other nations signed the North Atlantic Treaty that provided for their collective defense against an aggressor. A little more than a year later, that treaty was tested when Communist forces from North Korea invaded South Korea. In June 1950, President Truman ordered American forces to protect South Korea's independence against Communist aggression. By the end of the year, Chinese Communist troops

Christmas Greetings 1950. HARRY S. TRUMAN LIBRARY

had joined North Korea in the war. The Chief Executive knew that peace on earth would not last, but his goodwill toward the people of South Korea was a necessary part of his peacekeeping efforts.

His Christmas gift to his staff in 1950 reflected his goodwill and appreciation to those who faithfully and unobtrusively cared for his needs while he tended to the cares of the nation. *In Christmas Greetings 1950,* he reminded them that, "We need Christmas to bring us back to a due sense of spiritual values." The Government Printing Office produced 1,000 copies of the frameable keepsake. To his Cabinet and other close associates, the President gave a set of six crystal glasses engraved with the Presidential Coat of Arms.

Christmas Greetings
🎄 1950 🎄

AS 1950 EBBS TO ITS CLOSE OUR HEARTS TURN ONCE MORE TO BETHLEHEM AND TO THE COMING OF A LITTLE CHILD, THE DIVINE INFANT, THAT BROUGHT LOVE TO a weary world. This is the season of love—the season wherein our thoughts are of the love of friends, the love of home, the love of children, the love of all those little half remembered things which, although they make up the best portion of our days, are too often forgotten in the distractions of troublous times.

❧ We need Christmas to bring us back to a due sense of spiritual values.

❧ And so at this blessed season we are thinking of those faithful members of the White House staff who, day in and day out, have so quietly and with such unobtrusive efficiency performed their tasks and by their continuous and often unnoticed labors, lightened our cares and added pleasure to our lives.

❧ May Christmas Day be a day of joy to each and every one.

❧ It is not possible for us personally to know all those to whom we owe so deep a debt of gratitude. But to each we send this heartfelt message of affection and appreciation.

❧ May the Star of Bethlehem, which came so mysteriously and lingered so briefly, shine in our hearts and light our way to joy and peace even as it directed the steps of the Wise Men to the Manger in the City of David in the long ago.

❧ And may we, too, hear the song which the Angel Choir sang on the night of the first Christmas: "Glory to God in the highest and on earth, peace, good will toward men."

Harry Truman
Bess W. Truman

With U.S. troops engaged in combat in Korea, the White House received thousands of letters from citizens and church organizations requesting that the President proclaim a national day of prayer. In his Christmas message, taped in Washington before he went to Missouri for Christmas, Truman responded by urging the American people to renew their faith in God. He called for prayer based upon righteousness. Due to an assassination attempt in November, security was tight and no one was permitted on the White House grounds. Outside the iron fence, a crowd of 3,000 heard the broadcast and listened to the Marine Band. President Truman spoke by tape from Washington, but lit the tree by remote control from Independence.

Many of us are fortunate enough to celebrate Christmas at our own fireside. But there are many others who are away from their homes and loved ones on this day. Thousands of our boys are on the cold and dreary battlefield of Korea. But all of us—at home, at war, wherever we may be—are within reach of God's love and power. We all can pray. We all should pray.... The Nation already is in the midst of a Crusade of Prayer. On the last Sunday of the old year, there will be special services devoted to a revival of faith. I call upon all of you to enlist in this common cause. I call upon you no matter what your spiritual allegiance.

We are all joined in the fight against the tyranny of Communism. Communism is godless. Democracy is the harvest of faith–faith in one's self, faith in one's neighbors, faith in God. Democracy's most powerful weapon is not a gun, tank, or bomb. It is faith–faith in the brotherhood and dignity of man under God.

No one knew whether this Christmas was to be one more postwar Christmas or the last Christmas before war. All across the nation, people of all faiths joined in prayer for peace.

1951: *Blair House Memento*

During the renovation of the White House, from November 1948 until March 1952, President and Mrs. Truman lived in Blair House. For their Christmas gift to their staff in 1951, the Chief Executive directed the Government Printing Office to produce 1,000 copies of a photograph of the Blair House taken by the Signal Corps. With a total cost of $90, the gift was given to the staff by the President on December 22 at his annual pre-Christmas reception. One of the recipients, M.O. Carter, was a White House electrician who, over time, became close to the President. Years later he wrote on the back of his Christmas gift, "He would come downstairs and eat bean soup with several of the boys. We all liked President Truman alot [sic]." To his Cabinet and close personal friends, the President gave 60 bound, limited editions of his opening address at the Conference on the Japanese Peace Treaty in San Francisco.

Christmas Greetings from the President and Mrs. Truman

1951

The 1951 gift print of Blair House. HARRY S. TRUMAN LIBRARY

From his home in Independence, on Christmas Eve 1951, the President recalled the year 1941.

As we think of Korea, we should also think of another Christmas, 10 years ago, in 1941. That was just after Pearl Harbor, and the whole world was at war. Then almost every country, almost every home, was overshadowed by fear and sorrow.... Tonight we have a different goal, and a higher hope. Despite difficulties, the free nations of the world have drawn together solidly for a great purpose; not solely to defend themselves; not merely to win a bloody war if it should come; but for the purpose of creating a real peace–a peace that shall be a positive reality and not an empty hope; a just and lasting peace.

When we look toward the battlefields of Korea, we see a conflict like no other in history. There the forces of the United Nations are fighting–not for territory, not for plunder, not to rule the lives of captive people. In Korea the free nations are proving, by deeds, that man is free and must remain free, that aggression must end, that nations must obey the law.

Americans on the front lines in Korea experienced snow and sleet, but a quiet Christmas, with only an occasional rumble of Communist artillery. Efforts were made to serve turkey, dressing, cranberry sauce, mixed nuts, pie and coffee to all the troops. Francis Cardinal Spellman celebrated Mass for 3,000 Marines on the eastern front. Santa Claus, dressed in red and white or khaki green, also paid a visit to the frozen front. While delegates talked of peace at Panmunjom, the soldiers in the midst of war turned their thoughts to home.

1952: Last Christmas in Office

When the President of the United States went to Independence for Christmas, scores of people went with him, including White House staff members, secretaries, Secret Service agents, military aides, his airplane crew, the press, and many others. Harry Truman had gone home for Christmas six of the eight years of his Presidency. Aware of the personal sacrifice of all those who accompanied him, he announced, early in December, "I'm staying at the White House this Christmas. It's my last Christmas as President and Bess and I want to spend it in Washington." What he hadn't said was that, for a change, all his staff could spend the holiday with their own families.

The Trumans had moved back into the newly renovated White House in March. For Christmas they gave their staff a photograph of the historic mansion depicting the 1946 Truman Balcony. The Signal Corps shot the photograph and the Government Printing Office printed it. The gold

White House — View from the East Garden

Christmas Greetings from the President and Mrs. Truman, 1952

The Trumans' last gift print was reproduced by the Government Printing Office.

Presidential Seal in the lower left corner accented their sentiment. The reproductions in black and white cost 50 cents each, and in color, $2, and were presented at the annual reception in the President's office. Mrs. Truman and Margaret broke tradition by being on hand to exchange holiday greetings with the 350 members of the executive staff and the crews of the *Sacred Cow* and the *Williamsburg*, the Presidental yacht.

For the first time in five years, the President appeared in person to light the National Community Christmas Tree on the White House lawn. To a crowd of several thousand watching from outside the iron fence, he said: "As we pray for our men and women in Korea, and all our service men and women wherever they are—let us also pray for our enemies. Let us pray that the spirit of God shall enter their lives and prevail in their lands. Let us pray for a fulfillment of the brotherhood of man. Through Jesus Christ the world will yet be a better and a fairer place. This faith sustains us today as it has sustained mankind for centuries past."

God appeared to answer the Americans' prayers in an unusual way. The Korean War did not end overnight, but it did cease for a day, as the enemy joined in the celebration. The cannons on Sniper Ridge were silent while Communist loudspeakers played Christmas carols, after announcing a cease fire until noon, "in observance of your Christmas." The enemy left toys, dolls and candy on the front lines, along with banners that read, "Merry Christmas." On the Western front, Allied watchers were stunned to see a decorated Christmas tree and numerous signs bearing holiday greetings in English.

In January 1953 "the man from Independence" went home for good. Harry Truman had become President as World War II was coming to a close, and left office in the last days of the Korean War. He faced crucial decisions in both crises but remained constant in his pursuit of peace. For a man who had tried to dodge the nomination for Vice President, the responsibility of the Presidency was heavy. He said of his sudden entry into office upon the death of FDR, "I felt like the moon, the stars, and all the planets had fallen on me." Almost eight years later, the departing President summed up his performance: "I have tried my best to give the nation everything I had in me."

PRESIDENT ABRAHAM LINCOLN
FROM A PHOTOGRAPH
BY ALEXANDER GARDNER
TAKEN NOVEMBER 15, 1863

BY

Dwight D. Eisenhower

CHRISTMAS 1953

THE EISENHOWERS
Art From a Painting President

f ever a President took a personal interest in the gifts and cards that were sent from the White House, it was Dwight D. Eisenhower. Having had no formal training in painting, the President known as "Ike" allowed six of his own creations to be used as Christmas gifts to his staff during his administration. In a letter to Joyce C. Hall, president of Hallmark Cards, he wrote: "As you know I always hate to inflict 'art' on my friends and members of my staff, but Hallmark makes such a beautiful package job that I am, and I hope others are, distracted into the belief that the whole thing is a superior product."

While president of Columbia University, General Eisenhower began painting at the urging of New York painter Thomas E. Stephens. Interest had turned to fascination as Ike watched the artist work on a portrait of Mrs. Eisenhower. Before Stephens was finished, the General had borrowed paint, brushes and canvas from him and had begun his own portrait of Mamie, his wife. Thus was launched a new hobby for a man already in love with golf and fishing. Eisenhower always referred to his work not as art, but as "daubs, born of my love of color and in my pleasure in experimenting." Painting became a means of relaxation for him rather than an accomplishment. Consequently, the General gave his first painting to Stephens, who numbered it among his prized possessions. Having no deep attachment to his work, Eisenhower often created paintings that ended up as mementos for his personal friends or as thoughtful holiday gifts.

Facing page: Eisenhower's Abraham Lincoln, the 1953 gift print. HALLMARK CARDS

1953: The Abe Lincoln Portrait

When planning for their first White House Christmas, it seemed only natural to call on card expert Joyce C. Hall. The President had known the Hallmark chief executive since 1950, when Hall had been asked to serve on a committee to build the General's war trophies museum in Abilene, Kansas. That relationship grew over the years and resulted in a unique collection of Christmas cards unlike those of any other Presidential era. "Being an artist himself, Eisenhower was most challenging and imaginative to deal with," Hall said. "We felt strongly that he should use his own paintings on the cards, but he didn't think they were good enough. He had recently done a portrait of Abraham Lincoln which we thought was an excellent choice—a portrait of one President painted by another."

The President had begun work on the portrait of Lincoln while waiting for news of a Korean armistice. The Lincoln likeness was derived from an Alexander Gardner photograph of November 15, 1863. Hallmark reproduced the portrait and enclosed it in a white commemorative gift folder bearing the Presidential Seal. The President wrote to Hall: "Someone just showed me your reproduction of my laborious attempt to paint a portrait of Lincoln. I must say that if my work could only remotely approach the quality that is so evident in every part of your reproduction, the thing would be a real masterpiece. In fact ... I even like my head of Lincoln—except when I did it originally I did not realize I had allowed so much red to creep into the face tones. That was a mistake which one of these days I shall correct."

Of the 1,100 keepsake folders ordered that year, 516 were given to White House employees at the annual Christmas party in the East Room. Along with the gift print, each member of the staff received an official gift enclosure card with the words "Season's Greetings" engraved in gold.

In 1953, the list of Presidential Christmas card recipients was expanded significantly, with season's greetings going to American ambassadors abroad, foreign heads of state, government officials, members of the Cabinet and Congress. Thereafter, the Presidential greeting was to be the "official" White House Christmas card. In addition to the gift folder and gift enclosure card, Hallmark reproduced 1,100 official greeting cards for the Eisenhowers. The ivory white formal card for the year was designed with a blank embossed Presidential Seal and the words "Season's Greetings" engraved in gold. Inside, the black engraved message read, "The President and Mrs. Eisenhower extend their best wishes for Christmas and the New Year." A similar but less formal card was designed with embossed holly leaves and red berries. A simple engraved "Mamie and Ike," in Mamie's handwriting, was sent to 500 personal friends. The President wrote to Hall: "The Christmas cards are, of course, equally outstanding and both are completely appropri-

The 1953 official Presidential Christmas card. HALLMARK CARDS

ate to the purpose for which we intend to use them."

Greeting the American people on Christmas Eve from inside the White House, the Chief Executive reached the nation by radio and television, and his words were carried around the world in 34 languages by Voice of America radio. While applauding the cessation of fighting in Korea, the Commander-in-Chief acknowledged that a cold war still existed. He said: "For us, this Christmas is truly a season of goodwill—and our first peaceful one since 1949. Our national and individual blessings are manifold. Our hopes are bright even though the world still stands divided in two antagonistic parts." Following his message, the President and Mrs. Eisenhower were driven to the South Lawn, where he set aglow the 1,500 red and green lights of the National Christmas Tree. Seven hundred invited guests crowded around the tree, while 3,500 watched the ceremony from outside the fence.

In those days, the cost for printing the gift folders and cards that were sent by the President came out of his personal account. On January 23, Ike expressed his appreciation to Joyce C. Hall: "Your bill was not only nominal, it was practically nonexistent. I have some inkling, at least, of the enormity of my obligation to you.... Incidentally, you will be pleased to know that the obvious excellence of your work in reproducing and mounting my *Lincoln* elicited far more compliments from my intimate friends than did my own effort." Enclosed was a check for $139.50.

1954: *The George Washington Portrait*

By February, the President was already thinking ahead to the next Christmas. His secretary, Thomas E. Stephens, contacted Hall for advice. Said Hall: "I doubt if there is anything he could do that would be as interesting as a series of Presidents and it also seems to me that he has put them in exactly the right order—Lincoln, Washington, Jefferson, and Theodore Roosevelt." He added, "If the President were willing to paint a series of these, the recipients would each have a priceless collection and the originals would be an exhibit worthy of a room in any gallery. Every good critic of art who

The 1954 official gift enclosure.
HALLMARK CARDS

Eisenhower's George Washington, the 1954 gift print. HALLMARK CARDS

PRESIDENT GEORGE WASHINGTON
FROM A PAINTING
BY GILBERT STUART

CHRISTMAS 1954

saw the painting or the print has marveled at the President's ability as a por-trait painter."

Hearing indirectly later in the year that the requests for the Lincoln print had exhausted the supply, Hall authorized a second printing to be for-warded to the President. In a thank you note to Hall he wrote: "I think you would be gratified, as I must confess I have been, by the flattering comments I have had throughout the year about the Lincoln. Recently, when

The 1954 personal embossed wreath Christmas card, complete with hand-applied nail polish on the red holly berries. HALLMARK CARDS *Below:* The 1954 personal gift enclosure card that turned out to be the first in a series of "Mamie Bangs" variations. HALLMARK CARDS

Chancellor Adenauer was here, I was astonished to hear him express a desire for one, and of course I was delighted to have a copy to give him."

In September, while on a fishing trip near Fraser, Colorado, the President had painted the portrait of George Washington from Gilbert Stuart's famed work. Hallmark reproduced the artwork in lithography and put the print in a folder with a blank embossed Presidential Seal. Some of the prints were marked "this edition is a limited edition of 950." Hallmark also shipped 350 without the words "limited edition." To accompany each Washington print, the President ordered 1,300 official gift enclosure cards, designed with the Presidential Seal and "Season's Greetings 1954" with a red border.

The gift print and enclosure card were distributed to 664 office associates, Secret Service agents, White House police force, chauffeurs, telephone operators and domestic employees. Gift folders were also hand-delivered to Cabinet members and government departments within Washington. Accompanying each was a greeting from the President: "Last Christmas time I had the audacity to send you a lithograph of a reputed 'portrait' I had done of President Lincoln. While my effort of this year is not even up to the woefully low standard of last year, I thought you might like a companion picture. It is a reproduction of a painting of President Washington which I have just completed."

The 1954 official Christmas card was a smooth, white greeting card with a blank embossed Presidential Seal; a gold, hot foil eagle; and a red, white and blue silk screen shield. The White House ordered 1,300 greeting cards. Hallmark also designed two personal cards for the Eisenhowers. While extremely pleased with the white blank embossed wreath card with a red bow and red berries, the President and First Lady never learned of the challenge those 400 personal cards posed for artists at Hallmark.

On the morning they were to be shipped, it was discovered that the red ink from the berries on one card would smear onto the next one. Artists armed with bottles of clear nail polish were quickly pressed into service to apply a dot of polish to each and every berry. Rendered smudge-proof, the cards were shipped that afternoon on TWA. That year also, a Hallmark artist designed a personal gift card for the First Lady's use. Meant to be an affectionate holiday greeting for close personal friends, the informal card caricatured her hairstyle and was identified by its clever trademark as the "Mamie Bangs" card. "Mrs. Eisenhower adored them," wrote her social secretary, Mary Jane McCaffree. "Please thank the artist for his originality," requested the First Lady.

On December 17, instead of on Christmas Eve, President Eisenhower lit the 70-foot National Christmas Tree to open a 21-day celebration of what was to be the first Pageant of Peace. Taking place in a large cross-shaped park on the Ellipse, the unprecedented event included musical presentations on a 40-foot stage, Protestant services, Catholic Masses, a nativity scene and a children's corner featuring Santa and eight reindeer from North Pole, New York. The inauguration of the Pageant of Peace provided Washington with one of the most successful civic celebrations in the city's history. More than 300,000 spectators visited the festival over several days, and millions witnessed it from around the world.

Having been confronted with the possibility of military action in Vietnam earlier in the year, the President focused on peace: "This year, even as two thousand years ago, when the Prince of Peace was born into the world, the drums of war are stilled. In their silence, after a whole generation of almost ceaseless beating, many people—already become fathers and mothers—enjoy the first peaceful Christmas they have known. So—mankind's unquenchable hope for peace burns brighter than for many years."

1955: "Distance in the Mountains"

An avid fisherman who especially enjoyed the excellent trout fishing near Fraser, Colorado, the President, in mid-September 1955, began a new painting, *St. Louis Creek, Byars Peak Ranch*. He had been working on it only a week when he suffered his first heart attack and was rushed to Fitzsimons Army Hospital in Denver. "The painting was to be his Christmas card that year," recalled Joyce C. Hall, "and he asked me to visit him to discuss it since he wasn't sure he could finish it in time. When I got to the hospital he had already started working on it again. Can anyone doubt what great therapy painting was for him?"

Eisenhower's St. Louis Creek, the 1955 gift print. HALLMARK CARDS

On November 3, Hallmark received the painting. The message of Hall to the President in his Denver White House was, "We all think it is exceptionally well done, and particularly like your treatment of snow and how well you achieved a feeling of distance in the mountains. These are hard things to do, and you should be very proud of your result. Our opinion is that it will reproduce very satisfactorily, and within a short time after size is determined we will send proofs to show you just how it will finish. We are greatly pleased with the news of your splendid improvement and will be praying for it to continue."

Even with the President's "never satisfied, always-critical eye," he was pleased with the results. He responded to Hall: "This year, perhaps because of my illness, I am more than ever grateful for some of the wonderful kindnesses shown to me by my friends. The assistance and cooperation of Hallmark, in producing—in a very limited space of time—the lithograph of the St. Louis Creek scene, is right on top of my list." The White House had ordered 1,500 prints.

The official greeting card kept the same design as the previous year's card with the exception of a blue silk screen background and gold foil stars to enhance the appearance of the 1,300 cards. Again Hallmark designed a card to extend "Christmas Greetings" to the First Family's personal friends. A second "Mamie Bangs" gift card was designed for Mrs. Eisenhower's personal use.

On December 16, President Eisenhower touched a telegraph key in the office of the president of Gettysburg College to light the 65-foot spruce on the Ellipse. Speaking from Gettysburg, the President's Christmas message took on more personal overtones than in previous years. He said: "For me, this particular Christmas has a very special meaning, and has brought to me, really, new understandings of people. During the past three months, my family and I have received literally thousands—tens of thousands of mes-

The 1955 official Presidential Christmas card.
HALLMARK CARDS
Below: The 1955 "Mamie Bangs" gift enclosure card. HALLMARK CARDS

sages. Each of these has borne a sentence of good wishes and goodwill for health and happiness to us both. It has been heartwarming evidence that human understanding and human sympathy can surmount every obstacle—even those obstacles that some governments sometimes seem to raise in the attempt to divide us."

Having spent their first two Christmases in Augusta, Georgia, the President and First Lady decided to spend Christmas of 1955 at the White House. They were joined by their son, John, and three of his four children. John's wife, Barbara, remained in the hospital, having just given birth to the President's fourth grandchild.

1956: *Photographic Gifts*

In June the President underwent emergency surgery following an ileitis attack. Unable to spend much time painting, he decided to give the staff a portfolio of twin black and white pictures of himself and Mrs. Eisenhower. The President's photograph was taken by Willard Volz of Reni Photos at CBS at the beginning of the campaign for his second term in office. Mrs. Eisenhower's was a photograph of the Thomas E. Stephens painting of her in her pink 1953 inaugural gown.

The White House ordered 1,750 official gift enclosure cards along with the 1,750 gift portfolios, 200 of which were to be prepared blank so that a personal note could be added in longhand by the President and Mrs. Eisenhower. Just four days before Christmas, however, 175 of the blank folders were returned to Hallmark by air to add the engraving. The photographs to be inserted in the portfolio were likewise being returned by air from Rochester, New York. A wire to Joyce C. Hall from the White House queried

The 1956 gift print: twin photographs of the President and First Lady. HALLMARK CARDS
Left: The 1956 personal Christmas card: the front door at the Eisenhowers' Gettysburg farm.
HALLMARK CARDS

whether it would be possible to make this change for the President; it went on to say that it would be all right if the order was shipped after Christmas. Also, an additional supply of 200 cards was needed.

Stating that "a Christmas card received after Christmas is about as effective as 'last year's bird nest,'" the Hallmark president assured the White House that his staff would see to it that the order was completed before Christmas. On the Saturday before Christmas, a number of Hallmark personnel arrived to help with the Presidential project. The folders to be engraved arrived from Washington, but the plane from Rochester, New York, carrying the photographs had been grounded due to bad weather, and there was no hope of getting them in time. At Hall's suggestion, photographs were taken of the portraits, providing negatives from which replacement photos could be made. Other "Hallmarkers" responded with equal enthusiasm and the deadline was met.

After learning from a trade magazine that the Eisenhowers had selected Castleton china with a wide gold band for use in the White House, Hallmark artist Bette Johnson designed their 1956 official card with this in mind. It portrayed a gold, hot foil eagle on the blank embossed Presidential Seal, against a gold litho background with embossed "Season's Greetings

1956" on the front. The White House ordered 1,900 of these along with another 800 personal cards depicting the front door at the Eisenhower Farms near Gettysburg, Pennsylvania. The farm, purchased in 1950 upon the Eisenhowers' return from Europe, became the First Family's weekend get-away. It also was the only permanent home the General and his wife had ever owned.

On December 20, President Eisenhower formally opened the Pageant of Peace by setting aglow the 5,000 lights and 4,000 decorations on the 67-

The 1957 personal gift enclosure card: Ike and Mamie on a golf cart. HALLMARK CARDS *Below:* A Green Room photograph, the 1957 gift print. HALLMARK CARDS

foot spruce. The newly reelected Chief Executive extolled the spirit of Christmas in his remarks.

1957: *The Green Room Photo*

As their Christmas gift, the Eisenhowers chose to give their staff a color photo of the Green Room. An engraved message in the President's handwriting under the picture eliminated the need for the official gift enclosure that year. The White House ordered 1,950 gift folders. Almost without exception, the White House would order the same number of official Christmas cards as they did gift folders, but in 1957 they ordered 2,500 cards. The official card shape also changed. Hallmark placed a blank embossed Presidential Seal and gold, hot foil eagle and stars on the oblong white card stock. The Eisenhowers sent 800 personal cards depicting in silver foil their house at the Eisenhower Farms.

The President's favorite sport was golf, and his pride and joy was the putting green on the South Lawn that had been a gift from the American Public Golf Association. In 1957 Hallmark designed a "Mamie Bangs" gift enclosure card depicting Ike and Mamie in a golf cart loaded down with packages and a Christmas tree. The 400 gift cards would have been useful to a First Family that gave many gifts. Chief usher J.B. West, in his *Upstairs at the White House*, said: "Mamie Eisenhower was personally a most thoughtful First Lady." Besides remembering her employees' birthdays with a cake and a card, she also selected something for everyone at Christmas.

At the annual ceremony at the Pageant of Peace in 1957, President Eisenhower warned the audience of 9,000 that sweat and toil, courage and self-sacrifice would be needed to achieve and sustain world peace.

1958: *Deserted Barn*

The Christmas staff gift for 1958 was a reproduction of *Deserted Barn*, a painting done by the Chief Executive at the Gettysburg farm the previous summer. A recipient of one of the 2,150 gift folders that year was Major Donald Glew, Jr., the Chief Executive's physician at Walter Reed Army Hospital. Later, in a letter to him, the President told the story behind the gift print.

As you well know, I have had no instruction in painting. I know nothing whatsoever about technique and in the course in mechanical drawing I pursued at West Point I was such a failure that I ran the risk of discharge. Actually my great interest is colors. They intrigue me and I try to indulge my bent in this direction by applying myself to attempt in oils, a representation of any scene or person I can think of. Frankly, I don't even know how to mix colors decently. Sometimes it is a real effort to achieve the approximate color and value I seek.

So far as my latest reproduction is concerned, I started it merely as an imaginative sketch. I wanted to see whether I could, from memory, project the straight lines to their approximately correct vanishing points—and do so without the aid of any model or drawing. In order to make the exercise of some interest to myself, I wanted also to represent desolation or hopelessness if this could be done in a structure. The other items of the composition were put in there merely incidentally, so I might judge my success in achieving the effect of relative distance and of color.

Once I had finished with this particular exercise, I was on the point of throwing it away when other members of the family asked me not to do so. Later I found that they had decided a reproduction would make a nice Christmas memento, but in the meantime I had given the painting away to a friend [Walter A. West]. So we had to get it back—and that is the way the project got underway despite all the imperfections I could easily see in the thing. After 1961 I am going to start taking lessons.

Eisenhower's *Deserted Barn*: the 1958 gift print. HALLMARK CARDS

A 1958 contemporary card with an overlapping front and inside design. HALLMARK CARDS
Left: The 1958 personal card: a painting of the Eisenhower Museum in Abilene, Kansas. HALLMARK CARDS

The 2,100 official Christmas cards for 1958 bore the traditional design of an embossed gold foil Presidential Seal with a field of blue silk screening placed on ivory white card stock. For the family's personal card, Hallmark framed a painting of the Eisenhower Museum in Abilene, Kansas, with a green wreath made of holly, red berries and a red bow. Mrs. Eisenhower ordered 300 of them and 200 of an informal contemporary card Hallmark had designed especially for the First Couple. A red original "Mamie Bangs" card completed the order for the First Family. Hallmark art director Jeannette Lee wrote of the relationship between her company and the Chief Executive: "We're so pleased to be doing cards for the President and Mrs. Eisenhower again this year. The most excitement we have around here is hearing the results of what they like."

A 99-foot Engelmann spruce from Montana served as the National Christmas Tree in 1958. Trimmed to a mere 79 feet, the stately spruce was decorated with 5,000 lights, 1,200 balls, 108 red bells and 60 three-foot candy canes. As he lit the tree, President Eisenhower made a pledge to the

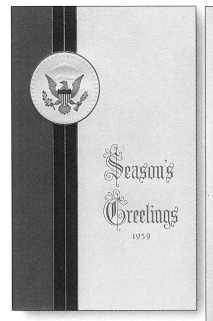

MOUNT EISENHOWER

Above left: The 1959 official Presidential Christmas card. HALLMARK CARDS
Above: *Mount Eisenhower*: the 1959 gift print. HALLMARK CARDS

7,500 present and to the millions in the television and radio audience. He said: "The United States is strong, and will remain strong, because that is the only way in today's world that the peace can be protected—but the United States will never use its strength to break the peace."

Participants that traveled the farthest for the Pageant of Peace were 14 reindeer and a caribou from north of the Arctic Circle. A Christmas gift to the nation from the Governor of Alaska, the herd traveled by plane, railroad, ship and truck to get to Washington, D.C. The biggest challenge of the long trip came when one of the reindeer became skittish and kicked open the door of the Alaskan Air National Guard plane at 2,000 feet. Despite the hair-raising incident, the animals arrived safely and retired to the zoo when the pageant was over.

1959: *The Year of Mount Eisenhower*

As their Christmas present in 1959 the White House staff received a reproduction of *Mount Eisenhower*, a painting of a tall rocky butte looming over Lake Louise with fir trees rising above the shore. At 9,390 feet, the mountain is located in Banff National Park in the Canadian Rockies, between Banff and Lake Louise, and was formerly called Castle Mountain. It was renamed on January 11, 1946, in appreciation of the leadership given to the Allied Forces in World War II by the Supreme Commander, General Dwight D. Eisenhower.

Sam Rayburn, longtime Speaker of the House, writing to the President in appreciation of his gift said, "I think the picture of the painting of Mount Eisenhower that you made is perfectly lovely. It will be framed and will find its way to the Memento Room of the Sam Rayburn Library in Bonham, Texas. Maybe you and I can do something sometime that people will remember us for, so I am putting a lot of you and me in the Library where it will be preserved always."

Hallmark printed 2,200 of the gift folders and 1,200 official gift enclosure cards. The 2,900 official Christmas cards took on a slightly different appearance with its red, white and blue silk screened borders. The Presidential Seal was also changed by Executive Order from 48 to 50 stars to reflect the recent addition of Alaska and Hawaii as states. The Eisenhowers' personal card featured a watercolor of the Little House at the farm, with a poem to describe it. For the First Lady's personal gift cards Hallmark turned out another "Mamie Bangs" creation using her favorite holly, red berries and bow to shape a hat.

Upon his return from a 19-day goodwill tour of 11 countries, the President spoke at the Pageant of Peace ceremonies on December 23 and said, "I wish that every American ... could see and hear what I have seen and what I have heard. The mutual understanding thereby created could in itself do much to dissolve the issues that plague the world."

1960: Church in Bavaria

Christmas of 1960 was the last one the Eisenhowers would spend in the White House. J.B. West recalled that Mrs. Eisenhower wanted this one "to be the most beautiful Christmas ever" and consequently "spread Christmas throughout the entire White House." Together with her social secretary, Mary Jane McCaffree, the First Lady scoured all of Washington's department stores for ideas and baubles. As elaborate as her 1960 preparations were, the 26 trees she had decorated in 1959 set a record that stood for many years.

On December 22, the President and First Lady gave their annual party for 1,000 members of the White House staff and employees. A reproduction of the President's painting *Church in Bavaria*, along with a gift enclosure card, was given to each person who had worked for them. Hallmark produced 2,225 gift folders and 1,200 official gift enclosure cards for the Eisenhowers'

Eisenhower's *Church in Bavaria*, the 1960 gift card. HALLMARK CARDS

last Christmas in the White House.

Church in Bavaria was the sixth in the gallery of paintings the President shared with his White House staff. Over the years, he had created more than a hundred portraits of friends and family, landscapes, pastoral scenes and an occasional still life.

Between 1953 and 1960, the list of recipients of the official Christmas card from the President had almost tripled, growing from 1,100 to 3,100. The last official card featured a blank embossed Presidential Seal on a white card, with 50 gold, hot foil stars, placed on a wide band of red silk screen. For their personal card, Mrs. Eisenhower loved the watercolor of the South Portico and its two staircases leading into the White House, because that was the entrance she most often used. The White House ordered 500 of the watercolor cards along with 100 of the "Mamie Bangs" gift cards.

Joyce C. Hall and Dwight Eisenhower had a unique working relationship. In eight years, Hallmark produced a prodigious 38 different Christmas cards and gift prints for the President and First Lady. No previous administration, nor any since Eisenhower's, has sent such a variety of holiday greetings from the White House. "I like Ike" was more than a campaign slogan; it was the essence of Hall's appreciation for the famed General. "When you care enough to send the very best" was more than an advertising slogan for the President; it was the epitome of what he had come to rely on as an outlet for the products of his newfound passion for painting. Earle Chesney,

The 1960 personal card, a watercolor of the South Portico. HALLMARK CARDS

Hallmark President Joyce C. Hall and President Eisenhower as caricatured by Earle Chesney. HALLMARK CARDS

Assistant to the Deputy Assistant to the President, captured their mutual admiration in an affectionate caricature.

On December 23, in his last Christmas message, Eisenhower called for a self-examination ..."to test the sincerity of our own dedication to the ideals so beautifully expressed in the Christian ethic.... One of America's imperishable virtues is her pride in the national ideals proclaimed at her birth. When danger to them threatens, America will fight for her spiritual heritage to the expenditure of the last atom of her material wealth; she will put justice above life itself. America will never cease in her striving to remove the blemishes on her own reflection...."

Together the President and First Lady pressed the button that lit the thousands of colored lights on the 70-foot Douglas fir tree from Oregon. More than 1,200 area citizens braved the 21-degree temperature to pay their respect to the President. When the Marine Band finished the National Anthem, the Chief Executive walked to the microphone and said, "For the last time as a part of this lovely ceremony, I wish you a merry Christmas and a very, very happy New Year—all of you."

With our appreciation and best wishes for a happy Christmas

John F. Kennedy   Jacqueline Kennedy

1961

CHAPTER VI

THE KENNEDYS
Art, History and Christmas

hen John F. Kennedy came to the White House in 1961, First Lady Jacqueline Bouvier Kennedy was astonished by its lack of tradition. There was no sense of history; no reminders of the great Americans who had lived there in the past. She decided to take on the task of making the world-famous building "a showcase of American Art and History." With that goal in mind she embarked on an ambitious project to restore the White House rooms to their rightful place in history and to transform the Executive Mansion into an historic museum, a repository of period furniture and art that would reflect the history of the Presidency. Despite her husband's fore-shortened administration, Mrs. Kennedy succeeded admirably in calling the nation's attention to the building's rich legacy.

1961: *The White House Ducks*
The American people have always been fascinated with the Kennedys. Volumes have been written and myriads of photographs have been taken of them. Consequently, when it came time to shop for a Christmas card idea, the subject matter had already been in the camera or the artwork was on the drawing board. It then became a simple matter of reproducing the image and gift wrapping it for the holidays.

For their first Christmas, the Kennedys gave their White House staff a photograph of the White House with Caroline's ducks in the fountain on the

Facing page: The Kennedys' first gift print to their staff in 1961. HALLMARK CARDS

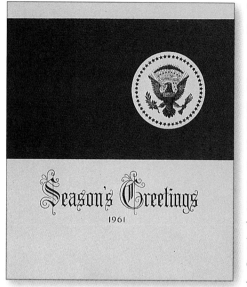

The 1961 official Presidential Christmas card.

Season's Greetings
1961

South Lawn. Chief usher J.B. West recalled, "With great glee, Mrs. Kennedy had me install a pen for the fluffy baby ducklings. Then as they grew, we acclimated them to the majestic fountain on the deep south lawn. But the ducks ate the tulips. And Charlie, the terrier, ate some of the ducks. And Caroline kept falling into the fountain, accompanied by great whoops from the tourists lined up at the fence." Before Caroline's ducks were transported to Rock Creek Park, Cecil Stoughton, the Presidents' personal photographer, recorded the familiar scene, including the fence that was put up not to keep the ducks in, but to keep Charlie out.

The photograph, taken in the spring, was given to General Ted Clifton, a military aide to the President, to pass on to the First Lady. The President and Mrs. Kennedy obviously appreciated having this memory recorded and chose to share it with their staff at Christmas. General Clifton, who had already been personally involved with Hallmark president Joyce C. Hall, asked if the card company would be willing to produce the gift print for the Kennedys. Hallmark agreed and placed the brilliantly colored photograph in a red folder, the front of which was embossed with a 50-star Presidential Seal.

The Christmas remembrance was presented to some 1,000 White House executive and military employees at an informal reception on December 13. Four-year-old Caroline Kennedy was the first of her family to arrive at the party, along with her four-year-old cousin, Stephen Smith. Oblivious to the guests, both children were intent on finding the children's tree in the Blue Room. For the first time, the tree was decorated around a theme—Tchaikovsky's *Nutcracker* ballet. To the delight of the children, the branches were laden with toy soldiers, sugar plum fairies, candy canes, lollipops, toy musical instruments, imitation mice, miniature toys and baskets of fruit.

The President and First Lady mingled and offered personal greetings to those who served them daily behind the scenes. Refreshments were served in both the State Dining Room and East Room. The Marine Band was set up in both rooms to play Christmas carols. A 68-voice choir from Howard University provided additional entertainment in the East Room.

Of special interest to all was the brief preview of the Red Room, which was being redecorated. Most of the French Empire red silk wall covering and furnishings had been donated by Secretary of the Treasury and Mrs. C. Douglas Dillon. A red and gold brocade Dolley Madison sofa and chair were grouped by the fireplace. A portrait of Thomas Jefferson hung over the mantel and a magnificent desk was placed between the two windows. While the room appeared to be complete, it was reportedly "far from finished."

Cards In; Telegrams Out

As for an official Christmas greeting card, the President had considered sending telegrams to the heads of governments around the world. Due to the high cost of transmission, though, it was agreed that the practice of sending Christmas cards should be continued. Hallmark designed a formal card, one very similar to the Eisenhower official card. On smooth white card stock with a wide green silk screen border, the Presidential Seal and the words "Season's Greetings 1961" were engraved, in gold. The sentiment read: "The President and Mrs. Kennedy wish you a Blessed Christmas and a Happy New Year."

Mrs. Kennedy's social secretary, Letitia Baldrige, ordered 800 of the official cards on December 13. As to the timing of the order, Jeannette Lee of Hallmark remarked, "When the President asks you to do something, you do it." Due to the various religions of the recipients, a New Year's greeting, without reference to Christmas, was ordered for 100 of the cards; 150 were designed to be personally signed by the President and Mrs. Kennedy. It was customary to sign cards to heads of state or the heads of government with whom there was a personal acquaintance.

By late November, the White House had not yet decided whether President Kennedy would participate at the Pageant of Peace ceremony, as every President had done since 1923. He did agree to speak, however, and the arrangements were set. Unfortunately, when the President's 73-year-old father, Joseph P. Kennedy, suffered a stroke, the First Family flew to Palm Beach to be with him. From Florida, the President proceeded with his plans to meet British Prime Minister Harold Macmillan in Bermuda. Representing the President at the Pageant of Peace on December 20 was Vice President Lyndon B. Johnson. He lit the 75-foot Washington State Douglas fir and delivered greetings to the approximately 4,000 people in attendance.

1962: The Red Room Painting

In little more than one year in the White House, Mrs. Kennedy and her Fine Arts Committee completed four rooms of her grand-scale restoration project. To stimulate the public's interest in the Executive Mansion, she also inspired the creation of the White House Historical Association. Its purpose was to research, produce and distribute educational materials of all kinds in

With our appreciation and best wishes for a happy Christmas 1962

John F. Kennedy   Jacqueline Kennedy

Edward Lehman's Red Room painting was the 1962 gift print. HALLMARK CARDS

order to preserve the history of the White House and its occupants. In 1962, the organization's first book, *The White House, An Historical Guide*, was produced in conjunction with the National Geographic Society.

On Valentines Day, the First Lady invited the nation into the State Rooms of the White House via CBS television. Weeks in advance of the one-hour special, photographs of the rooms had been sent to the press. Barbara Barnes, home furnishings editor of the *Philadelphia Bulletin*, rejected the photographs and requested that she be allowed to send Edward Lehman, an advertising-illustrator artist, to sketch some renderings of the rooms. Permission was granted.

At the White House, Lehman was drawing his initial sketches in black and white when Mrs. Kennedy came in with fresh flowers for the room and said, "You must be Edward Lehman?" They talked briefly and established an instant rapport. She showed considerable interest in his work. "In art you create interest and feeling, an impression," said the artist. "You can't beat a photograph for detail, but seldom does a photo tell the warmth and create an impression an artist can make." Later, back in his studio, Lehman finished the drawing and delivered it to the newspaper.

On February 9, Lehman's sketches were published in the *Philadelphia Bulletin* and immediately caught the attention of Mrs. Kennedy. According to the artist, shortly thereafter, Mrs. Kennedy called to express her appreciation of his fine work. Assuming that the original sketches had been done in color, she asked if she might be able to obtain them, particularly the one of the Red Room. Lehman explained that due to the process of publishing the sketches in the newspaper, the originals would be of no value. Not wanting to disappoint Mrs. Kennedy, Lehman offered to return to the White House. When he did so, he painted a 20 x 30-inch watercolor of the Red Room, which, upon completion, was sent to the Executive Mansion. The task was sheer pleasure, he reported. "My first impression of the Red Room was love at first sight. My favorite color is red and I found it to be the most stimulating of all the rooms." Lehman later gave a watercolor of the Green Room also to Mrs. Kennedy.

The President and Mrs. Kennedy were so pleased with the results, there was little doubt that the painting of the Red Room would be reproduced by Hallmark and gift wrapped as the 1962 Christmas keepsake for their staff. The 15 x 17-inch gift prints were mounted in a red folder and facsimile signed by the President and First Lady. The 2,000 mementos were handed out at the annual staff Christmas party on December 12. As a special gift, the Kennedys also gave to the Cabinet and to members of their executive staff about 50 red leather-bound copies of the *The White House, An Historic Guide*.

The Chief Executive and First Lady gave gift prints of the Red Room for Christmas, and the artist gave the original to Mrs. Kennedy as a gift. On July 27, she sent him a thank you note. "You can't imagine how much I love the watercolors of the Red and Green Rooms, or how touched I am by your giving them," she wrote. "We are giving a picture of the Red Room one to all the people who work at the White House as a Christmas present this year. That shows you a little bit how much we treasure it. How I envy you being able to do that. I thought I would try to paint some rooms, but put it off as I couldn't face the disappointment I knew my efforts would give me. Now I don't have to bother! Thank you so very much." Lehman was surprised to hear the news but pleased to receive such a personal note from the First Lady. For a man who had never had an art lesson in his life, to be recognized by an art connoisseur such as Mrs. Kennedy was "a rare thrill."

A Cecil Stoughton photograph of a February sleigh ride on the White House lawn became the subject of the 1962 official Presidential Christmas card. HALLMARK CARDS

An Action Photograph Card

For their second official Christmas card the Kennedys chose a personal photograph of Mrs. Kennedy and the children taking a sleigh ride on the South Lawn of the White House. On February 13, after an unusual Washington snowfall, the First Lady had called for the sleigh and Caroline's pony, Macaroni, to be brought in from their farm in Glen Ora, Virginia, so she could take Caroline and her playmates sleighing. With Mrs. Kennedy at the reins, the one-horse open sleigh, complete with sleigh bells, traversed the grounds. After unhitching Macaroni, she took 14-month-old John John for a ride and then led the pony up to the outside of the Oval Office for a visit with the President.

Upon arriving that morning, CBS White House correspondent George Herman saw Mrs. Kennedy and the children enjoying the newly fallen snow. In violation of an agreement with press secretary Pierre Salinger that the media were not to disrupt the children's private lives by stealing photographs of them through the fence, Herman instructed cameraman Bruce Hoertel to film the sleigh ride. This CBS "exclusive," consequently, caused quite a disturbance among the press. Not subject to the privacy embargo, the Presidents' personal photographer, Cecil Stoughton, also recognized the photographic potential on that snowy day. With an artist's eye, he captured this unusual romp in the snow in classic Currier and Ives fashion. Salinger then released an official photograph of the sleigh ride to the press so all could cover the story.

Having herself once served as a fledgling photographer for the *Washington Times-Herald*, Mrs. Kennedy was pleased to have the picture of this "moment to remember." Later that year, she and the President decided to use the wintry picture for their official White House Christmas card. This informal setting was a great departure from their previous formal card, especially considering the fervency with which the Kennedys protected the children's privacy. Mrs. Kennedy did request that it be touched up a bit, however. Russell Armentrout, an airbrush artist, attested to the fact that the photograph was "airbrushed within an inch of its life." Whereas the original picture revealed tracks in the snow, cars and a horse trailer, the Christmas card did not.

The 1962 official Christmas card was produced by Hallmark with varied messages: 1,000 "Christmas Greetings and Best Wishes for a Happy New Year" with facsimile signatures; 700 "Christmas Greetings and Best Wishes for a Happy New Year" without a signature; 100 "With Best Wishes for a Happy New Year" with facsimile signatures; 50 "With Best Wishes for a Happy New Year" without signature; and 100 "Season's Greetings" with facsimile signature.

The White House made a token payment to Hallmark of $800 for the 1,950 Christmas cards and 2,000 gift folders. Hallmark's policy had always been to take extra special care of the President's Christmas order. Their production cost ran upward of $20,000 that year. Mrs. Kennedy expressed her appreciation to Joyce C. Hall in a note dated December 7. "The President and I are more than grateful for the magnificent job Hallmark did on our Christmas Staff present and on our official Christmas card. Both of them were technically difficult to execute, and the taste and skill with which they were done will be appreciated by everyone who receives them. Our deepest thanks to all of the people who worked on these projects and our best wishes to you and your family for the holiday season."

The Pageant of Peace was held on December 17 at 5 o'clock. As fate would have it, 1962 was the only year when President Kennedy would address the nation at Christmas. With indirect reference to the Cuban missile crisis a few weeks earlier, he said:

With the lighting of this tree, which is an old ceremony in Washington and one which has been among the most important responsibilities of a good many Presidents of the United States, we initiate, in a formal way, the Christmas Season.... It is the day when we remind ourselves that man can and must live in peace with his neighbors and that it is the peacemakers who are truly blessed.... We greet each other at Christmas with some special sense of the blessings of peace. This has been a year of peril when the peace has been sorely threatened. But it has been a year when peril was faced and when reason ruled. As a result, we may talk at this Christmas, just a little bit more confidently of peace on earth, goodwill to men. As a result, the hopes of the American people are perhaps a little higher. We have much yet to do. We still need to ask that God bless everyone. But yet I think we can enter this season of goodwill with more than usual joy in our hearts....

1963: *Tragedy Changes Everything*

Mrs. Kennedy began planning for the 1963 gift print as early as February. Pamela Turnure, Mrs. Kennedy's press secretary, sent the following letter to Lehman: "The staff present this past Christmas of the reproduction of your Red Room picture was such a success, that Mrs. Kennedy is thinking of continuing the series for future Christmas presents. You have already been more than generous but I wonder if you would possibly be able to come to Washington sometime late this Spring or Summer to do additional watercolors of the newly completed Blue Room and Green Room, which has new fabric on the walls?"

The Green Room Painting

In the middle of summer Lehman personally delivered the Green Room painting to the White House. Hallmark reproduced 2,300 gift prints for the Kennedys' Christmas present for their staff. A total of 2,000 were shipped and 100 were retained by Hallmark. The White House also wanted 200 prints without the greeting and without the folder. For whatever the apparent urgency, Hallmark art director Jeannette Lee sent a telegram to Pamela Turnure that the 2,000 Green Room folders and

With our appreciation and best wishes for a happy Christmas 1963
John Kennedy   Jacqueline Kennedy

Edward Lehman's Green Room painting was the Kennedys' 1963 gift print. Mrs. Kennedy gave it to the White House staff for Christmas after the President's death.

HALLMARK CARDS

200 prints without the facsimile had left Kansas City on November 22, the day of the assassination, and would arrive at Washington's Friendship Airport at 1:38 that afternoon.

The Blue Room for 1964

In the last week of August, Ed Lehman came to the White House at the request of Mrs. Kennedy. With him was the finished painting of the Blue Room that the First Lady intended to use for the 1964 Christmas gift. Pamela Turnure met Lehman and extended an invitation from the President and First Lady to spend Christmas in Virginia at the Kennedys' newly built home near Rattlesnake Mountain. They wanted Lehman, if he was interested, to paint the First Family around their Christmas tree. The prospect was exciting and Lehman agreed. The President arrived shortly and greeted the artist with comments of admiration for the newest painting. "The Blue Room is my favorite of the public rooms," the President said. The events of November, however, ended the possibilities for either a family portrait or a 1964 Christmas gift.

Despite her personal pain, Mrs. Kennedy decided to give the gift prints of the Green Room to the White House staff as planned. "I know it will have more meaning than ever at this particular time," wrote Nancy Tuckerman, Mrs. Kennedy's social secretary. In a White House memorandum that accompanied the gift, she told the employees:

Mrs. Kennedy has asked me to express her deep appreciation to The White House Staff for their faithfulness during the past three years. She is especially touched by your untiring devotion during the past two weeks and your loyalty at this sad time has been a great source of comfort to her. Unfortunately, circumstances prevent Mrs. Kennedy from

Edward Lehman's Blue Room painting was to have been the Kennedys' 1964 gift print—the third in a planned series of State Room Christmas gifts.

thanking each of you individually. However, it is with the warmest feelings that she gives each of you the painting of the Green Room, which was chosen by The President as this year's Christmas present. It is Mrs. Kennedy's hope that this will serve as a continual reminder of The President.

Following the assassination, in January 1964, Lehman received a copy of the Green Room painting with this handwritten note: "The President was the one who chose this picture to give to the White House staff this year. He loved it so much. Thank you for making him so proud of the Christmas present he would give to those who made his life so happy the past two years. With deep appreciation, Jacqueline Kennedy."

Mrs. Kennedy also decided to go ahead with a special gift she and the President had planned to give their executive staff for Christmas—reproductions of an engraving of W.H. Bartlett's painting, *The President's House, From Washington*, mounted on a handmade French mat. Each was dated and signed, "With deepest appreciation, John F. Kennedy, Jacqueline Kennedy." A favorite of the President, the engraving had hung in his office.

The Collectors' Cards

Unlike the gift folder that was distributed, the 1963 official Christmas card was never sent. The card, *Creche in East Room, The White House*, featured a color photo of a nativity scene. Beneath the gold embossed Presidential Seal appeared the engraved message "With our wishes for a Blessed Christmas and a Happy New Year" on 1,500 facsimile-signed; "With our wishes for a Blessed Christmas and a Happy New Year" on 700 without signature; "With best wishes for a Happy New Year" on 100 with facsimile signature; and "With best wishes for a Happy New Year" on 50 without signature. [The order for 750 cards without signature was placed with Hallmark on August 23, but only 500 were shipped in November. It is not known whether the White House later reduced the order or if 250 were held in reserve.]

In a letter dated November 14, Jeannette Lee informed Presidential aide General Clifton that "within the next day or two the five hundred blank cards you wanted will be shipped directly to you" pending notification of how to proceed with the billing. A separate order for 2,000 Green Room folders and 200 prints left Kansas City on November 22 and arrived in Washington only minutes after the President's death in Dallas. Obviously, having received the 500 blank Creche Christmas cards before departing for Texas, the President and Mrs. Kennedy had begun to sign them at their convenience through November 20. Jacqueline Kennedy signed in blue ink. John Kennedy boldly signed in black ink. The next morning they flew to

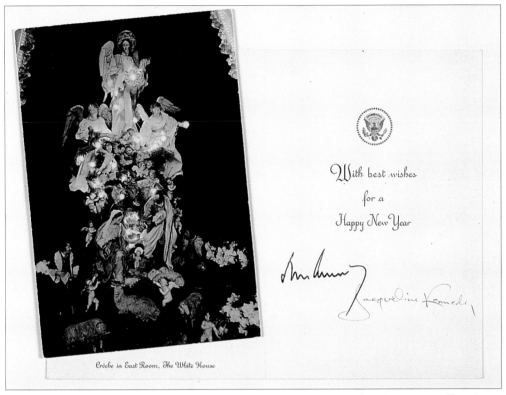

Crèche in East Room, The White House

A photograph of the creche in the East Room was the art for the 1963 official Presidential Christmas card that was never sent. Before departing for Dallas, the President and First Lady signed less than 30 of what were to become rare collector's items. HALLMARK CARDS

Texas, where they were to experience, according to Raleigh DeGeer Amyx, of American Heritage Autographs and Collectibles, an "unspeakable tragedy ... that negatively changed the history of the world." At the time, there was no official record of these authentically signed Christmas cards.

Amyx later offered an explanation. "This rendition of the 1963 Presidential Christmas card is the rarest known Christmas format ever signed by a President and First Lady.... These dual-signed Christmas cards were not located until 1985. Of the maximum 30 dual-signed cards, perhaps as many as half did not have the words imprinted 'Blessed Christmas.'" The remaining cards bore the sentiment "With Best Wishes for a Happy New Year." Once rediscovered, these rare cards "were quickly absorbed in other personal collections." The existence of these collectibles was unknown even by the Kennedy Library, he added.

The Jacqueline Kennedy Cards
Hallmark produced two other Kennedy Christmas cards in 1963. These were not *for* the Kennedys but were painted *by* Mrs. Kennedy and

Jacqueline Kennedy painted two watercolors, T*he Journey of the Magi* and *Glad Tidings*, as art for Christmas cards. Proceeds from their sale went to build what was eventually to become Washington's Kennedy Center for the Performing Arts. HALLMARK CARDS

donated to help raise $30 million for the proposed performing arts center. Officials at the center had arranged for the First Lady's art to be produced on holiday cards and distributed by Hallmark. Their design had been discussed as early as June when Hallmark's art director Jeannette Lee and design stylist Alice Ann Biggerstaff met with the First Lady at Camp David.

Lee recalled, "Her hair was in a pony tail and her bare feet were in sandals. Mrs. Kennedy was picking up after her son, John, who was taking a nap. She couldn't have been more gracious or offered a warmer welcome. We talked about her painting for a couple of hours. Alice Ann showed her how to mix her paint, sponge the background and let it dry before she put ink on it. Mrs. Kennedy was delighted.

"At the time, she was pregnant with her third child, Patrick. It was late afternoon, and she suggested that we spend the night and have dinner with her," continued Lee. "When I mentioned that my belongings were at the hotel in Washington, the First Lady offered to send someone to get them. The cabin to which we were assigned was very beautiful and rustic. Mrs. Kennedy picked us up for dinner in an old stationwagon and drove us back to her house. Together we watched President Kennedy on television from her bedroom as he delivered a speech from Bonn, Germany. After dinner we talked about the difficulties she encountered redecorating the White House. We were completely charmed by her," said Lee. "Alice and I met with her as representatives from Hallmark. She didn't have to spend the whole evening with us, but she couldn't have been nicer. It was a remarkable day for us!"

Mrs. Kennedy, who had been painting since childhood, completed the two watercolors at Squaw Island on Cape Cod in July. As her personal interpretation of the true meaning of Christmas, one represented the three wise men on their way to Bethlehem and was entitled *The Journey of the Magi*. The other, *Glad Tidings*, depicted a golden-haired angel announcing the birth of Christ. Both works carry the initials "JBK" at the bottom.

These original tempera paintings are said to have been the first greeting cards ever designed for sale by a member of the First Family. Hallmark's Joyce C. Hall said of the project, "We are pleased to ... cooperate in this fashion with the National Cultural Center. Mrs. Kennedy's work is in excellent taste." The originals now reside at the Smithsonian Institution.

Shortly before the disaster in Dallas, Jacqueline Kennedy was asked to write a Christmas greeting as an introduction to a story about "Christmas at the White House" for the December 31 issue of *Look* magazine. In retrospect her message was insightful:

> *Even though the White House is often the center of national attention—a public building—during the Christmas season it is the home of an American family sharing in the anticipation of the joy of this festival. The world around us is a complicated and troubled place. But through Christmas, we keep unbroken contact with the simple message of the redemption and love that God sent into the world so many years ago. To many of us, Christmas has a deep religious significance. To all of us, it celebrates the most profound hopes for the comradeship of man.*

With our warm wishes for a joyous Christmas
and a New Year full of happiness,

Lyndon B. Johnson

Lady Bird Johnson
December 1964

CHAPTER VII

THE JOHNSONS
Presidential Plantings on Parchment

The tragedy that occurred in their beloved state of Texas on November 22, 1963, changed forever the lives of Lyndon and Lady Bird Johnson. One hour and 39 minutes after the death of John F. Kennedy, Lyndon Baines Johnson, aboard *Air Force One*, was sworn in as the 36th President. From that turmoil, through the transition, the ensuing days were filled with shock and sadness, but life had to go on. Protocol was followed to keep the White House on track, even when emotions would have led the primary figures to do otherwise.

1963: Last-Minute Arrangements

On November 27, Angier Biddle Duke, the Chief of Protocol at the State Department, sent a memorandum to the new President: "Unless you and Mrs. Johnson prefer not to do so this year, I recommend that you send holiday greeting cards to certain groups of top level government officials." He suggested that cards be sent to all foreign chiefs of state with whom the United States had relations, foreign ministers and heads of government that the President had met. He specifically mentioned the top ranking officials of delegations that had attended the Kennedy funeral. Walter Jenkins, LBJ's chief of staff, approved the recommendation on December 1 and notified Duke to forward the appropriate lists to the White House.

Hallmark had just finished shipping the remaining Kennedy Creche Christmas cards to the White House on November 22. Now, the card company was called upon again to produce an official Christmas card for a second President in the same year. The major difference was the emotional climate under which they worked to provide a card "for such a time as this." The simple official card was printed on textured white card stock with a blank embossed Presidential Seal and red silk screen band along the bottom.

Perhaps, when reflecting on a similarly late request from the Kennedys in 1961, designers at Hallmark decided to borrow the 1961 sentiment for the Johnsons' first card: "The President and Mrs. Johnson wish you a Blessed Christmas and a Happy New Year." A second message read: "The President and Mrs. Johnson extend Season's Greetings and Best Wishes for the New Year." Due to the devastating circumstances that caused its creation, the undated 1963 card was historically forgotten for 30 years. It was not until late in 1995 that Christmas card collector C.L. Arbelbide came upon it and, through the research of Claudia Anderson, senior archivist at the Lyndon B. Johnson Library, identified the red-bordered card as the first official Christmas greeting of President and Mrs. Johnson.

Dated December 16, 1963, a memo found at the LBJ Library listed the groups to whom the Christmas cards were sent. Included on the list were heads of state of foreign countries and a few other high officials whom the President had met, chiefs of mission in Washington, American ambassadors abroad, U.S. Senators and Representatives, Governors, the Supreme Court, the Cabinet and "Little Cabinet" members, and top officials of various independent government agencies. Newspaper clippings dated December 19, 1963, from the *Washington Post*, which pictured the Johnson card, and from the *New York Times* also confirmed the existence of the undated 1963 Christmas card.

Since the assassination, the Johnsons had received thousands of holiday messages from home and abroad. Acknowledgments were not ordinarily sent in response to every card or letter. Ivan Sinclair, an assistant in the Correspondence Office, requested that Walter Jenkins make some decision regarding Christmas cards, however. It would be most expedient, Sinclair suggested, to issue across-the-board acknowledgments rather than trying to be selective or pursuing missing addresses.

Forthwith, Sanford Fox of the White House Social Entertainment Office was instructed to ask Hallmark art director Jeannette Lee to design an appropriate card to express the President's appreciation. A complimentary card, smaller than the Christmas card, was made on textured white card stock with natural deckle enhanced by a small, blank embossed Presidential Seal and green silk screen border. The message read: "Thank you for your holiday greeting And best wishes For your happiness in the New Year," signed "The President and Mrs. Johnson." Approximately 30,000 of these Presidential thank you cards were mailed out after the first of the year.

The State Department approached President Johnson only five days after he entered office to learn his wishes about a holiday card. The Johnsons sent this simple greeting card for their first White House Christmas. HALLMARK CARDS

To mark the end of a month of official mourning for John F. Kennedy and the beginning of the Christmas holidays, a candlelight memorial service for the slain President was held at the Lincoln Memorial on December 22, just hours before the Pageant of Peace began. In his remarks at the memorial service, President Johnson said, "On this eve of Christmas, in this time of grief and unity, of sadness and continuity, let there be for all people in need the light of an era of new hope and time of new resolve. Let the light shine and let this Christmas be our thanksgiving and our dedication."

Moving later to the Ellipse for the Pageant of Peace ceremonies and the lighting of the 71-foot red spruce from West Virginia, the President spoke about the transition. "Tonight we come to the end of the season of great national sorrow, and the beginning of the season of great eternal joy. We mourn our great President, John F. Kennedy, but he would have us go on. While our spirits cannot be light, our hearts need not be heavy.... On this occasion one year ago, our beloved President John F. Kennedy reminded us that Christmas is the day when all of us dedicate our thoughts to others, when we are all reminded that mercy and compassion are the really enduring virtues, when all of us show, by small deeds and by large, that it is more blessed to give than to receive...."

Surprise Party

The following day, the President's simple suggestion for sharing was demonstrated by a kind of Texas hospitality characteristic of the new administration. About noon, the impetuous Lyndon Johnson decided he would invite members of Congress who were still in town to a 5 o'clock reception at the White House. Bess Abell, Mrs. Johnson's social secretary, exclaimed to the White House staff: "Hold on to your hat, President Johnson has just invited all of Congress and their wives over to the White House this afternoon ... What can we do?" Some White House staffers declared it just couldn't be

President and Mrs. Johnson, Lynda Bird (left) and Luci Baines in a family portrait they gave to close friends and employees for Christmas in 1963. LYNDON B. JOHNSON LIBRARY

done. But Lady Bird Johnson—who had been schooled over the years to expect the unexpected from her husband—as well as those who had worked previously for the Johnsons, knew it could and would be done. One of them replied, "You just move ahead and do the impossible. He likes 'can do' people around him, and he expects you to do what he asks."

Immediately, the kitchen staff began making finger sandwiches and arranging cookies and fruitcake on trays. Concocting tubs of punch and making urns of coffee, the butlers enlisted reinforcements from other divisions of government to help. Gone was the black mourning crepe that had been draped over the doorways and around the chandeliers. The White House came alive as florists replaced crepe with holly, wreaths and fresh flowers. The Blue Room was transformed by the addition of a decorated 12-foot balsam fir from Vermont and a lighted nativity scene. With snow blowing outside, the fires crackling in every fireplace created the perfect setting for the most impromptu Christmas party in the history of the White House.

About 200 members of Congress battled the elements to come. Some had flown back from their homes to cast their vote on the crucial foreign aid bill before Congress, while others circled the skies above Washington in bad weather—landing too late to vote, but in time for the reception. The President and Mrs. Johnson received their guests in the Blue Room in full view of the National Christmas Tree. It was undoubtedly one of the happier moments for the new administration. Standing on a gold-cut velvet chair in the State Dining Room, the genial host greeted his guests with the colorful phrase, "You have labored through the vineyard and plowed through the snow."

The reception came off like a charm. The next morning, on December 24, the House of Representatives passed the foreign aid bill. By 9:30, the First Family was headed for Austin and Christmas at the ranch. On Christmas

Day, 50 to 75 members of the press appeared at their doorstep to report to the world on the new First Family's holiday. Even though dinner was ready to be served, the President conducted a press tour of the house and gave all the reporters ash trays as gifts.

1964: *The Willow Watercolor*

By the middle of May 1964, Bess Abell was thinking ahead to Christmas. She inquired of Gen. C.V. Clifton about the possibility of his friend at Hallmark, Joyce C. Hall, making an offer to produce the card. "I am sure that Mr. Hall will be delighted to do the Christmas cards for us," replied Gen. Clifton.

American Greetings Corporation, in Cleveland, was also introduced into the Presidential Christmas card arena at this time. Abell received a letter from Raymond Nathan, of Ruder and Finn Incorporated, who affirmed that his client, American Greetings, "would be honored if they could have the privilege of supplying without charge, the greeting cards to be used by the President and Mrs. Johnson this year." In fact, Gen. Clifton confirmed that Ruder and Finn had tried on behalf of their client to "get the contract or part of it" for the previous three years. Irving I. Stone, president of American Greetings, had been a strong supporter of the administration and had contributed heavily to the Democratic National Campaign Committee. Cognizant of Hallmark's generosity over the past 11 years, Clifton suggested the situation be handled very delicately.

President Johnson decided to go with American Greetings Corporation. On July 9, Harry H. Stone, executive vice president of American Greetings, and Ed Pakish, his assistant manager of creative art, met at the White House with Mrs. Johnson's social secretary. Speaking for the First Lady, she suggested that the artwork somehow incorporate the mansion and its historical landscaping, specifically the commemorative trees planted by past Presidents. The Johnsons had lived in Washington since 1934 and had always appreciated the beautification project started by Thomas Jefferson in what had become known as the "President's Park."

The greatest challenge would be to get the right kind of artwork for Mrs. Johnson, who liked trees combined with softness. Of six artists submitting numerous samples, staff design consultant Robert H. Laessig seemed to have just the right touch. Having painted flowers for American Greetings for nearly 16 years, Laessig had won several national prizes for his work. Pakish now invited him to go to the White House to get inspiration for the task. Together they viewed the White House lawn from roof tops and every vantage point, taking pictures and making sketches of the landscape. Laessig believed that nature was only the beginning for his work. He refused to duplicate an object as seen by the eye. "Anyone can do that," he said. "I have to put in something of myself," he told the Cleveland *Plain Dealer*. "There has to be a mystery to what you see."

Among the three paintings Laessig produced for the President was a watercolor in which he created a Southwestern willow—the tree the Johnsons would plant on the South Lawn later that fall—set against the backdrop of the White House. Exercising his artistic license, Laessig imagined it as a mighty oak, the way future Presidents would view it in later years. As a center of interest, the artist added two girls to represent the Johnson daughters, Lynda and Luci, and the two Johnson beagles, Him and Her. Mrs. Johnson suggested only minor adjustments to the "woebegone" tree on the right, but was very pleased with his realistic style and the softness of color. In Laessig's judgment, "it was not bad."

American Greetings reproduced 4,500 of the paintings on a 14 x 18-inch textured paper. The gift was presented in a folder with a blind embossed Presidential Seal on the cover and again inserted into a white envelope with cardboard stiffeners for protection. A red sateen ribbon and a large gold foil Presidential Seal completed the outer packaging. To accompany each print, Mrs. Johnson enclosed a personal message penned on parchment by Sanford Fox. In 1964 it read: "One of our happiest family times was the planting of two oaks—a Darlington and a willow—on the White House lawn in October, 1964. Beginning with Thomas Jefferson, thirty Presidential families have followed this tradition. At this season when friends and families occupy our thoughts, we hope—with this watercolor—your thoughts may turn to the passage from James Russell Lowell, 'Each year to ancient friendships add a ring, As to an oak....' "

By this time the White House staff had grown to about 1,500 and now included the White House Communications Agency, and the Bergstrom AFB and Marine helicopter pilots assigned to the White House and Camp David. The Social Office sent each guest a memorandum and card they could exchange for their gift print from the President and Mrs. Johnson at the annual Christmas party. What a surprise for each recipient of the commemorative print to find it gracing the December 28 cover of *Newsweek* as a backdrop for a portrait of Mrs. Johnson.

Lyndon Johnson was a giver of many kinds of gifts and gadgets. "No matter how much planning ahead we do," Mrs. Johnson wrote in her *White House Diary*, "about five or six days before Christmas, Lyndon gets frantic, thinking about all the things he wants to do for all the people he loves, and heaping work on all those around him, and issuing orders, 'Recheck the names! Plan gifts! Get it done!' I know this results in many midnight hours for secretaries, merchants, picture framers, parcel post deliverers—and me.

But after more than thiry years I, at least, should know what to expect." Among the gifts the Johnsons gave to about 200 of their executive staff was a framed French-matted engraving by Robert Cruikshank entitled *The President's Levee of All Creation Going to the White House.* The cherished gift was personalized, signed and dated by the President and First Lady.

For their second official Christmas card, President and Mrs. Johnson chose a small black and white rendering of Laessig's painting of the willow oak. The Christmas card was designed with different messages. "With our wishes for a joyous Christmas and a Happy New Year" appeared on 2,904 facsimile-signed cards and 225 unsigned cards. "Season's Greetings and best wishes for the New Year" was ordered for 175 cards without a signature. The President continued to acknowledge those who had sent him a holiday greeting; 25,003 prints of the card designed by Laessig carried the message "Thank you for your holiday greeting and best wishes for happiness in the New Year."

Janice Ingersoll, who had worked in the Social Entertainment Office since the Eisenhower Administration, was the keeper of the Christmas card list. Said Bess Abell: "As far as I was concerned, Jan was a miracle person.... She knew who was married, divorced or had moved away, and she knew how to get anyone's address. After the President had given his input, she put the Christmas card list together."

All of the staff at American Greetings—artists, writers, lithographers, production people and management—had taken great pride in being able to design and produce the 1964 official Christmas card and gift print for the President of the United States. At a special White House ceremony, the executive vice president, Harry H. Stone, design consultant Robert Laessig and art director Ed Pakish presented the original painting for the gift print to the First Lady upstairs in the living quarters at the White House. Mrs. Johnson had liked the painting so much, Mr. Pakish said, that she wanted it for the ranch in Texas.

On December 18, when the President flipped the switch to light the National Christmas Tree, the 5,000 red and white lights gleamed in the night. The beautifully shaped 72-foot white spruce from New York's Adirondacks was surrounded by 53 other trees, each representing a state or territory. Extending best wishes, President Johnson addressed the crowd of 7,000 and spoke optimistically of peace: "At this Christmas season of 1964, we can think of broader and brighter horizons than any who have lived before these times. For there is rising in the sky of the age a new star—the star of peace...."

On December 23, President Johnson also sent Christmas greetings to the American troops in Southeast Asia:

You who carry freedom's banner in Vietnam are engaged in a war that is undeclared—yet tragically real. It is a war of terror where the aggressor moves in the secret shadows of the nights. Murder and kidnapping and deception are his tools. Subversion and conquest are his goals.... But your sacrifices are known and honored in American towns and cities more familiar to you, for you are meeting your country's commitment to a world of justice....

1965: *The White House in Winter*

By May, work had already begun on the 1965 Christmas gift print. Continuing the theme of Presidential plantings, Robert Laessig chose to focus on the Jefferson mounds on the South Lawn of the White House. When John Adams moved into the mansion in 1800, it reportedly was surrounded by barren land strewn with rubbish. Thomas Jefferson moved in the following year and developed a landscape plan that included tree-covered mounds on the South Lawn to provide privacy. Each new family that occupied the White House left its own mark on the landscape, and the barren expanse eventually became a "President's Park."

Having visited the White House only in the spring and summer, Laessig had to imagine the two tree-covered mounds as a winter scene. He confessed, "I never even thought about the history. I was more concerned about getting the trees and landscaping right." Given photographs of the dogs, he figured that they were important and added people taking them for a walk. When Mrs. Johnson received the nostalgic watercolor, she wrote him, "The President and I appreciate your lovely Christmas greeting. Seeing your card made me wonder if you had drawn family and home into the background of your Christmas scene."

Each gift print of Laessig's paintings for the First Family was accompanied by a parchment scroll—the only way to learn about the Presidential plantings. In 1965, it stated: "First to develop a plan for landscaping of the White House was our third President Thomas Jefferson. In his attempt to make the terrain of the South Lawn more interesting, he directed the placement of the two tree-covered mounds which slope gracefully toward the center of the President's Park. This winter scene of the White House is viewed from the East Mound." American Greetings produced 2,760 gift prints of the nostalgic *Winter at the White House* scene. Because of a high percentage of spoilage in production plus a request for all additional prints to be sent to the White House in January 1966, there were no prints held in reserve that year. The 950 White House employees were presented their gift at a staff Christmas party on December 17. A second engraving, entitled *Washington From the President's House* by W. H. Bartlett, framed with a French mat, was given to 200 of the executive White House staff.

Artist Robert Laessig focused on the Jefferson mound on the South Lawn in winter for the 1965 Christmas card and gift print. AMERICAN GREETINGS

Winter at the White House was also used as the 1965 official Christmas card. American Greetings printed it with different messages. "With our wishes for a Joyous Christmas and a Happy New Year" appeared on 2,000 facsimile signed cards and 200 unsigned cards. "Season's Greetings and Best Wishes for the New Year" was ordered for 200 unsigned cards. "Thank you for your holiday greeting and best wishes for happiness in the New Year" appeared on 27,800 facsimile signed reciprocating cards.

On December 17, President Johnson illuminated the 6,250 lights on the Nation's Tree, an 85-foot blue spruce donated by the White Mountain Apaches of Arizona. The crowd of several thousand listened to the President's words:

> *As in other Christmas seasons in the past, our celebration this year is tempered by the absence of brave men from their homes and from their loved ones. We would not have it so. We have not sought the combat in which they are engaged. We have hungered for not one foot of another's territory, nor for the life of a single adversary. Our sons patrol the hills of Vietnam at this hour because we have learned that though men cry "Peace, peace," there is no peace to be gained ever by yielding to aggression. That lesson has been learned by a hundred generations. The guarantors of peace on earth have been those prepared to make sacrifices in its behalf.*

1966: The North Portico

A night view of the North Portico of the White House would be the third in a series of Laessig watercolors of Presidential plantings. The 1966 selection depicted the tall American elm planted by President Wilson in 1913. The accompanying parchment read: "Tall and graceful, with fan-shaped crowns of finely subdividing branches, the American elm has long

The Johnsons' 1966 Christmas card featured the American elm planted by President Woodrow Wilson in 1913. AMERICAN GREETINGS

been favored as an ornamental, stately shade tree. A few days before Christmas 1913, President Woodrow Wilson took a moment from the affairs of State to plant this symbol of peace and serenity which today shades the North Portico of the White House."

A total of 3,000 prints were lithographed in six different colors on high-quality text paper and enclosed in a folder embossed with the Presidential Seal. The gifts were presented to the White House staff at a party on December 15. The executive staff also received a French matted engraving, *President's House* by August Kollner.

The official Christmas card kept the same design as the gift print. American Greetings printed a total of 2,400 of the cards with Christmas as well as nonsectarian verses, as had been requested in the past. The administration discontinued the large order for thank you cards of previous years.

Early in the afternoon of the 15th, the East Room was the scene of a holiday reception for 125 recuperating Vietnam veterans from five Washington hospitals. Serving as hostesses were the Johnsons' daughter Lynda Bird; Muriel Humphrey, wife of Vice President Hubert Humphrey; and the wives of the Cabinet. President Johnson, who stopped by to salute the men, some on stretchers and many on crutches, said that "no guests had ever been more welcome in the White House.... I hope you have a good Christmas," he told them, "You deserve it more than anyone I know."

Rounding out his busy schedule that day, the Chief Executive ushered in the Christmas season at the ceremony for the Pageant of Peace. The 65-foot red fir from California's Sierra Nevada Mountains blazed in the glory of its 2,500 red and yellow lights. Speaking on the 175th anniversary of the Bill of Rights, the President greeted the American people in a somber tone.

Exactly 175 years ago today America sent another light into the world. That light—and that promise—was America's Bill of Rights. Few documents in all the history of freedom have ever so illuminated the paths of men. Today, the light of that great charter guides us yet.... I know, as you know, that we face an uncertain future.... Here at home, in our own land, more than 20 million Negroes still yearn for the rights and the dignity that the rest of us take for granted..... In Vietnam, the tide of battle has turned. No one can say just how long that war will last. But we can say that aggression has been blunted, and that peace, with honor, will surely follow. The months ahead will not be easy ones. They will require great sacrifice, patience, understanding and tolerance from each of us....

1967: *The Blue Room Tree*

Much planning and forethought went into Christmas when the Johnsons lived in the Executive Mansion. This was especially so in 1967 with daughter Lynda Bird's wedding scheduled for December 9. That year the First Lady decided to depart from Presidential plantings and suggested an interior painting of the Christmas tree that traditionally graced the Blue Room. As he had done each year, Robert Laessig prepared several rough drafts of scenes appropriate for the gift print and official card. Mrs. Johnson finally settled on the Christmas Tree in the Blue Room for both the gift print and Christmas card. She also requested that the artist complete a winter scene she particularly liked and used that print as a special Christmas gift.

The White House ordered 2,600 official Christmas cards and 3,000 lithographs of the Blue Room. The accompanying parchment message read: "The first White House Christmas tree was introduced in 1889 by President Benjamin Harrison, a custom he asked 'be followed by every family in the land.' It is the hope of the President and Mrs. Johnson that the lights which blaze on this tree and the trees throughout our nation rekindle the ancient promise of the Christmas season, 'Peace on earth, goodwill to men.'" The print and scroll were enclosed in a blue envelope and secured with a gold ribbon and Presidential Seal. Executive staff members again received the French matted engraving Mrs. Johnson had selected for them. This year it was *Mill's Colossal Equestrian Statue of General Andrew Jackson*, signed and personalized for each recipient.

Because of Lynda Bird's wedding, Christmas came early to the White House in 1967. Decorators, florists and technicians mixed bridal white with Christmas reds and greens, turning the historic mansion into a winter wedding wonderland.

"The Christmas decorating is done so exquisitely here that I try to fill the house with people who would enjoy it," the First Lady was quoted in the *Washington Post*. Of particular interest to all who visited that year was the 30-piece, 18th-century antique Baroque creche, valued at $25,000, that was presented to the White House by Mr. and Mrs. Charles W. Engelhard, Jr., of Far Hills, New Jersey. Mrs. Johnson received it at a ceremony on December 15.

Artist Robert Laessig's Blue Room card and gift print painting showcased the official White House Christmas tree in 1967.
AMERICAN GREETINGS

Later that day, President Johnson greeted the 4,500 attending the 44th annual lighting of the National Christmas Tree, a 70-foot balsam fir from Vermont's Green Mountain National Forest. He referred in his message to the military activities in Southeast Asia. "Today, a young soldier, in the prime of his life, was killed in the central highlands of Vietnam.... Half a million brave American men—who love their country and are willing to die for their land—will be celebrating Christmas in a strange land, surrounded by the weapons of war.... A part of every American heart will be with them."

Christmas 1967 was the first one in seven years that the Johnsons spent at the White House. "I know that my husband prefers to be in Texas," the First Lady said, "but the 'family council' decided that this time they would gather in the White House." The family had increased by two: the President's first grandchild, 6-month-old Patrick Lyndon Nugent, and Lynda's new husband, Chuck Robb.

1968: The White House in Spring

As early as May 1967 Bess Abell was already suggesting to American Greetings an idea for the following year's Christmas print. She related that Mrs. Johnson would like to have a spring or summer scene encompassing the South Lawn looking beyond to the monuments, with the color and the species of the flowers as true to life as possible. It was the view enjoyed by the First Lady from her second floor bedroom window on the south side of the house. Robert Laessig came to Washington in the spring and drew several sketches. Again the artist was able to so please the First Family that they chose two scenes, one for the Christmas print and the other for their official card, something they had not done previously.

The 1968 Christmas print was a nostalgic springtime view from the South Portico of the White House. The First Lady recalled that, "this beautiful setting in the midst of the rushing city" provided her with "a constant serenity." In an article in the December 1968 issue of *McCalls*, she further said, "Calm has followed crisis on so many occasions…. In any season, this view, frosted with the luminous glow surrounding the Jefferson Memorial and Washington Monument across the Ellipse at evening, always restores a sense of peace and proportion in turbulent times."

The White House ordered 3,680 Christmas prints of the watercolor. The parchment scroll that accompanied the gift to the White House staff, associates and friends read: "We have loved sharing the history and beauty of the White House these past five years. One of the memories we carry with us is the view from the South Portico, across the grounds to those great white memorials that rise between the White House and the Potomac River. The Washington Monument symbolizes the pride and steadfast faith of the American people in the principles of the founders of our nation. The

Washington from the South Portico was Mrs. Johnson's favorite view, especially in the springtime. It became the subject of the 1968 gift print. AMERICAN GREETINGS

For their last official Christmas card, the Johnsons chose another Robert Laessig winter view of the South Portico. AMERICAN GREETINGS

Jefferson Memorial commemorates our strength in the democratic ideals. May this season refresh our spirit and devotion to the eternal goal of peace on earth, goodwill to men." The White House Executive staff received the last of the French matted engraving series, *The President's House, Washington,* by H. Brown.

For their official Christmas card, President and Mrs. Johnson chose a winter scene by Robert Laessig depicting the South Portico of the White House as seen through the branches of a snow-laden fir tree. The Christmas verse on 2,300 of them read: "With our wishes for a joyous Christmas and a Happy New Year." Another 300 were printed with the nonsectarian sentiment "Season's Greetings and Best Wishes For the New Year." As in the past, the card was sent to some 1,500 dignitaries at home and abroad.

As chief stylist of American Greetings, Robert Laessig experienced great satisfaction from designing seven different images for Christmas gift prints and official cards for the President and First Lady. No other artist has had that distinction. Reflecting on this honor, he said humbly, "I'm pleased that I was chosen to do it, but so much depended on where you were at the time. I wasn't always satisfied with my paintings, but I painted to try to please the First Lady." To express his appreciation for that privilege, the "posy painter" sent Mrs. Johnson an original painting of wildflowers.

At his last lighting ceremony of the National Christmas Tree on December 16, President Johnson spoke indirectly of the War on Povery with which he had kicked off his full term in office; its last two years had been painfully punctuated by urban unrest and rioting. He said, "We have had to preserve a dream; to work day and night to close the gap between promise and reality, so that all would have equal opportunity to fulfill the talents that God granted them; and to do so in an environment which protected the rights of all, including the right to expect that the law will be obeyed by everyone among us. We cannot say that we have triumphed in this endeavor. But we have begun—at long last."

A Second Surprise Party

At the last minute before the family's last Christmas Eve in the White House, Mrs. Johnson decided to throw a party. With the Johnsons' short-notice first Christmas party now a faded memory, Mrs. Johnson said of this one: "Never was a party at the White House put together so quickly and informally! I made most of the calls myself. By 4, all the fires were burning, and the spirit of Christmas and real joy was as strong as I have ever felt it." She invited longtime Washington friends, their children and grandchildren.

After the guests left, the Johnsons adjourned to the Yellow Oval Room in the family's quarters. There, hanging on the mantel, were personalized Christmas stockings, each illustrating important events in their lives. The symbols on the President's stocking included the Presidential flag, a scroll listing his public offices, a shape of Texas, a picture of the LBJ ranch, his horse Old Blue, *Air Force One*, the National Christmas Tree, the dove of peace and his dogs, Him and Yuki. "My sentimental Lynda had put small gifts for Christmas morning in all of them," Mrs. Johnson said.

The party came at the end of what the First Lady described as "this most awful year." Yet some good things had happened as well during 1968. Unemployment was at a 15-year low; the captured crew of the *Pueblo* had returned home; and three astronauts had circled the moon. While both sons-in-law were in Vietnam that holiday, both were safe and spent the day together near Da Nang. By telephone the First Family talked with Charles Robb of the Marine Corps and Patrick Nugent of the Air Force.

"Christmas of 1968 was a particular time of joy for us," according to Mrs. Johnson. "There was a special feeling of closeness to family and friends, and reflections on jobs done with heart and hope along with expectations about the time to come. We were looking forward to going home to the ranch with its fields of wildflowers to renew us—and for Lyndon to start afresh. He eagerly looked forward to having time for family and self and, perhaps, to teaching again and helping young people prepare for their future. That Christmas, our last in the White House and in Washington, was a glorious chapter in our lives that was drawing to a close. So many changes had taken place while we lived there. Truly, we counted our blessings."

THE NIXONS
White House as Open House

Before we came to the White House, our friends always looked to us to see what surprises we were going to give them at Christmas, with our decorations, our 'open house' party. We've always tried to make Christmas special and different. At the White House we enjoy giving surprises, too," admitted Mrs. Nixon in a *House and Garden* interview. "Because we want to share the house with as many people as possible, we've started a tradition of candlelight tours." Among other special surprises Richard and Pat Nixon shared with the nation at Christmas were the rare and authentic acquisitions for the State Rooms, the televised specials of holiday festivities and decorations, the exterior lighting of the White House, and the first-ever Christmas gingerbread house. At Christmas, the Nixons, more than any previous First Family, allowed their private home to become the most public house in America.

Candles and TV Cameras

Their first Christmas in the White House, President and Mrs. Nixon began candlelight tours of the mansion. With so many people visiting the nation's capital at Christmastime, the Open House offered an opportunity to enjoy the President's house as well. Chandeliers were dimmed, fires were set ablaze in the fireplaces and music was played throughout the house. The First Lady recalled that from their private quarters, they'd "hear people

Facing page: Gilbert Stuart's George Washington, the first in a series of Nixon portraits of Presidents, was the gift print for 1969. HALLMARK CARDS

Julie Nixon Eisenhower plays tour guide for CBS-TV's Charles Kuralt and Marya McLaughlin and the rest of the nation on the Christmas Eve 1971 special, "Christmas at the White House." NIXON PRESIDENTIAL MATERIALS PROJECT/NATIONAL ARCHIVES

breaking into song ... that's so nice, to know they are enjoying it," she told a *House and Garden* writer. "I suppose of all the places we've spent Christmas, the White House must be our favorite," the First Lady continued. "To be in this historical house with the memories of all the other families who've been here means so much—and to realize that we, in our way, are making a moment of history, too."

While becoming a popular Nixon tradition, the candlelight tours could be enjoyed only by those able to travel to Washington. For the rest of the nation there were the TV specials. "Christmas at the White House" aired on Christmas Eve in 1969 and featured an interview of Mrs. Nixon and daughter Tricia by *Time* magazine reporter Bonnie Angelo. Mrs. Nixon discussed family traditions and White House decorations, reminisced about Christmases past and, like all Americans, hoped for true "peace on earth." Shortly before Christmas of 1971, NBC aired "December 6, 1971: A Day in the Presidency," with correspondent John Chancellor as commentator. On Christmas Eve, Charles Kuralt and CBS television crews, escorted by the Nixons' daughter Julie Nixon Eisenhower, went where tourists can't—to the family quarters—for a candid visit with the President and the rest of the family. When Kuralt asked about a favorite Christmas, the Chief Executive replied, "Christmas is always a rich and a happy day.... For me, it's a time of children, a time of family, a time of music and a time of wonderful Christmas decorations."

The First Lady's Agenda

While the President's early months in office were devoted to restoring peace to the Far East and bringing American troops back home, Mrs. Nixon quietly went about a major restoration project at the White House. With a million and a half tourists visiting the mansion each year, and with countless millions looking in by way of television, she felt a responsibility to keep the house in perfect condition for the "guests." Many areas had simply been worn out since Mrs. Kennedy's renovation in 1962. "Dick and I want this to be the most beautiful house in America," she informed newly appointed White House curator Clement E. Conger, according to the *Providence Sunday Journal*. Together, the First Lady and her curator embarked on a "campaign that would restore the White House to its golden age, the first quarter of the 19th century."

Mrs. Nixon acquired things for the White House that others had not. Gilbert Stuart's portraits of George Washington and Dolley Madison were two paintings that were rescued when the British burned the White House in 1814. Dolley, wife of President James Madison, refused to flee until she was certain that the canvas bearing Washington's portrait had been removed for safekeeping. Her own portrait was also snatched from the flames, though without fanfare.

During the Nixon Administration, Conger located the portrait of Dolley Madison in the basement of the Pennsylvania Academy of Fine Arts. So thrilled was Mrs. Nixon that she persuaded the Academy's board to loan it to the White House. In 100 years the Academy had never permitted any piece to go on loan outside Philadelphia. Conger pointed out that "Dolley Madison saved George Washington and Pat Nixon saved Dolley."

Of the 14 First Lady original portraits that were missing when the Nixons moved to the White House, seven were acquired during their administration, as well as six original portraits of former Presidents. Many American paintings and sculpture pieces, nine period chandeliers, 13 period rugs, three gilded beechwood chairs from the Monroe era and several pieces of Duncan Phyfe furniture were all added during the Nixon years. Conger noted that the 10 pieces of the Monroe furniture found in the basement of the Philadelphia Museum was "the greatest retrieval of White House furniture in the history of the White House."

According to the *Providence Sunday Journal*, White House historian William Seale noted that "The Nixon era was the greatest single period of collecting in White House history. The great collection of White House Americana today is the long shadow of Mrs. Nixon. The impulse, the idea and the energy were hers."

1969: First President Graces a First Christmas

An admirer of his great predecessors, President Nixon was presented with the idea of giving a reproduction of a Presidential portrait to the staff for Christmas. The first year it was Gilbert Stuart's famous portrait of George Washington. The portrait was photographed by *National Geographic* and sent to Hallmark, which produced 3,500 mementos for the President. Hallmark framed the colored print with a linenlike mat on which a small gold plaque bore the words: "George Washington by Gilbert Stuart, The White House Collection from The President and Mrs. Nixon, Christmas 1969." The keepsake portrait was enclosed in a red velour folder with the blank embossed Presidential Coat of Arms on the front. A parchment frontispiece with gold lettering described the painting and protected the portrait. It noted, "The White House Collection's portrait of George Washington hangs in the President's Oval Office. It is a replica by Gilbert Stuart of his 'Athenaeum' portrait, the best known likeness of our first President. It was painted in 1796, the last year of Washington's Administration." The gift was signed, "With our best wishes, The President and Mrs. Nixon At Christmas 1969."

For their official Christmas card, the Nixons used a blank embossed engraving of a south view of the White House, a design submitted by James Hamil of Hallmark. The elegant creation was enhanced by a red and gold lithographed border. Of the 40,000 cards printed by Hallmark, 37,000 were sent to members of Congress, government officials, governors, foreign ambassadors, heads of state, business executives and friends.

Before the first guest arrived for the first Nixon Christmas party, the White House, under Mrs. Nixon's personal supervision, had been dressed in all of its holiday fin-

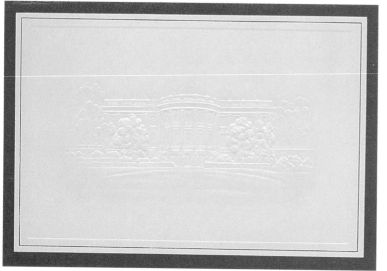

The 1969 Christmas card featured a south view of the White House.
HALLMARK CARDS

ery. More notably decorated than in previous years was the Great Hall, where the main White House tree was a 19-foot fir covered with huge ornate ornaments representing each state's flower.

The most spectacular sight was the gilded chandelier in the State Dining Room, laden with holly and red electrified candles and an enormous red bow. Gone were the portraits of Daniel Webster and Martin Van Buren to make room for the two holly-filled gilded wall sconces taken out of storage and returned to their original position adjoining the six other matching sconces in the room. In the State Dining Room a first-ever, three-foot, 45-pound gingerbread house was on display. Created by White House assistant chef Hans Raffert, it would be followed for each of the next 23 Christmases by a different Hansel and Gretel confectionery castle.

For the first time in 25 years, green wreaths and red candles were hung in the 16 windows facing Pennsylvania Avenue. "We love to decorate; you can't overdo at Christmas," Mrs. Nixon was quoted in an *Evening Star* account of her first White House tour for the press. Some who viewed the decorations described them as "the most colorful in many years."

On December 16, the President was scheduled to speak at the Pageant of Peace on the Ellipse. Prior to his arrival, park police had arrested eight adults and one juvenile for disorderly conduct. In contrast to the 65-foot Norway spruce donated by the town of Glen Falls, New York, the hecklers had brought their own tree, decorated it with soft drink cans and tin foil peace emblems. After the President began his remarks, the group of 50 to 200 hecklers, mostly students from the D.C. Moratorium Committee to End the War in Vietnam, shouted "Peace Now" and "Stop the War." A few unfurled Viet Cong flags, while others lined the fence separating them from the ceremony. Their chants required the President to raise his voice as he delivered his remarks to the crowd of several thousand and expressed hope for "peace for all people in the years to come." Other than that, he appeared unperturbed by their demonstration over the war he had inherited with the Presidency; he spoke of a bygone time when the nation was not at war.

> ... *Above everything else in this Christmas season, as we open this Pageant of Peace and as we light this nation's Christmas tree, our wish, our prayer, is for peace, the kind of peace that we can live with, the kind of peace that we can be proud of, the kind of peace that exists not just for now but that gives a chance for our children also to live in peace.... There is an old saying about Christmas trees.... May a Christmas tree be as sturdy as faith, as high as hope, as wide as love. And I could add, may a Christmas tree, our Christmas tree, be as beautiful as peace.*

The heckling continued intermittently throughout the President's remarks, but when he lit the National Tree, the jeers were drowned out by the joy of the rest of the crowd.

1970: The Jefferson Portrait and a New China Room

On November 25, Mrs. Nixon pushed a button that illuminated the exterior of the White House and transformed it into a monument within a city of monuments. Formerly only a lighted chandelier in the North Portico was visible to the approximately 35,000 cars that passed the White House each day. Speaking to more than 1,000 staff and their families, President Nixon said, "The lighting of the White House is being given as a gift to the nation. Once the White House is lighted at night it will be seen by millions of Americans as a symbol...." In actuality, the "gift" came from funds left over from the Republican Inaugural Committee.

Completed by Christmas on the inside of the house was the China Room with its new acquisitions of Presidential porcelain, hand-woven carpet and an English chandelier. The most striking surprise was the creation of a new ground floor "Map Room" reception area—where FDR had kept his war maps. The rare American Chippendale furniture and Heriz rug donated by private citizens were in place well before the holidays.

The Thomas Jefferson portrait by Rembrandt Peale was the Nixons' choice for their Christmas gift to their staff in 1970. Hallmark reproduced 4,000 of the gift print, which was enclosed in a green velour folder. The parchment page protecting the Presidential portrait described it as follows: "Rembrandt Peale's portrait of Thomas Jefferson hangs in the Blue Room of the White House. The painting was done from life in 1800, one year before he became President. It has been called 'the true Jefferson—the man, the statesman, and the serene human being.'" The greeting read: "With our best wishes, The President and Mrs. Nixon At Christmas 1970."

For the Nixons' official Christmas card, Hallmark was asked to create a design featuring the North Portico of the White House. Hallmark spokesperson Sally Guyton, who coordinated the project, said: "The card we created is a gold embossed representation of the portico, set off by a green embossed foil wreath on a green silk-screen background. The engraving is very close to the real thing. The famous chandelier on the portico is authentic. The number of windows, their size, and the spacing, are all accurate." Hallmark printed 45,000 Christmas cards for the Nixons in 1970.

In the East Wing corridor where visitors began their tour of the White House, two special cases displaying past and present Christmas cards of the President of the United States formed part of Mrs. Nixon's Christmas decor. The first included cards from Presidents Hoover, Roosevelt, Truman,

Rembrandt Peale's Thomas Jefferson was the subject of the 1970 gift print.
HALLMARK CARDS

Below: The 1970 Christmas card featured a Hallmark representation of the North Portico of the White House.
HALLMARK CARDS

Eisenhower, Kennedy, Johnson and Nixon; a card from Prime Minister Churchill to President Truman; and three Christmas cards received by Rutherford B. Hayes during his 1877–81 Presidency. The second case featured Presidential Christmas ornaments representing each of these administrations. Also on display was the 1866 edition of Dickens' *A Christmas Carol* read by President Roosevelt to his family every Christmas Eve; a red fire engine given as a Christmas gift by President Hoover to the sons of his secretary as a memento of the fire that shortened his 1929 Christmas Eve dinner party; the Eisenhower grandchildren's script for a "Children's Pageant of the Birth of Christ"; and the large doll house made for Fanny Hayes, daughter of Rutherford B. Hayes, by White House carpenters for her first Christmas in the White House.

While the National Christmas Tree ceremony on December 16 was dampened by rain, the spirit of Christmas prevailed as the President expressed, to a live audience of about 1,000 and a television audience of millions, his high hopes for peace in the world.

On Christmas Eve the President said, "Let us put aside what divides us and rediscover what unites us—concern for one another, love of liberty and justice, pride in our own diversity. Let us resolve to work together."

Acting upon his concern for the national family, President Nixon personally delivered season's greetings to the residents of the Washington Home for Incurables on Christmas Eve. The surprise visit was the first ever by a President. The patients were deeply touched by his gentleness and his unhurried chats, and were thrilled to shake his hand. Though speechless that night, many of them would for the rest of their lives talk about their Christmas Eve visit from the President, who was, in turn, inspired by their courage and optimism.

1971: The Lincoln Portrait and New Red and Green Rooms

Yuletide visitors were in for a surprise as the Red and the Green Rooms were open to the public just in time for the holiday open house at the White House. "The rooms are so full of beauty they just need a little dressing up for Christmas. I love the aroma of fresh flowers and plants—pines, firs, and spruce," Mrs. Nixon told *House and Garden*. "It was my idea to have lots of things in pots that can be watered easily. Potted miniature ivy makes marvelous garlands across the mantels, and the greenery helps to hide the pots holding the poinsettias. Red and white poinsettias all through turned out to be a great success." For the First Lady it was a constant challenge to beautify the house, which she described as "so full of history and now aglow with the magic and spirit of Christmas."

For Christmas, President and Mrs. Nixon gave members of the White House staff a reproduction of George Healy's 1869 portrait of Abraham Lincoln, the Civil War President for whom Richard Nixon had a special regard. Enclosed in a royal blue velour cover, the portrait was described as follows: "George P.A. Healy's portrait of Abraham Lincoln hangs in the State Dining Room of the White House. Lincoln sat for Healy in 1864 as one of the subjects in 'The Peacemakers,' a painting which also included Lincoln's military advisors, General Grant, Admiral Porter, and General Sherman. The portrait shown here, painted in 1869, is one of four based on the likeness of

George P.A. Healy's Abraham Lincoln was the subject of the 1971 gift print. HALLMARK CARDS

Below: N.C. Wyeth painted *Building the First White House* for a patriotic poster for the Pennsylvania Railroad. Depicting George Washington and architect James Hoban inspecting the uncompleted building, it became the art for the Nixons' official Christmas card in 1971. HALLMARK CARDS

Lincoln as depicted in 'The Peacemakers.'" The greetings read: "With our best wishes, The President and Mrs. Nixon At Christmas 1971."

The Nixons' official Christmas card was a reproduction of a painting N.C. Wyeth did for a patriotic poster for the Pennsylvania Railroad in 1930. The company originally planned a series of 12 historical posters to identify that railroad with national growth, but only four were completed. Poster No. 4 was called *Building the First White House* and depicted George Washington and the architect James Hoban inspecting the uncompleted building. The White House ordered 50,000 cards in 1971.

With President Nixon in Key Biscayne, Florida, preparing for talks with British Prime Minister Edward Heath, Vice President Spiro Agnew pushed the button to light the National Christmas Tree on December 16.

1972: Theodore Roosevelt and the Blue Room

"Change that works" was the slogan used to sum up the President's first term in office. The cold war had diminished. There were 25,200 troops in Vietnam as compared to a half million when Richard Nixon had entered office. Mrs. Nixon's major refurbishing of the state rooms had been completed with the opening of the Blue Room. It was there that the First Lady chose to place the 1972 White House Christmas tree, a 20-foot Noble fir from Washington State.

Apparently thrilled with the prospect of having their state tree displayed in the White House, an unidentified party in Tacoma requested that it be returned after Christmas. Just the thought of such a task brought out social secretary Lucy Winchester's sense of humor. She said, "Unfortunately, the tree—like the Social Secretary—is a dried up, shattered wreck after Christmas. Neither one of us could be sent to Tacoma, as both of us are carried out in vacuum cleaner bags after the festivities."

For their 1972 Christmas gift folder to their staff, President and Mrs. Nixon chose the portrait of Theodore Roosevelt by John Singer Sargent. Nixon greatly admired the former President and created the Roosevelt Room in the West Wing of the White House in his honor.

The description of the portrait as recorded on the parchment page of the gift folder read: "Theodore Roosevelt posed on a White House stairway for this 1903 portrait by John Singer Sargent. The painting now hangs in the Red Room and is one of the finest Presidential portraits in The White House Collection. Roosevelt preferred it. In 1918 he wrote, 'I care even more for the Sargent, which seems to me to have a singular quality, a blend of both the spiritual and the heroic.'" Hallmark prepared 5,000 of the keepsakes for the White House. In addition to the gift print, the Nixons also gave their household staff a 2 x 3-inch marble paperweight on which is adhered a brass seal of the President of the United States in red, white and blue. Beneath it was a small brass plate bearing the names Richard Nixon and Patricia Nixon in script and "Christmas 1972" in block letters. Mrs. Nixon gave a chatelaine pin to the women on her staff and Dion cuff links to the men.

For their official Christmas card, the President and First Lady reproduced an 1839 etching of the White House by English artist William Henry Bartlett. *View From the Tiber*, as it was called, depicted the lush foliage on the south grounds of the White House with Tiber Creek in the foreground. Filled in during the 1880's, the creek today runs under Constitution Avenue.

The 1972 gift print was John Singer Sargent's Theodore Roosevelt.
HALLMARK CARDS
Below: In 1839, English artist William Henry Bartlett created the White House etching *View From the Tiber*. The Nixons selected it for their 1972 official card.
HALLMARK CARDS

This painting was one that was acquired during the Nixon Administration and hung in the Oval Office. Hallmark framed the card with a green and antique gold hot foil border and produced 60,000 for the Nixons.

The lighting of the National Christmas Tree was held on December 14, amidst a chilly rain but heated controversy. Due to legal action against the National Park Service, the Christmas star that had traditionally adorned the top of the National Tree was to be substituted with a newly designed emblem. An even greater controversy had been brewing over the presence of the nativity scene at the pageant. It, however, was allowed to stay. In the absence of President Nixon, Vice President Spiro Agnew again brought Christmas greetings from the President.

1973: Old-Fashioned Christmas Saves Energy

In the throes of a national energy crisis, a Monroe Christmas was the theme for Christmas 1973. James Monroe, who had served as President from 1817 to 1825, had already influenced the Nixon White House in a number of ways. Many of the original pieces of furniture of the Monroe era, for instance, had been returned to their rightful place. The Monroe furniture in the Cross Hall had been a recent acquisition and added to the history and authenticity of the mansion. Because Monroe and his staff had used vermeil for their White House, the modern decorations included lots of natural greens and pine cones, accented by shiny gold.

In keeping with the Monroe Christmas theme, the President and Mrs. Nixon decided to give a reproduction of President James Monroe by Samuel F.B. Morse as their Christmas gift to their staff in 1973. *National Geographic* photographed the portrait and Hallmark placed it in a white velour folder. The description included with the gift print read: "This portrait of James Monroe, fifth President of the United States, was painted in the White House by Samuel F.B. Morse in 1819. Born in Virginia in 1758, Monroe served in the American Revolution and later became a United States Senator, U.S. Minister to France, Governor of Virginia, and U.S. Secretary of State. He was elected President in 1816. The portrait hangs in the Green Room of the White House." The sentiment on the keepsake was the following: "With our best wishes, The President and Mrs. Nixon At Christmas 1973."

The official card for that year was a reproduction of a 19th century view of the *President's House*, a painting by the German artist August Kollner. Hallmark framed the print with a gold antique hot foil border against a red silk-screened border. The black engraved message below a blank embossed Presidential Seal read: "With all best wishes for a Merry Christmas and a Happy New Year, The President and Mrs. Nixon." The 60,000 cards were sent to heads of state, American and foreign diplomats, government officials, friends and close supporters of the First Family.

The 50th anniversary of the lighting of the National Christmas Tree was held on December 14. What might have been slated as a major celebration was unusual in many ways. For the first time in 20 years, the committee had reverted to using a live tree, a 42-foot Colorado blue spruce grown in Pennsylvania and presented by the National Arborist Society. Planted on the Ellipse, the 40-year-old tree was expected to live another 150 years. Due to

James Monroe, the fifth President, as painted by Samuel F.B. Morse, was the subject of the 1973 gift print.
HALLMARK CARDS

Below: The official Christmas card for 1973 featured the White House as depicted by the German painter August Kollner. The 19th century view from Lafayette Park shows the bronze statue of Thomas Jefferson placed on the north lawn by President James Polk in 1847.
HALLMARK CARDS

the energy crisis, a drastic energy reduction of 81.9 percent over the previous year would be achieved by the use of one electric light on the tree and four spotlights on it from the ground. The surrounding 57 smaller trees would have no lights at all.

Another difference from Christmases past was that the traditional nativity scene would be eliminated from the Pageant of Peace due to a U.S. Court of Appeals ruling stating that it constituted "excessive entanglement" of the government in religion and violated the First Amendment. The controversy, lodged by five plaintiffs, had been in the courts for four years. A lower court decision ruled the nativity scene could stay, but a higher one ruled it had to go. As a result of many protests, a private organization was granted a permit to erect a nativity scene near but not on the Pageant of Peace complex.

To many the most significant difference was the fact that this would be the first Christmas in 12 years that the United States would not have troops committed in a military conflict around the world. The Vietnam War had concluded. In his Christmas message to the nation on the 50th anniversary of the lighting of the National Community Christmas Tree, President Nixon reflected on the affairs of the nation as he shared from his heart.

> *... This year Christmas will be different in terms of lights, perhaps, all across America. Instead of having many lights on the tree as you will see over there in a few moments, there will be only one on it, the star at the top, and the other lights you see will simply be the glitter from the ground lights which are around the tree. And in a way, I suppose one could say with only one light on the tree, this will be a very dreary Christmas, but we know that isn't true, because the spirit of Christmas is not measured by the number of lights on a tree. The spirit of Christmas is measured by the love that each of us has in his heart for his family, for his friends, for his fellow Americans and for people all over the world. And this year, while we have a problem, ... the problem of energy.... This year we will drive a little slower. This year the thermostats will be a little lower. This year every American perhaps will sacrifice a little, but no one will suffer.*

One young man who rejoiced at the lighting of the lone star on the tree was 9-year-old Scott Stewart of Middlefield, Ohio. Writing to the President after the ceremony, he said, "Dear President Nixon; My Dad made the star on your Christmas Tree. We were afraid you wouldn't light it, But you did! I told all the kids in my room my Dad made the star but they wouldn't believe me. A lady from the paper came and took our picture. She wrote about how my Dad made the star. I thought you would like to see it. We love you and Mrs. Nixon too. Have a happy Christmas. Your friend, Scott Stewart. P.S. Hope Santa brings you a nice present.

Without a doubt, the one present Richard Nixon would have liked to have received never came. While he had brought peace to the world, there was no peace on Capitol Hill. Several Nixon loyalists had broken into the Democratic National Headquarters at the Watergate complex in an attempt to discover the Democratic campaign strategy, and Nixon was implicated in efforts to cover up the scandal. Impeachment was the talk of the time. Even during Christmas, the President's lawyers worked long hours to defend their client against a myriad of charges involving "Watergate." As it turned out, this would be his last Christmas message to the nation. At his first tree ceremony, he had to talk above the shouts of hecklers: "Peace Now—Stop the War." At his last ceremony, sections of the audience waved signs, "God loves America, God loves Nixon." When his message was finished, they chanted, "We want Nixon" and "We want the President."

A Somber Christmas

For Richard Nixon, Christmas 1973 was a time of family. It was a somber occasion, daughter Julie Nixon Eisenhower said: "All of us in the family were discouraged and frankly overwhelmed by the repeated blows of Watergate." She recalled: "My father made several Christmas phone calls ... to the small- and big-town heroes and heroines across the country. As my parents and their guests enjoyed a turkey dinner in the Red Room, my father became nostalgic." He talked about the kindness of one of his Duke University law professors who had invited him and another student to his home for Christmas because they couldn't afford to return to their own homes for the holidays. "The conversation became more nostalgic," the daughter said, "especially about his foreign policy triumphs—the trip to China, the meetings with Mao and Brezhnev, the conversations with Golda Meir at the time of the Yom Kippur War and the military alert."

"As I look back," the President said, "while it has been a rough game, it has been worth it. I might not want to do it again, but I would not have missed it.... I know I have lived for a purpose, and I have at least in part achieved it. You must live your life for something more important than your life alone. One who has never lost himself in a cause bigger than himself has missed one of life's mountaintop experiences. Only by losing yourself in this way can you really find yourself."

In his last message to the American people as President, Richard Nixon said, "We think sometimes when things don't go the right way, when we suffer a defeat, that all has ended. Not true. It is only a beginning, always. Greatness comes when you are really tested, when you take some knocks, some disappointments, when sadness comes. Because only if you have been in the deepest valley can you ever know how magnificent it is to be on the highest mountain. Always give your best. Never get discouraged, never be petty. Always remember, others may hate you, but those that hate you don't win unless you hate them, and then you destroy yourself."

NEW ENGLAND SNOW SCENE

GEORGE DURRIE (1820-

Wishing you a Joyous Christmas and a Happy New Year
THE PRESIDENT AND MRS. FORD
1974

HALLMARK CARDS

CHAPTER IX

THE FORDS

An Old-Fashioned Christmas

*P*resident and Mrs. Gerald Ford brought to the White House an informality that reflected their unique style and personality. Prior to Richard Nixon's resignation, Betty Ford was quoted in *U.S. News and World Report*, "If I go there, I'm going to make it fun. I couldn't stand to live there unless it were happy, free and open. Because we are that kind of people and we're not going to change." And they didn't. The ambiance of the Ford White House was warm and folksy, simple and low-key. Mrs. Ford described it as kind of "down-home-like." Especially at Christmas, the First Lady was able to define her independence and leave the distinctive mark of an old-fashioned Christmas on the White House, a tradition the Ford family had always enjoyed.

Gerald Ford had served in the House of Representatives since the Truman days. Mrs. Ford said, "My husband was so dedicated to this country, having first visited Washington as an Eagle Scout, that his devotion rubbed off on me. My desire throughout the time we served in the White House was to present an American feeling." She insisted that every event have a theme and portray American arts and crafts, American antiques and artists.

1974: A Patchwork Theme

Preparing for Christmas would be a challenge for any administration that had just come into being at the end of summer. Despite the turmoil of Watergate, plus the trauma of major surgery within her first few months in the White House, Mrs. Ford's outlook was courageous. She said, "Having been in Washington for 25 years, I had the advantage of being at the White House for quite a few Christmases. I had seen how others had served the President and First Lady. I knew a lot of people and felt a part of the whole thing." In addition to being an insider, she added, "I had a very good staff and I leaned on them."

In fact, the topic of Christmas didn't even surface until November, recalled Mrs. Ford's press secretary, Sheila Weidenfeld, in her book *First Lady's Lady*. The Johnsons and the Kennedys had taken their holiday decorations with them. The Nixons' tree ornaments were available, but they were not Mrs. Ford's style. She preferred handmade ornaments or ones that had a sentimental attachment. Her idea of a Christmas tree was that it "should be warm and personal and familial, even if it is 19 1/2 feet tall and stands in the middle of the White House." In her enthusiasm, she actually considered using decorations made by everyone who wished to do so. When the reality of the moment sunk in, Weidenfeld said, they decided to compromise and asked specific groups to participate in the project to make ornaments for the White House tree.

Coordinating with Washington florist William Dove, Mrs. Ford chose a patchwork theme for the mansion. Patchwork ornaments were made by the Blue Ridge Cottage Industries in North Carolina, the Quilters Workshop in New York and the Farm Women's Cooperative Market in Bethesda, Maryland. The 19 1/2-foot concolor fir that had been coincidentally selected the previous year from the Fords' home state of Michigan was swagged with blue moiré lined with calico. The base was accented with a prize-winning patchwork quilt and fabric-wrapped packages.

Mrs. Ford's "old-fashioned handmade theme" emphasized thrift and simplicity amidst a recession-time holiday; choosing a piece of lace that had sentimental value, she decorated an ornament created for her. Daughter Susan, using scraps from her sewing basket, also made ornaments for the White House tree. High prices "affect my budget and everyone else's," the First Lady said, and encouraged families across America to save money by getting together to make their own Christmas ornaments from scraps. She even offered a White House how-to pamphlet on patchwork Christmas tree ornaments. While it was intended that these hand-crafted ornaments would be more economical than the ostentatious decorations of previous years, Mrs. Ford was surprised when she received the bill, according to a *Washington Post* account. "Patching up the White House tree" was simple but costly after paying the craftspeople for their labor. It was, however, an investment the First Lady was happy to make, because it created work for many senior citizens.

Mrs. Ford's personality and thinking were also reflected in the kind of

An 1831 engraving of the White House, after a drawing by English artist H. Brown, was used on the 1974 official Presidential card. HALLMARK CARDS

gifts she chose. "When I think of Christmas, I always think of snow," she said. "For years our family has spent time together between Christmas and New Years in the mountains of Colorado." The Fords admired the beautiful prints in the White House collection of snow scenes in America. In 1974, they chose George Durrie's *New England Snow Scene* as the First Family's Christmas gift print to their staff. While it was a departure from the formal portraits of previous Presidents, the 19th-century Durrie represented the folksy atmosphere of the Ford White House. This particular painting hung on the second floor of the White House and had been acquired for the mansion during the Nixon Administration. Hallmark Cards reproduced 5,000 of the Christmas gift print.

Before Gerald Ford had become President, the Fords customarily had sent a family photograph as their Christmas card. This tradition, however, was now complicated by the fact that the family was too scattered to take a picture. Also, concerned that such an informal card would not be appropriate for foreign dignitaries, the President and Mrs. Ford asked Hallmark to reproduce an engraving entitled *The President's House, Washington* for their official 1974 Christmas card. Hallmark printed the lithograph on clearform silk, edged with a gold bronzed line and green lithographed border. A notation on the back said: "The pastoral atmosphere of the nation's capital in the early 19th century is shown in 'The President's House, Washington.' This engraving published in 1831 depicting a French style garden was made by Fenner Sears and Company, London, after a drawing by the English artist, H. Brown." On the inside was a blank embossed Presidential Seal. The green engraved message read: "With best wishes from our family for a Merry Christmas and a Happy New Year, The President and Mrs. Ford." The White House ordered 50,000 Christmas cards, which were personally paid for by the President.

On December 17, the President participated in the lighting of the National Christmas Tree. Sharing the platform with the University of

Michigan Chorus, he greeted those present: "My fellow Michiganders, my fellow Americans ... I would like to share with you my personal list of Christmas wishes. At the top of my list are peace, economic well-being for all, and a caring climate that will permit everyone to achieve the fullest potential of their human gifts. And I wish this nation a strong future out of a very proud past. And I wish everyone of us the realization of love and belonging...."

Mindful of the economy, social activities at the White House that Christmas were limited, but those that were held were warm and cheerful, just as Mrs. Ford had planned. "It had occurred to me that while the White House looked so beautiful during the holidays it would be an ideal time to entertain the Congress with a great black-tie gathering." The Fords hosted the first annual Christmas Ball in years for their Cabinet and members of Congress. The gala event, held after the lighting of the National Christmas Tree, was one that dispensed with protocol and included both sides of the aisle. "It was healthy for us all," said the First Lady. "I had in mind to bring everyone together for food and dancing in an effort to lighten up the spirit. I think the country was in need of that because we had gone through a very traumatic and difficult time."

Addressing the crowd, President Ford compared himself to the White House tree. "That tree and I have a lot in common. Neither one of us expected to be in the White House a few months ago. Both of us were a little green, both of us were put on a pedestal," he said. "And I'd like to add this as a postscript—we've both been trimmed a little lately." Many of the 900 guests were friends that the President had served with for a quarter of a century. "We live here but my heart is really up there," said the President referring to members of Congress who came to help him celebrate his first Christmas in the White House. One guest, according to *U.S. News and World Report*, described the reunion as "warm and genial—like a party in a private house, not a formal function in an official residence."

The First Family, believing that "A family that skis together stays together," then left for Vail, Colorado, as was their Christmas custom. Invariably their holiday gifts revolved around their favorite sport. Even after he had become President, though, the Gerald Ford who had always been proud of his thrifty habits continued to encourage his children to go careful with money. I'm "still a Ford," he was quoted in the Sunday *Globe Democrat*, "and not a Lincoln and don't go overboard on gifts." Having always enjoyed a more casual Christmas, the Fords were able to set an example for a country brought, earlier in the year, to the brink of impeachment and whose economy had been stymied by war. A time of healing and rebuilding was needed before the country could move forward.

1975: A Colonial Christmas

Mrs. Ford recalled, "I loved Christmas of 1975, when we were preparing for the Bicentennial of our country. It was a very exciting time. The preparation for that got underway early in the year. We had been to Williamsburg for Christmas several times. I was so impressed with the trees and candles and the beauty of Williamsburg at Christmas. I figured we could get a lot of help from the people there and that is the way it turned out."

Advised by the staff of the Colonial Williamsburg Foundation, the Fords opted for another old-fashioned Christmas. Their second Christmas tree, an 18-foot Douglas fir from New York, was decorated with 3,000 ornaments reminiscent of those used in early American homes. Reflecting her personal preference for natural and hand-crafted ornaments, which she had used on her family's trees for many years, Mrs. Ford chose an early American theme for the eve of America's Bicentennial. The Williamsburg advisers suggested such ornaments as "corn dollies," pine cone angels, felt and wooden animals, crocheted snowflakes, paper cutouts, baskets filled with dried flowers, gingerbread cookies and garlands of popcorn, cranberries and red peppers. All the decorations were constructed from easily accessible and inexpensive materials. Natural materials such as peanuts, acorns, pine cones, dried fruits and flowers replaced the sequins and glitter to preserve a theme steeped in tradition and heritage. The task of "taking out the tinsel" was left to 75 professional florists who had volunteered to help decorate the White House for Christmas.

For their Christmas gift to their White House staff as well as for their official greeting card, the President and Mrs. Ford chose another George H. Durrie snow painting, one entitled *Farmyard in Winter*. Durrie, growing up in New Haven, Connecticut, shunned the crowded city life in favor of the solitude of rural America, which became the setting for his best works. Many of his paintings were reproduced as lithographs by Currier and Ives.

In 1971, the Richard King Mellon Foundation gifted Durrie's original oil painting of *Farmyard in Winter*, done in 1858, to the White House as part of Mrs. Nixon's restoration project. She had it hung in the Green Room. The Fords liked Durrie's work in general

Mrs. Ford chose an old-fashioned Christmas as the theme for the White House tree on the eve of the American Bicentennial. GERALD R. FORD LIBRARY

A second George H. Durrie painting, *Farmyard in Winter*, graced the 1975 official Christmas card and gift print.
HALLMARK CARDS

and asked Hallmark to reproduce this snow-covered Connecticut farmyard for both their Christmas gift and card. The First Family ordered 5,000 of the keepsakes and presented them to their White House staff. The Fords mailed 35,000 Christmas cards bearing Durrie's *Farmyard in Winter* painting and framed it with a red hot foil border.

In preparation for America's Bicentennial, the Pageant of Peace in 1975 was inspired by Colonial America. The National Christmas Tree was decorated with 4,600 red, white and blue ornaments and illuminated by 12,000 low-watt minibulbs. A specially designed four-foot gold and green replica of the Liberty Bell, donated by the General Electric Company, was placed atop the 45-foot Colorado blue spruce. The National Tree was surrounded by 13 smaller trees representing the 13 colonies. The 44 other trees representing states and territories were placed in a row leading up to it.

With the mercury plummeting, President Ford ushered in the holiday season on December 18 by switching on the tree's lights. About 7,500 chilled people were on hand to hear his Christmas message and watch the performance of Colonial Williamsburg Dancers and the Mount Vernon Fife and Drum Corps. Members of the Colonial Congress were characterized by actors portraying Benjamin Franklin, Thomas Jefferson, John Adams and Richard Henry Lee. Against this backdrop, the President greeted the American people:

> *In our 200 years, we Americans have always honored the spiritual testament of 2,000 years ago. We embrace the spirit of the Prince of Peace so that we might find peace in our own hearts and in our own land, and hopefully in the world as well.... Yes, we have endured economic difficulties, but our Nation and we in the American family can now look forward to a more prosperous new year. And on this eve of our Bicentennial year, liberty and justice still burn brightly as guiding stars of our Nation.*

1976: The Bicentennial Christmas

The "natural look" of flowers and evergreens was the main emphasis of decorations used by President and Mrs. Ford their last Christmas in the White House. The 20-foot balsam fir from Black River Falls, Wisconsin, was decorated with more than 2,500 handmade flowers, including the state flowers of all 50 states. The flowers, crafted by garden clubs, art classes and senior citizens across the nation, were made of silk, felt, beads, shells, ribbon, seeds, bamboo, cornhusks, metal, porcelain and glass. Baby's-breath and small baskets of dried flowers hung on the tree along with tiny white lights. A nosegay of flowers topped the tree. Dolls, quilts, pillows, stuffed animals, a hand-carved dove and other gifts sent to the White House to commemorate the Bicentennial were arranged under the tree. Unveiling it to the press, Mrs. Ford said that the inspiration for the decorations was in "the spirit of love that is Christmas." To express this, she hung two turtledoves on the tree to set the mood.

That mood changed dramatically, though, at the party for Washington diplomats' children, many in native costume, as they marched around the tree to the music of the Army's Brass Band. Awed by the toys and decorations, their initial polite restraint was soon dissolved by the antics of Big Bird and his "Sesame Street" friends. Santa Claus only added to the children's wild excitement. According to one report, "Thomas Jefferson and James Madison rocked in their frames—the Christmas tree in the Blue Room teetered—Santa Claus wiped his brow and staggered back— The children's invasion of the White House was over for another year."

Appropriately chosen for the First Family's Bicentennial Christmas gift to the staff at the White House was a reproduction of Ferdinand Richardt's painting *Philadelphia in 1858*, which hung in the Green Room. White House curator Clem Conger tells an incredible story of how the painting came home to the Executive Mansion. Richardt, an artist from Denmark, sketched the Philadelphia scene while he was in America painting Niagara Falls, for which he became quite famous. Moving on to London, he apparently finished the painting there and signed it "Reichardt," as his name was spelled in England. In 1863, he held an exhibition in his studio in which New York and Philadelphia street scenes were on display. The Philadelphia scene was purchased, probably by Saler Jung, who had extensive holdings in Hyderabad, India, as well as a museum that he gave to the city of Hyderabad.

It was in Hyderabad that Albert Nesle, a New York antiques dealer involved in liquidating the estate of Saler Jung, noticed it at one of the auctions. In a letter to Conger, he wrote:

It looked interesting to me. The steeple, the architecture of the building in the

Philadelphia in 1858, a painting once purchased for $7, was reproduced as the 1976 gift print. HALLMARK CARDS

background, the people, made me to believe it to be of Colonial America, or somewhere in England. The canvas was in shocking condition. Anyway, I purchased it for $7 and had it shipped to New York with my shipment of many things. Upon its arrival, I showed it to one or two of my friends, especially a man named Jack Treleaven of Needham's. We discussed the possibility of restoring it, but we thought it too expensive, and I subsequently sold it to Kennedy [Galleries, Inc., in New York] for a very modest figure. It was later illustrated in the "Antique Magazine" and a few months later was considered a great discovery. Anyhow, Mr. Conger, now you have it and that is the story. I feel I have done a nice thing by rescuing it from the junk pile.

Thus it was that this piece of American history, also known as *Independence Hall in Philadelphia*, became known as "the greatest bargain in American paintings in the history of the world," according to Conger. Mr. and Mrs. Joseph Levine later purchased it and gave it to the White House in memory of the late John F. Kennedy. Hallmark reproduced the painting and published 5,000 folders for the Fords' 1976 Christmas gift.

President and Mrs. Ford liked the work of George Durrie. For their third Christmas card, they chose a third snow painting, entitled *Going to*

Going to Church, a third George H. Durrie painting, was featured on the 1976 official Presidential Christmas card. HALLMARK CARDS

Church. On the back of the card is the following description. "In his classic painting 'Going to Church,' George Durrie (1820–1863) beautifully captured the mood of winter in his native Connecticut. Reproductions of this work were widely circulated, making it a familiar scene to nineteenth century Americans." The original painting was presented to the White House in 1963 by collector George Freling-huysen. The Fords sent out 35,000 Christmas cards that year.

On December 16, no less than 10,000 people witnessed the annual lighting of the 1976 National Christmas Tree. It was the last ceremony for President Ford and the last for the 44-year-old Colorado spruce that had served as the nation's tree since 1973. Having lost most of its bottom branches, the tree would have looked scrawny without a "transplant" of 50 healthy branches wired on to the barren trunk and covered with ornaments.

The focus of the ceremony, however, was the Bicentennial. The President said: "As our Bicentennial year comes to a close, it is especially appropriate to gather once more around the traditional symbol of family ties and friendly reunions, our Nation's Christmas Tree. In doing so, we combine our year-long celebration of historical events with a personal rededication to timeless values."

Looking back over their last year, Mrs. Ford said, "It was such a wonderful, historically exciting kind of period. It was very demanding, but very interesting. The Bicentennial year was tremendously busy. I always said it was like having a revolving door with one head of state going out, while the next one was coming in. I never expected to meet so many important figures, but they all wanted to pay their respects to our country. Each one was a buildup to the Queen's visit, which was the icing on the cake. Historically, it was a great privilege to represent America during its Bicentennial!"

THE CARTERS
The President's House

President and Mrs. Carter were "Sunday painters" who appreciated American art. Jimmy Carter first became interested in art history as an education officer in the Navy. In time, he and his wife, Rosalynn, studied the great masterpieces together, "not to become experts," she explained, "but for enjoyment." When they moved into the mansion of the Governor of Georgia, they found in it a wonderful collection of Federal period furniture. Taking up residence in the White House, the Carters realized their marvelous opportunity to surround themselves not only with the furniture of former Presidents but also with great works of art. The task of selecting art for their personal residence was one Mrs. Carter compared to Christmas. "Here were all these great paintings and you could pick any you wanted," she was quoted in the *New York Times Magazine*. The Carters' preference was American impressionist.

Remarked White House curator Clement E. Conger: "The Carters knew more about American furniture and American art than any other First Family in the twentieth century." During the Carter Administration a great many pieces were added to the White House collection, 150 of which were acquired on loan. To share their love of art and the honor of living at 1600 Pennsylvania Avenue, the Carters' Christmas card each year while there presented a painting of the President's House.

Facing page: The First Family poses in front of the White House tree. Its ornaments were handmade by retarded adults and children from across the country. JIMMY CARTER LIBRARY

The White House · Christmas 1977

Harvey Moriarty's *The President's House* was the art used on the 1977 Christmas card and gift print. HALLMARK CARDS

1977: South Portico Drawing

"As a friend of two of my sons," Mrs. Carter later said, "Harvey Moriarty was in and out of the Governor's Mansion often when my husband was Governor of Georgia. I thought Harvey was very talented, and I have one of his paintings in my dining room. When you are at the White House," she continued, "you get so busy doing so many things that when it got close to Christmas, Harvey was just there. We asked him to draw us a picture of the White House for our Christmas card. We let him do whatever he wanted. He came up with a pen and ink detail drawing of the South Portico, and I was very pleased, because that's the view of the White House most people in our country associate with."

Hallmark reproduced the image in sepia and lithographed it on ivory paper with a deckled edge. The engraved message read: "With best wishes from our family for a Merry Christmas and a Happy New Year. The President and Mrs. Carter." Early on, Paul Sullivan, executive director of the Democratic National Committee (DNC), suggested to the President that he send Christmas cards to the 1976 campaign workers and donors not only because it would be a good way to show appreciation for their past efforts but also because it could solicit support for his current programs and the 1980 campaign. The advice was received favorably and the strategy was adopted. The Carter White House ordered 60,000 Christmas cards—more than any previous administration had ever ordered—and sent the bill to the DNC. Hallmark also produced for the Carters 5,000 gift prints, which featured the same Moriarty drawing. The sepia memento was titled: "The White House - 1977." Facsimile signatures of the President and First Lady appeared below the inscription.

In preparation for 11 straight days of holiday entertaining, the President's House was dressed with all the usual trappings of Christmas, but not to the lavish extent of previous administrations. The Carters' style consisted of simple ornaments handmade by retarded children and adults all across the country. The 2,500 ornaments adorning the Blue Room's 20-foot Noble fir from Washington State varied in size, material and design, and according to the skill of their makers. Mrs. Carter explained in a *Washington Post* story, "We wanted to show that retarded citizens have talents, and we recognize their right to develop them fully." The First Lady sent each person a certificate recognizing his or her contribution to the First Family's first White House Christmas.

The modest decorations in the President's House were consistent with the Chief Executive's approach toward conserving energy and halting inflation. Following in the steps of Franklin Roosevelt and Harry Truman, President Carter also called upon the nation to set aside a National Day of Prayer, encouraging the people to pray for world peace and for guidance for themselves and their leaders. The day of prayer, December 15, coincided with the opening of the Pageant of Peace. The President addressed the nation and spoke of, among other things, his American family theme: "... I hope that we'll make every effort during this Christmas season not only to bring our immediate family together but to look at the family of all humankind, so that we not any longer cherish a commitment toward animosity or the retention of enemies but that we forgive one another and indeed, form a worldwide family where every human being on Earth is our brother or our sister...." With the help of daughter Amy, the President lit the live, newly transplanted 30-foot Colorado blue spruce and its 2,000 low-wattage green lights.

After a full schedule of holiday entertaining, the President and Mrs. Carter returned to Plains, Georgia, for a quiet Christmas. While the tourists had long since departed, now hundreds of farmers descended on the President's hometown to protest low farm prices. His only word, however, was a warm wish to all Americans on Christmas Eve. "Our country has been especially blessed throughout our history," he said. "In this season of hope we seek, as individuals and as a nation, to serve as instruments to bring the ancient promises of peace and goodwill closer to fulfillment for all the peoples of the earth...."

When Mrs. Carter came upon a hand-colored wood engraving of the White House, it became the first of the historic White House scenes to adorn the Carters' official Christmas cards and gift prints. AMERICAN GREETINGS

1978: *Carriages at the North Portico*

On January 26, just weeks after the tree-lighting ceremony, the tree that had served as the 1977 National Christmas Tree was knocked down, twice in the same day, by brutal winds. Having been ripped out of the frozen ground by its roots, it was not expected to live and ended its days as a yule log. After a National Park Service search of 2,000 miles of back roads north of Washington, D.C., a "perfect" 26-foot Colorado blue spruce was found quite by chance in the front yard of the York, Pennsylvania, residence of Mr. and Mrs. William E. Myers. The National Park Service purchased the tree and moved it to the Ellipse, where, so far, it has served as the National Christmas Tree for four administrations.

In the summer, while redecorating the third floor solarium, Mrs. Carter began exploring ways to furnish it. "It was really exciting for us to wander through the White House warehouse where all the unused furniture and paintings are kept. We brought in Harry Truman's desk for one of our sons; a table that Mary Lincoln had bought; and John F. Kennedy's bed," she said. Then she discovered a hand-colored wood engraving of a photograph of the Executive Mansion by L.E. Walker that had originally appeared in *Harper's*

Weekly in 1877. It portrayed guests arriving at the North Portico of the White House in horse-drawn carriages. Becoming aware of a number of other historic White House scenes, the First Lady decided to continue to depict the President's House on the Carters' official Christmas card.

A change in vendor was made, however. American Greetings Corporation, with its "union label," was selected to reproduce the print Mrs. Carter had selected. Because the original engraving lacked the color she thought would reproduce appropriately, American Greetings artists were instructed to enhance the color before final printing.

A woman for details, Mrs. Carter also noticed that "her flowery script didn't match the precise, minutely executed pen of her husband. She addressed the apparent different look, asking him to redo his name to better match the look of the inside of the card," a spokesperson for American Greetings noted. No year appeared on the card, only the Presidential Seal and the Carters' greeting: "With best wishes from our family for a happy holiday season."

The initial White House order was for 60,000 Christmas cards and 5,100 Christmas gift prints. By mid-September, there was a new request for a second run of another 40,000 cards, a total increase of 67 percent over the previous year. Much effort, meanwhile, was being put into the compiling of an accurate master Christmas card list and purging the list of duplications and address errors. Volunteers were enlisted to address, stuff and stamp. The Christmas card project became a major undertaking at the President's House. Volunteers included some men, but mostly women, from various clubs in the Washington area. The White House Correspondence Office sent representatives to speak with organizations as they were setting their schedules for the coming year. Christmas card volunteers represented nearby Andrews Air Force Base; Fort Meade, Maryland; Fort Myer in Arlington, Virginia; the Minnesota State Society; former Eastern Airlines stewardesses; B'nai B'rith, and various Democratic Clubs.

To complement her 1877 card, the First Lady decided also to decorate the White House with holiday memorabilia from a century of Christmases. To adorn the 20-foot Veitchii fir from New York State, the Margaret Woodbury Strong Museum of Rochester, New York, loaned 2,500 antique dolls, toys and furniture from their collection, even sending along seven museum staff members to create a Victorian nostalgia in the Executive Mansion, according to *Antique Monthly.* In place of the traditional gingerbread house, a 42-inch Victorian doll house and about 40 other large toys were arranged along the base of the tree in the Blue Room.

Simplicity was the keynote of the second Carter Christmas. Red candles, pine cones and evergreens enhanced the mantels. Pink and white cyclamen and small undecorated cedar trees stood in the crosshall. The creche in the East Room was positioned in the window so that the draperies could be pulled during other functions. Joy Billington of the *Washington Star* wrote that it seemed to harken "back to less troubled times ... when china dolls wore lace and rocking horses had manes and tails of real horsehair, when halls were decked with boughs of holly, when first families lived more like other families and plastic hadn't been invented."

Mrs. Carter admitted that living in the White House was a humbling privilege for her family. "At first you are awed by being there and then after a busy day you sit down to eat dinner off the plate of a former President. Sometimes, you'd think, I can't believe this is happening to me. It was all very exciting. But also the White House was a haven for our family. Amy was little, Chip lived there, as did Jeff and his wife. Whenever the First Family went out in public, there were always people who wanted your photograph or your autograph because we were the family of the President," she continued. "But the times we really treasured were the times we could be home upstairs in the White House and just be normal people. We had lots of stories to share because Jimmy always made us feel that we were a part of what he was doing. It really drew our family close together."

With a new live Colorado blue spruce serving as the National Christmas Tree, President Carter spoke at the Pageant of Peace ceremonies on December 14, having just announced that he had decided to recognize mainland China and was working to bring about peace between Israel and Egypt. Addressing a crowd of about 10,000, the President expressed his hope that these two ancient enemies could "turn their energies and talents away from war and death ... to building, instead of preparing to destroy."

When asked what the Carters wanted most for Christmas, the First Lady replied, according to *U.S. News and World Report*, "A Mideast peace settlement. You especially hope for peace in the world at Christmastime, but this year it's more significant than ever."

1979: South View of 1860 White House

The year 1979 was full of challenges—the Iran crisis, the hostage crisis and the continuing energy crisis to name but a few. To some members of the White House staff, even the Christmas card project proved a challenge. Anticipating the need to mail twice as many Christmas cards as in the previous year, there was a recommendation made for the creation of a separate Christmas card management team to alleviate the tremendous burden on the Correspondence Office.

Evaluation of the whole Christmas card project was necessary due to the "tight financial position" taken by the DNC with regard to the bill. An

The historic print selected for the 1979 gift print and official Christmas card is Lefevre J. Cranstone's *The President's House, Washington*. AMERICAN GREETINGS

The President's House, Washington   by Lefevre Cranstone 1860

investigation was even made as to whether Presidential Christmas cards justified the use of appropriated funds. Because they did not, however, and were regarded as the personal expense of the person sending them, the DNC finally approved the purchase of the 105,000 Christmas cards.

Mrs. Carter chose Lefevre J. Cranstone's 1860 watercolor of the south view of the White House as the art for the 1979 Christmas card. Titled *The President's House, Washington*, the painting had been a gift to the White House from Wilmarth Lewis that had hung in the Lincoln Bedroom. The greeting from the Carters read: "With best wishes from our family for a happy holiday season." Five thousand gift prints were also ordered for the First Family's Christmas present to their staff. American Greetings provided an extra 2,000 prints for the Carters' personal use.

The crisis with Iran in late November resulted in one of the most critical challenges to the Carter Presidency. After the transfer of American allegiance from the Shah of Iran to the Ayatollah Ruhollah Khomeini in his rise to power, Khomeini's followers had unexpectedly attacked the U.S. Embassy in Iran on November 4 and took the 50 Americans there hostage. Aides to the President suggested that the Chief Executive consider canceling all holiday festivities, but, according to a *U.S. News and World Report* account, he countered with the statement that "canceling Christmas would be giving the Iranians more power over events here than they ought to have."

The halls of the Executive Mansion were decked for Christmas against a subdued national backdrop. Fine arts students from the Corcoran School of Art, inspired by the folk art of the American Colonial period, crafted 500 ornaments, including rocking horses, angels, ships, fruit and birds. Students from the Ceramic Department created such objects as ballet slippers, a tiny grand piano, a teddy bear, a ski boot and duffel bag—all displayed under Plexiglas at the base of the 18-foot Douglas fir from West Virginia. A reporter for the *New York Times* described them as the most "avant-garde decorations ever to grace the White House." While unveiling them to the press, Mrs.

Carter said, "It's a special time of the year. Christmas is still Jesus' birthday—a time to come together, to count your blessings and to pray for the hostages," reported *U.S. News and World Report*. A highlight of the holidays in 1979 was the State Dinner held for British Prime Minister Margaret Thatcher.

Since November 4, the hostage crisis was on everyone's mind—especially the President's, as he came to speak at the lighting of the National Christmas Tree on December 13. He said:

> ... *I think it would be appropriate for all those in this audience and for all those listening to my voice or watching on television to pause just a few seconds in a silent prayer that American hostages will come home safe and come home soon—if you'd please join me just for a moment. [Pause for silent prayer.] Thank you very much.*
>
> *Nineteen seventy-nine has not been a bad year. Many good things have happened to us individually and have also happened to our Nation. Not far from here, on the north side of the White House, we saw a remarkable ceremony, headed by a Jew, the leader of Israel, a Moslem, the President of Egypt, and myself, a Christian, the President of our country, signing a treaty of peace. This peace treaty was a historic development, and it was compatible with the commitment that we feel so deeply in the religious season now upon us.... We've seen divisions among people because of religious beliefs. The recent events in Iran are an unfortunate example of that misguided application of belief in God. But I know that all Americans feel very deeply that the relationships between ourselves and the Moslem believers in the world of Islam is one of respect and care and brotherhood and goodwill and love.*
>
> *So, we do have disappointments; we do have suffering; we do have divisions; we often have war. But in the midst of pain, we can still remember what Christmas is—a time of joy, a time of light, a time of warmth, a time of families, and a time of peace.*

Amy Carter threw the switch to light the National Christmas Tree. Only the Star of Hope on the top and the blue lights on the 50 Christmas trees around the periphery lit up—one small tree for each hostage. The President announced that the rest of the lights would be turned on when the hostages came home.

There had been no warning that the National Christmas Tree would not be lit. Mrs. Carter said, "We had talked it over and Jimmy decided it was the right thing to do!" The audience was touched by the President's dramatic gesture to identify with the hostage crisis. One father remarked, "It makes it more meaningful to see a darkened tree. It symbolizes the suffering of the hostages." Another in the audience of 7,500 said, "I thought it was super. It was a warm effort to signify the hostages' plight." After a moment of silence, the crowd broke into applause, reported the *Washington Post*. The decision of the President marked the second time since World War II that the National Christmas Tree had not been lit during the Christmas season. War restrictions had prevented the use of electricity for the lights on the tree from 1942 to 1944. In 1973, due to the energy crisis, only the star at the top and four spotlights from the ground were lit.

Concern over the hostages in Iran changed the Carters' plans for Christmas. As the First Lady would later explain, "We always went home for Christmas except the one year when the hostages had just been taken. That year we had Christmas at Camp David. We thought any day the hostages would be coming home. My husband didn't want to be too far from the White House. The whole family came and it was really wonderful."

Two days after Christmas, the peace among nations had eroded as Russia invaded Afghanistan; by the following December, reports of Soviet aggression against Poland posed an additional threat to "peace on earth." At home, inflation, recession and unemployment caused a disillusioned electorate to speak their mind in November. The economy and foreign affairs dealt President Carter a decisive blow in his bid for reelection. Sarah Booth Conroy of the *Washington Post* concluded that "even in the times of sadness to the occupants of the White House—when elections have been lost, or scandals threatened resignations, the Christmas celebration goes on, with only a bit of poignancy for the Spirit of White House Christmases Never-to-Be." While it was difficult to project a Merry Christmas, Mrs. Carter was determined to make their last Christmas in the White House a memorable one.

1980: The Andrew Jackson White House

Planning actually began as the decorations came down from the previous Christmas, remarked Gretchen Posten. "We decided that this year would be our romantic, old-fashioned Christmas," the First Lady's social secretary is quoted in the *Washington Post*. "Mrs. Carter has been especially interested in adding to the White House's painting collection. So all year, she's kept her eye out to pick out the painting to use on the Christmas card." The First Lady finally chose a romantic 19th century painting of *The President's House*. In the foreground the unknown artist placed Sunday sailors and straw-hatted fishermen in boats on the serene, but smelly, Tiber Creek. What now flows through a channel under Constitution Avenue was then known to be a "home for dead cats." On a knoll in the background was the White House as it appeared in the days of Andrew Jackson.

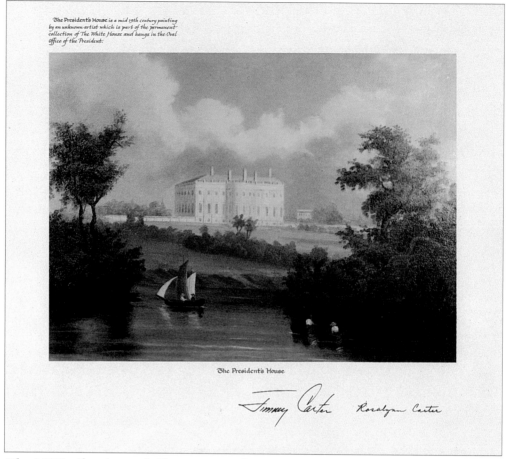

The President's House is a mid 19th century painting by an unknown artist which is part of the permanent collection of The White House and hangs in the Oval Office of the President.

The President's House

The 1980 gift print and Christmas card. AMERICAN GREETINGS

On the back of the card, American Greetings printed a description of the artwork. "This romantic mid 19th century painting of the President's House was executed by an unknown artist after a drawing of the White House by the English artist William H. Bartlett. Bartlett first visited North America in 1836 and steel engravings based on his drawings began appearing in 1837. These engravings were published in England, Germany, France and the United States. They were immensely popular and served as the source for oil paintings and watercolors by many American and European artists. The origin of *The President's House* is unknown." The painting was given to the White House in 1967 by Mr. and Mrs. Hawley S. Simpson. President Carter enjoyed it so much, he chose it to hang in the Oval Office.

The cards were printed by American Greetings Corporation, whose artists began working on the design in the spring and who carefully inspected each card individually. Shortly after receiving the envelopes, 1,000 volunteers began addressing the record number of 120,000 Christmas cards. The message, "With best wishes from our family for a happy holiday season," was intended to be a holiday greeting to those on their official list, as well as a political thank you and good-bye to those who had supported and worked on their 1980 and 1976 campaigns. Mrs. Carter later recalled all the people, all around the country, who campaigned so hard for the President. "It was such a warm, wonderful feeling to have people help you. They would do just about anything for you. We really tried to thank them as we went along, but we also realized how important it was for someone to receive a letter or a Christmas card from the White House. It meant so much to people and we were happy to be able to send it."

The romantic, old-fashioned theme was carried throughout the Executive Mansion. The fantasy of ecru lace and old rose pink was found in the velvet and moiré bows on the wreaths and in the ornaments on the tree. Louis Nichole, a craftsman and interior designer from Hartford, Connecticut, coordinated the Victorian-style decorations. The tree was covered with reproductions of 19th century dolls with porcelain heads; parasols; miniature hats and fans; balls decorated with tapestry and lace; baby's-breath; tassels and 1,000 miniature lights. Under the tree, Nichole and his family re-created a Victorian street scene with their handmade Victorian houses and toys. "I always thought our Christmas decorations were the best in the White House. It was always so beautiful," Mrs. Carter said.

As a real change of pace, President and Mrs. Carter offered snow and Southern hospitality on the South Lawn of the White House to some 4,000 White House staff members, military personnel, Secret Service agents and their families. Using snow made for the occasion, there was a snowman-making contest that was judged by the President himself, with prizes for the winners. A special ice rink was constructed for a performance by Olympic skater Peggy Fleming and a skating snowman. Carolers from churches and schools sang as the White House staffers munched on hot dogs and popcorn and drank hot chocolate and cider. The evening was special, but "the end was spectacular," recalled Gretchen Poston, referring to the final, huge fireworks "Christmas card saying 'Merry Christmas, Jimmy and Rosalynn.'"

White House employees each received one of the 7,000 gift prints of *The President's House* that had been ordered in 1980. Some staffers received, in addition, a leather-bound copy of the President's book *Why Not the Best?*, which he had written on the campaign trail in 1976. As a special parting gift of appreciation in December 1980, the Carters gave a print of Howard Watson's painting of the White House to their staff, senior administration officials and Carter friends. Each print was inscribed and signed by the President and the First Lady.

The last Christmas at the White House was a melancholy time for the Carters. Their social obligations for the season brought them face-to-face

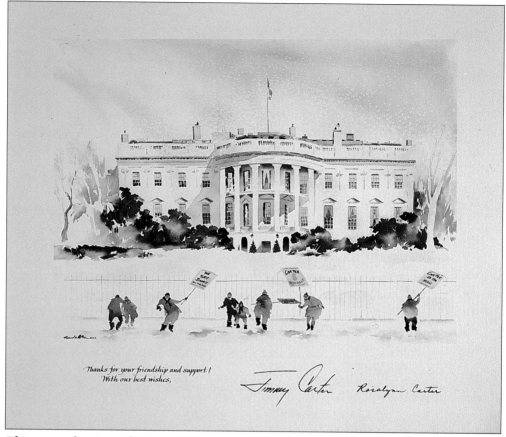

Thanks for your friendship and support!
With our best wishes,

Jimmy Carter   *Rosalynn Carter*

This reproduction of Howard Watson's painting was a special parting gift to the staff, senior administration officials and friends. JIMMY CARTER LIBRARY

with folks they had come to know over the past four years. The First Family took time out to be photographed with each one who had worked for them. President Carter spent his days preparing the last budget he would submit to Congress, while, according to one official, "a kind of aimlessness" set in on those who no longer found it necessary to plan beyond the next month. It was disappointing to the President that the hostages had not yet been released; it was disenchanting to contemplate his future as a former President. In his remarks at the lighting of the National Christmas Tree on December 18, he alluded to both.

> *... Last year, we had a very sober Christmas, and we all were hoping that there would be an early release of the American hostages. And along with that we prayed that their lives would be spared, that they would stay in touch with all Americans who love them, and that we would not be forced to give up either our hope or our faith in God.... Our American hostages have not*

yet come home. But most of our prayers have been answered. They have stayed in touch with their families. So far as we know, they are safe and their lives have been spared....

Last weekend the families of the American hostages met here in Washington to have a briefing by the State Department officials, including the Secretary of State, about the status of the negotiations for their release and to receive the information that we have about how those hostages are getting along. I asked the families of the hostages whether or not they wanted all the lights on the Christmas tree to be lit tonight, or whether they wanted us to light just the Star of Hope on top of the tree and then all Americans to pray that the hostages would come home.... The hostage families asked me to do this year the same thing we did last year. And that is just to light the Star of Hope and to hold the other lights unlit until the hostages come home. And they also asked me to ask all Americans to continue to pray for the lives and safety of our hostages and for their early return to freedom....

For a second straight year the National Christmas Tree remained darkened pending the return of the 50 American hostages. Special recognition was paid to the hostages by the National Association of Broadcasters, who lit the tree for 417 seconds, one second of light for each day in captivity. Christmas came and went. Finally, on the morning of January 20, Inauguration Day, the Carter White House got word that the hostages would be released after 444 days in captivity and put on a plane to leave Tehran. The plane sat on the runway, however, until Ronald Reagan had been sworn in as President of the United States. At noon, the new President got the official word that the plane carrying the hostages was no longer in Iranian air space and that they were on their way to Germany. Jimmy Carter was on his way to Georgia. It was not until then, on January 20, that the National Christmas Tree was fully lighted. Altogether it was a bittersweet day for the former President.

CHAPTER XI

THE REAGANS
Years of Young Artists

Christmas in Illinois, where both Ronald and Nancy Reagan grew up, was a sharp contrast to their Christmases in Washington. In his autobiography, *An American Life*, the President recalls that his family never had a really fancy Christmas. His father, a salesman, struggled to provide for his family, especially during the Depression. When the family couldn't afford a Christmas tree, his mother would decorate a table or make a cardboard fireplace out of a packing box. "Those Christmases when we didn't have much money ... our home radiated with a love and a warmth that meant a lot more to me than packages wrapped in colored paper," said Reagan. While young Reagan learned the value of hard work from his father, it was the faith of his mother that kept the family going during the disappointments of life. She raised her son to believe that God had a plan for everyone and that even the most disheartening setbacks were part of that plan. In the end everything would work out for the best.

As President, Ronald Reagan was to draw upon the faith of his mother when, in an address to the nation on December 23, 1981, he shared some thoughts about Christmas: "Like the shepherds and wise men of that first Christmas, we Americans have always tried to follow a higher light, a star, if you will. At lonely campfire vigils along the frontier, in the darkest days of

Facing page: The Reagans commissioned a number of young artists to produce art for their official Christmas cards and gift prints. The first, *Christmas Eve at the White House*, was painted by Jamie Wyeth. HALLMARK CARDS

the Great Depression, through war and peace, the twin beacons of faith and freedom have brightened the American sky. At times our footsteps may have faltered, but trusting in God's help, we've never lost our way."

The future First Lady, formally named Anne Frances Robbins, was born into a world of change. Her father left shortly after her birth. Her actress mother took Nancy, as she was called, with her from theater to theater, until deciding it would be better for the child to live with her sister. When her mother remarried, Nancy suddenly had a father, a brother, a home in Chicago and a new last name, Davis. "I was indoctrinated early to love Christmas," she said, fondly remembering the old-fashioned tree decorated with all the ornaments she and her brother had made in school. Little Nancy would stay awake Christmas Eve listening for the sound of reindeer on the roof and waited anxiously to see if she had received what she had requested in her letter to Santa.

As First Lady, Nancy Reagan was much less dependent on Santa. "Christmas at the White House was truly magical," she recalled. "We worked out a theme and it was so much fun. The huge tree in the Blue Room was very beautiful and the trees in the East Room looked like they were standing in snow with tiny white lights on them. I remember going in there with the family alone to look at the decorations right after they were finished. Everything was just beautiful. I loved Christmas at the White House even though it was a very busy time."

1981: A Jamie Wyeth White House

To share the aura of the White House at Christmas, the Reagans decided to invite young artists to paint scenes of the Executive Mansion for their Christmas cards. "I thought that people would want to see the different rooms in the White House and that's what we did," explained the First Lady. To introduce the series, social secretary Muffie Brandon recommended the young artist Jamie Wyeth, whose grandfather, N.C. Wyeth, had provided the artwork for one of the Nixons' official Christmas cards.

Jamie Wyeth came to Washington in September to get inspired. "I was given free rein to do whatever I wanted, which was very nice," he said. As he wandered around the White House, he saw that it was more than a people's museum; it was a President's home. "We tend to forget that the First Family actually lives here. They prepare for Christmas, late at night, just like everyone else," he explained. He decided to try something instructive and different—to symbolize by a single light that this is Christmas Eve at the President's House. "I literally went down and sat on the lawn of the White House and began to paint. A large part was done right there, because I don't work from photographs," he said. "I drove down to Washington a couple other days and painted some more and the rest was done back at my farm."

Evoking his powers of imagination, Wyeth sketched the White House under a blanket of snow and, with the magic of his brush, cast a spell of indigo. Using a mixed medium on a toned board, he revealed the mystery of night through the star-studded sky and his single White House light. When he took his work to the White House for the unveiling, the President and Mrs. Reagan both came into the Red Room to see it. The First Lady got the message. It looked, she said, like "everyone else had gone to bed and I was still up in my dressing room wrapping presents and doing all those things you do the night before Christmas. I loved it!"

Entitled *Christmas Eve at the White House*, the Wyeth work required eight color separations and was reproduced by Hallmark. The artist was most pleased with the rich color of the finished product. "Jeannette Lee was wonderful to work with; Hallmark did a terrific job," he said of the company and its veteran consultant. The White House ordered 65,000 cards, slightly more than half of what the Carter Administration had sent the previous year. The engraved message in deep blue script read: "The President and Mrs. Reagan extend to you their best wishes for a joyous Christmas and a peaceful New Year." A blank embossed Presidential Seal appeared above the message, the year 1981 below it. A commemorative postage stamp honoring James Hoban, the architect of the White House and the subject of N.C. Wyeth's 1971 card, was used on the Reagans' first Christmas greeting.

The Reagans' gift to their staff was a keepsake version of Jamie Wyeth's artwork for the Christmas card. A simple enclosure read, "With special holiday wishes, The President and Mrs. Reagan 1981." Mrs. Reagan also gave her East Wing staff a silver-framed photograph with the engraved message: "Merry Christmas 1981, Nancy Reagan." In addition, signed photographs were given to the resident domestic staff. As holiday party favors, the White House ordered 5,000 four-inch brass tree ornaments with the inscription "Merry Christmas, The White House 1981."

The holiday season was ushered in by the first snowfall of the winter. Mrs. Reagan's old-fashioned American Christmas decor reflected the nostalgia of a simpler life, with wreaths in windows, boughs of holly, magnolia leaves, and red and white poinsettias decking the halls of the White House. The 19-foot Fraser fir in the Blue Room was decorated with 200 ornaments by eight craftspeople who had been selected by the director of the Museum of American Folk Art. They had created animals from tin, fabric and wood; some were painted with sponges dipped in color; others arrived with hand-painted faces. The White House menagerie roaming the branches of the tree represented the animals that spoke at midnight and shared the stable with the Christ child. Inspired by Edward Hicks' *The Peaceable Kingdom*, where beast of the field and farm came together in friendship, Muffie Brandon planned the display. At the very top, a nearly two-foot angel Gabriel watched over the flock.

International Posturing Hits the Front Pages

Events of the President's first year in office put a damper on the peaceful holiday mood. Only 70 days after his inauguration, Reagan had received a gunshot wound in an assassination attempt. When, shortly before the holidays, rumors surfaced that a Libyan hit squad had been sent to assassinate the President and other officials, the threat was taken seriously. As a precautionary measure, Ronald Reagan did not appear at the Pageant of Peace and the lighting of the National Christmas Tree on December 17. Instead he remained in the East Room and, by remote control before an audience of 25 children, lit the living Colorado blue spruce on the Ellipse—the same tree that had served in this capacity since 1978. In his televised speech, the Chief Executive alluded only briefly to the international crisis and opted to talk of Christmas traditions and how peace could be achieved. He said: "I know there are some who celebrate this day, the Christmas Day, as the birthday of a great teacher and philosopher. To others of us, he is more than that; he is also divine. But to all of us, he taught us the way that we could have peace on Earth and goodwill to men, and that is if we would do unto others as we would have others do unto us."

Unfortunately, for security reasons, Ronald Reagan was never to attend a tree-lighting ceremony in person. For the eight years of his administration, the Secret Service kept him at least one block from the tree and the crowds.

Disturbing news from Poland also interrupted the mood of Christmas at the White House in 1981. In what was supposed to be a Christmas speech to the nation on December 23, the President sent a strong message to the Soviets condemning their action in Poland and suggesting a way for Americans to make a personal statement. "Yesterday," he said, "I met ... with Romuald Spasowski, the distinguished former Polish ambassador who has sought asylum in our country in protest for the suppression of his native land.... Ambassador Spasowski requested that on Christmas Eve a lighted candle will burn in the White House window as a small but certain beacon of our solidarity with the Polish people. I urge all of you to do the same tomorrow night, on Christmas Eve, as a personal statement of your commitment to the steps we're taking to support the brave people of Poland in their time of troubles."

On Christmas Eve, the candle flickering in the window of the North Portico stood as a symbol of solidarity with the Polish people in their time of crisis. Confined to the White House on Christmas Day because strict security measures would have interfered with the worship of others, the First Family did not attend church services. Instead, they spent their first Christmas in the Executive Mansion quietly among family and friends.

1982: A James Steinmeyer Red Room

For their second official Christmas card, the Reagans continued their idea of commissioning a young American artist to showcase the White House. After seeing his work in *House and Garden* magazine, Mrs. Reagan selected James Steinmeyer, an illustrator noted for his interior renderings, to do the Red Room. The First Lady later admitted her particular fondness of

The Red Room was the subject of illustrator James Steinmeyer's 1982 official Christmas card and gift print for the Reagans. GIBSON GREETING CARDS

that room. It was where she and Soviet leader Mikhail Gorbachev's wife, Raisa, would have coffee and talk; where the Soviet Foreign Minister Andrei Gromyko asked her, "Does your husband believe in peace or war?" "Peace," she said. "You're sure?" "Yes, I'm sure," the First Lady answered. "Well, then, you whisper peace in his ear every night," he instructed her. "I certainly will, and I'll also whisper it in your ear too!" she replied.

Steinmeyer painted in his studio from detailed photographs he had taken of the overall room and its furnishings. Focusing on the fireplace, he meticulously documented the periphery, then added a holiday touch by placing evergreens and pomegranates on the mantel along with magnolia leaves in vases. At a Christmas open house in December, he finally met the Reagans, and the First Lady told him how pleased she and the President were with his warm rendering of the subject. Said Steinmeyer, "The Red Room is a pretty room and the decorative Empire furniture was fun to paint." Reimbursed for his work, the artist gave the painting to the White House. A press release noted that Steinmeyer's gouaches were reminiscent of early 19th century watercolors that reproduced every object in the room in detail while conveying fully the sense of light and shadow.

For the first time, Gibson Greeting Cards, Inc., reproduced the official Presidential Christmas card. That was quite a coup for Gibson, which is just one quarter the size of Hallmark. While printing the Presidential card doesn't enhance a company's finances, "It is nice to be able to say the President uses our card," admitted Ward Cavanaugh, chief financial officer of Gibson. "That puts us in pretty good company," he was quoted in the *Wall Street Journal*.

The White House ordered 65,000 cards and 6,000 gift prints in 1982. These keepsakes were accompanied by an enclosure card bearing the message: "With all best wishes for a joyous Christmas and a peaceful New Year from the President and Mrs. Reagan 1982."

Because in 1981 the White House Historical Society had begun offering for sale to the public a White House Christmas ornament (a Christmas angel in '81 and a dove of peace in '82), there was no need for the Reagans to duplicate the effort as a holiday party favor. Mrs. Reagan did give the press a home-made, red-wrapped present—Monkey Bread, a traditional family favorite at Christmas dinner.

The Reagans kept the theme of a simple old-fashioned American Christmas. Dominating the house were red and green decorations with accents of white. Because of the First Lady's deep involvement with the war against drugs, she enlisted volunteers from Second Genesis, a local rehabilitation center, to help make 2,000 silver and gold metallic ornaments, wrap 100 pounds of California walnuts in lace and trim the White House Christmas tree. The group began working October 29 in the Executive Office

Building. Sidney Shankman, executive director of Second Genesis, wrote Mrs. Reagan to thank her for giving these young people the opportunity to assist her. They were delighted and in awe of having been asked. He said, "Our kids, once they graduate from the program, will not have easy lives. But those who worked with you last Friday will carry with them always the memory that the very gracious First Lady of the Land took time to show them her concern and her love."

Unfortunately, the tree in the First Family's private quarters was lacking its usual nostalgic decorations. "By mistake all our ornaments were sent to storage," Mrs. Reagan lamented in a *Washington Home* article. "I'd have to go through everything to find them, and I'm not in California." A sentimentalist, she had always treasured the decorations her children made in school, as her own mother did. "One year they both did a green cut-out star with silver pasted on it that said 'Merry Christmas, Mom.' They made clay stars too. I kept those things for years. One of the clay ornaments finally broke, but I would keep getting it out, and they would tease me and say, 'Oh, Mom, you don't want to put that on the tree again.'"

The year 1982 also saw the launching of "Christmas in Washington," a TV special bringing the American people into the White House at Christmas as well as providing the First Family a vehicle to communicate their Christmas wishes directly to the nation. Underwritten by NBC, such a holiday musical extravaganza had long been a dream of George Stevens, Jr., founding director of the American Film Institute. Mrs. Reagan showed the taping crew of NBC the White House Christmas tree and gave a history of Christmases in the house for her segment of the special. Then President Reagan talked to a group of children about the real meaning of Christmas and told one of his favorite stories, "One Solitary Life," a piece about Jesus. Said the President:

> *He never wrote a book. He never held office. He never owned a home. He never had a family. He never went to college. He never put his foot inside a big city. He never did any of the things that usually accompany greatness.... Nineteen wide centuries have come and gone, and today He is the centerpiece of much of the human race. All the armies that have ever marched; all the navies that ever were built; all the parliaments that ever sat; all the kings that ever reigned, put together, have not affected the life of man upon the earth as powerfully as this One Solitary Life.*

On December 16, at the lighting of the National Christmas Tree with its 1,500 green, gold and white bulbs, the President made a plea for *all* Americans in the spirit of charity to reach out to others; for neighbor to help neighbor, for employed to help the unemployed, for the fortunate to remember the less fortunate. "They are not statistics, they are people" who have a need, said the President. He was delivering his speech from the Rose Garden of the White House to the crowd at the Pageant of Peace on the Ellipse as well as to the nation at large.

Unemployment had been a troublesome issue for the Reagan Administration. With 12 million Americans out of work, the President looked forward to signing a gas-tax bill to provide more than 320,000 jobs but denounced the temporary "make work" programs that suited the pork barrel needs of Congress. While growing up in Dixon, Illinois, he had seen how ordinary people had solved the problems of their community.

"Whether it was my mother bringing a meal to a family that was down on its luck, my dad canvassing the county in search of work for the jobless, or a group of neighbors getting together to help rebuild a farmer's barn lost in a fire," the President recalls in his autobiography, *An American Life*, "I witnessed how people helping one another could be a far more effective means of solving a community's problem than government giveaway programs." His memories of the Great Depression were too personal and too vivid for him not to show empathy with the plight of the unemployed. He admitted, "I prayed a lot during this period, not only for the country and the people who were out of work, but for help and guidance in doing the right thing."

1983: A Mark Hampton Green Room

Planning for the 1983 official Christmas card began with a search for a watercolorist to paint the Green Room. Shelia Tate, the First Lady's press secretary, said, "It's very difficult to find artists who do such detailed work in watercolor. The Reagans are fond of that style." In the end, five artists were asked to submit samples. Mrs. Reagan chose Mark Hampton's style from a preliminary watercolor of the room. While the First Family had not met Hampton, he was well known as a New York interior decorator, and he had refurbished much of the official residence of Vice President and Mrs. Bush.

Painting from sittings in the Green Room and from photographs, Hampton captured the fine detail of the French crystal chandelier and the Duncan Phyfe secretary. The 1767 portrait of Benjamin Franklin by David Martin was clearly discernible over the fireplace. Holiday greens, red candles, flowers and a wreath in the window added a touch of Christmas. Hampton summed it up: "The Green Room, because of its color, its paintings and its furniture, is one of the most loved of the White House drawing rooms. Furthermore, the Green Room Christmas card served as a pendant to the Red Room Christmas card; that their colors relate to Christmas is obvious." Titled *Green Room at the White House*, the original watercolor was

A watercolor of the Green Room by Mark Hampton became the art for the Reagans' 1983 gift print and official Christmas card.
HALLMARK CARDS

reproduced by Hallmark, which printed 100,000 Christmas cards and 7,500 gift prints.

Addressing the cards for President and Mrs. Reagan was a diverse group of approximately 20 men and 380 women who had volunteered at the Office of Presidential Inquiry. Beginning in November, as reported in a *Los Angeles Times* story by Betty Cuniberti, the "pen-pushers"— as they were affectionately described by the director of volunteers, Joan DeCain—addressed envelopes at an average rate of 30 per hour and 150 per day. Many, using their best penmanship, addressed more than 700 each. Nothing left the White House unless neatly presented. Explains DeCain: "I like it done right. We have a firm policy. Everything is spelled out. We use black ink, and we don't abbreviate the states." A volunteer would choose a favorite pen from a half dozen types and insert a darkly lined "cheat sheet" into an envelope to avoid a downhill slant. A list of the 50 states was taped in front of each volunteer, just in case the brain shut down in the middle of *Mississippi*.

The Republican National Committee picked up the tab for the President's stamps and cards, but duplication was still a concern. "A computer isn't good enough for me. We find we are more accurate," declared DeCain in explaining why volunteers checked names by hand against ZIP codes. Volunteers also stamp the envelopes. "We hand-place the stamps with moisteners, but some of the old-timers lick," admitted the director. Professional calligrapher Kathlyn Peake addressed the envelopes to members of the Senate, the House of Representatives, the Supreme Court and the past Presidents. Her work is a form of art. She managed about 20 an hour. That was a lot of work with no recognition from the VIP, because it was probable that such mail was opened by a staff member who discarded the envelope. "You can only hope that whoever sees it might appreciate it," said Peake.

At the 1983 Pageant of Peace ceremony on December 15, President Reagan was assisted by seven-year-old Amy Benham of Westport, Wash-

"I wish so much to help President Reagan turn on those Christmas lights," wrote seven-year-old Amy Benham to the Make a Wish Foundation. At the Pageant of Peace in 1983, her wish came true.
RONALD REAGAN LIBRARY

ington. A victim of Hodgkin's disease, Amy had written a letter to the National Make a Wish Foundation to explain her dream. She wrote, "Dear Make a Wish, The Christmas tree that lights up for our country must be seen all the way to heaven. I wish so much to help President Reagan turn on those Christmas lights. In my school we learned only about Presidint Washington and Presidint Lincoln. I would like to meet our now Presidint because he is the one that we trust now. He isn't done but I trust him because he loves Jesus just like I do. Love Amy."

Before the lighting of the National Christmas Tree from the South Portico of the White House, President Reagan drew again from the "One Solitary Life" story he liked so well and then introduced Amy, declaring that very shortly "the whole world will know that Amy Benham lit up the skies, sending America's love, hope, and joy all the way to heaven and making the angels sing." Amy's wish came true when 3,600 clear and magenta lights came to life.

On Christmas Eve, in a radio address to the nation, Reagan spoke of the Christmas of 1776, the country's first year as a nation. He said: "The image of George Washington kneeling in prayer in the snow is one of the most famous in American history. He personified a people who knew it was not enough to depend on their own courage and goodness; they must also seek help from God, their Father and Preserver."

1984: A Jamie Wyeth North Portico

For the fourth Christmas at the White House, the Reagans invited Jamie Wyeth back to create an image for a second official Christmas card. Having had such a pleasant experience working with Mrs. Reagan in 1981, Wyeth agreed to paint again if he could do something out of sequence. Capturing the essence of a room did not personally interest him. "She was very open to any interpretation I would do," he recalled.

Wyeth returned to Washington during the fall to get inspired for Christmas. Contemplating the task, he thought, "The White House has so much history. It is a remarkable building, but I have already painted the

Jamie Wyeth's second painting for a Reagan official Christmas card and gift print was this 1984 *Christmas Morning at the White House*. HALLMARK CARDS

With special holiday wishes
The President and Mrs. Reagan
1984

whole house. This time I want it to be more of an intimate interpretation." As he wandered around, he noticed the squirrels. "President Reagan even fed them while I was with him. He kept a bag of acorns right in his office," he observed. Right then and there, he knew he had found that intimate moment; he had his inspiration. When finished, Wyeth had created, in oils, a peaceful view of the North Portico blanketed by newly fallen snow. An American flag unfurled gently in the breeze over the residence of the President. Garlands covered the chains of the lantern, while Christmas trees flanked the front door and wreaths hung in the windows. Only a lone squirrel had left its calling card—little paw prints winding through the fresh snow at dawn.

Nancy Reagan loved it! It reminded her of their weekends at Camp David. "My husband and I would go up every weekend we could. He would gather up nuts for the squirrels at the White House and put them in front of the door by the Oval Office. The squirrels began to know the nuts would be there and they would come every Monday. One weekend—there weren't any nuts—I don't know what happened. The squirrels came to the door of the oval room and they were very upset—very upset and they made their feelings known," she recalled.

After a successful bid for reelection in 1984, the Reagans had need for more Christmas cards and gift prints to appropriately thank people. Hallmark reproduced approximately 125,000 cards and 7,000 gift prints at cost. Both of the original works painted by Jamie Wyeth for the Reagan

Christmas cards were loaned to the White House during the President's term of office. They were later returned to the personal collection of the artist.

The nativity scene, which had been part of the federally sponsored Pageant of Peace until 1973, returned to the Ellipse on December 11 for the first time in 12 years. At the South Portico of the White House, President Reagan spoke of the meaning of the nativity in his remarks at the Lighting of the National Christmas Tree on December 13.

1985: A Thomas William Jones Blue Room

Thomas William Jones was chosen to paint the Reagans' Christmas card in 1985. Lloyd M. Taggart, a member of the President's Committee for Arts and Humanities, had viewed Jones' work at an invitational "Artists in America" exhibition in Denver, Colorado, and made a presentation to the White House on his behalf. The Reagans liked what they saw and asked the artist to paint the Blue Room as part of their series of cards of the White House at Christmas.

The artist first came to the White House in June 1985. For three days he studied photographs taken of Christmas and sketched several scenes of the oval room. His thoughtful approach was to choose a portion of the mantel or a window with a wreath that suggested the Blue Room, but which would not be overwhelmed by the Executive Mansion's tree. White House curator Rex Scouten showed Jones' sketches to the First Lady, who really wanted a panorama of the room. "I loved the Blue Room," she said. It was the only State Room she refurbished by adding furniture that had been kept in storage. It was also the room where she and the President received guests at Christmas and after State Dinners.

As Scouten's trips to the private quarters became more

Thomas William Jones created *The Blue Room at Christmas* for the Reagans' 1985 official Christmas card and gift print, little suspecting that this was to lead to a four-year engagement.
HALLMARK CARDS

frequent, Jones' painting became more encompassing. Together they agreed to a rendering of the room that included the fireplace, two windows and a table, all adorned with simple decorations to capture the holiday spirit, but which would balance Christmas with the character of the room. "It was very interesting listening to the staff excitement about how things are decorated at Christmas and the magic that the White House takes on," said Jones. "It's a very special and exciting time and the spirit and the enthusiasm of the project very rapidly caught up with me."

Jones spent about two months on the painting trying to get every detail right. While he normally employed a looser, freer flowing movement in his paintings than was required for this illustration, his main goal was to please the First Lady. Behind closed doors, the artist rearranged furniture to simplify the composition. He softened edges and utilized underpainting to build textures and suggest detail in areas like the rug and on the wall while actually softening the overall effect.

Was the First Lady pleased? "She was very pleased," he said. "It was a challenge, really, to please a lot of people. I think I did that and I pleased myself," he added. "It's a nice opportunity to do something like this and have the appreciation given to your art." Hallmark reproduced 125,000 Christmas cards and 8,000 gift prints of *The Blue Room at Christmas*. The Republican National Committee paid $27,000 for the printing and mailing.

Having returned from an historic first summit meeting with Soviet leader Mikhail Gorbachev in late November, President Reagan came to light the 1,200 red and gold bulbs on the National Christmas Tree on December 11 with renewed hope for a lasting peace in a nuclear age. At the Geneva summit, the two most powerful men in the world had come together to establish a personal working relationship with each other. Proceeding to that end, Reagan invited Gorbachev to Washington for a future summit meeting. Speaking from the South Portico of the White House to an audience of 12,500 on the Ellipse, the Chief Executive gave "thanks for an America abundantly blessed, for a nation united, free and at peace."

NBC's 1985 "Christmas in Washington" on December 15 focused on children. The First Lady's taped White House segment included a feature on the annual Christmas party for the children of foreign diplomats. The President, with an apology to NBC News correspondent Tom Brokaw, read a contemporary news account of the event in Bethlehem 1,985 years earlier. He quoted:

"And there were in the same country shepherds abiding in the field, keeping watch over their flocks by night. And, lo, the Angel of the Lord came unto them, and the glory of the Lord shone round them; and they were sore afraid.

NBC News correspondent Tom Brokaw and singer Pat Boone are joined on stage by President and Mrs. Reagan for the network's "Christmas in Washington" extravaganza.
RONALD REAGAN LIBRARY

And the Angel said unto them, Fear not; for, behold, I bring you good tidings of great joy, which shall be to all people. For unto you is born this day in the city of David a Savior, which is Christ the Lord."

So it's appropriate that in the Christmas season we honor the little children. Like the Savior, who first appeared in this world a helpless infant, our children, in their vulnerability, innocence, and trust, carry the light of the world in their hearts.

1986: The Jones East Room

Within a week after the Reagans' 1985 Christmas card was revealed to the press, Thomas William Jones was asked to paint the 1986 image. He would be honored to offer his talent to the Reagans for their next card, and he agreed on the condition that he be allowed the freedom to simplify the composition and interpret his own emotions toward the subject.

As in the previous year, Rex Scouten was to be the liaison. "Rex was very cordial to me from the beginning and we developed a friendship," Jones said. When the artist returned to the White House that Christmas, Scouten laid out the plan for the next three years! Mrs. Reagan wanted to make an historical statement by showcasing the East Room, the State Dining Room and the North Entry Hall. None of these had ever been the subject of a Presidential card before. Jones was given a complete vote of confidence; he was free to paint his own impressions of the rooms.

When Tom Jones and his wife, Carrie, walked into the East Room, it looked like a winter wonderland—eight trees covered with tiny white lights, tinsel and a synthetic product called "Real Snow." The mantels were nicely decorated with turn-of-the-century dolls engaged in winter activities. The artist's first impression of Christmas at the White House was collected in a quiet moment and stored in the recesses of his mind. Said Jones, "I don't try to duplicate what's there; I try to duplicate my emotional impression. I seek

The Thomas William Jones 1986 card and gift print art: *The East Room at Christmas.* HALLMARK CARDS

to put on paper what is in my mind. If a branch is too geometric, I paint it the way I want it to be, rather than the way it is. I take a lot of liberties in my painting, but most are very subtle."

The East Room at Christmas was a study of visual simplicity. With a progression of movement, Jones captured the reflection of the room in the mirror, the children playing on the mantel, the crackling fire and the snow-covered trees. Through his use of light and shadow, he directed the viewer's attention to Gilbert Stuart's painting of George Washington—the focal point of the painting and the entire East Room as well. Jones was thoroughly pleased with his watercolor. He later admitted that it was his favorite of the four cards he designed for the White House. Hallmark reproduced 125,000 Christmas cards and 7,200 gift prints for the Reagans' fifth Christmas at the White House.

President Reagan delivered his 1986 Christmas message for the lighting of the National Christmas Tree on December 10 from the Diplomatic Reception Room of the White House. On hand to throw the switch was eight-year-old Byron Whyte, of Prince Georges County, Maryland, with "Big Brother" Francis Hutton. Saluting that program, the President said, "the greatest gift we can give each other is the gift of ourselves."

1987: The Jones State Dining Room

Thomas William Jones returned to the White House during the Christmas of 1986 to sketch preliminary studies of the State Dining Room and the North Entry Hall. The decorations carried the same traditional feeling from year to year, so it was possible to plan the composition of the Christmas cards for the next two years on that visit. For 1987, he painted *The State Dining Room at Christmas.* The fireplace and the painting of Lincoln were draped with boughs of evergreen and red bows. A single poinsettia flanked by brass candelabra adorned the mantel.

To offer a choice, Jones made two preliminary studies of the room. One was an angled view of Lincoln from an opened door; the second focused

The State Dining Room at Christmas was the Thomas William Jones art for the Reagans' 1987 official Christmas card and gift print.
HALLMARK CARDS

straight ahead on the portrait. The Reagans chose the latter, which concerned the artist, because everything was so symmetrical. By incorporating lights and diagonal shadows, however, he worked the opposing elements together to create spontaneity and direction. To simplify the composition, the artist decided to remove the dining room table from the image; when he related that to Scouten, the curator literally had the table moved while the artist painted.

Because Jones likes the elusiveness that watercolor gives his work, he is one of the few artists using it as his primary medium. In the State Dining Room, he was challenged by the hard edges in the architecture. Like an oil painter, he used underpainting to create tonal qualities in the rug and softened the paneling behind Healy's portrait of Abraham Lincoln. Hallmark reproduced 6,600 gift prints and 125,000 Christmas cards of *The State Dining Room.*

The Pageant of Peace was held earlier than usual in 1987 because of a previously scheduled summit meeting with Soviet leader Mikhail Gorbachev and a State Dinner for him and Mrs. Gorbachev. Speaking from the South Balcony of the White House, the President shared his hopes for the summit with the 12,500 people who had gathered on the Ellipse. He said:

Two hours ago, General Secretary Gorbachev's plane touched down on American soil.... He and I will meet in hopes of promoting peace for our peoples and all the people of the Earth. I hope the General Secretary is watching this on TV. I'd like him to see what we're celebrating, because for us, Christmas celebrates the cause of peace on Earth, goodwill toward men. Peace on Earth, goodwill toward men—I cannot think of a better spirit in which to begin the meetings of the next several days. As a small reminder of that spirit, the Star of Peace atop the National Christmas Tree will be lit day and night during the time our Soviet guests are here. And as we look out from

Soviet General Secretary Mikhail Gorbachev and his wife, Raisa, are honored guests of President and Mrs. Reagan at a State Dinner at the White House on December 8, 1987. RONALD REAGAN LIBRARY

the White House during our discussions, let the star remind us why we've gathered and what we seek.

In Luke, chapter 10, verse 5, we read: "Peace be to this house." That blessing is most appropriate over the next several days.

The following day President Reagan and General Secretary Gorbachev took a giant step toward peace by signing an historic treaty that would hopefully eliminate an entire class of nuclear weapons. In the years that followed, Reagan's policy of "peace through strength" led to the demise of the Soviet empire and the end of the cold war.

1988: *The Jones North Entry Hall*

The Reagans' final White House Christmas card art was titled *North Entry Hall at Christmas*; like the three before it, it was designed by Thomas William Jones. The unique view from the Cross Hall, through garland-draped marble columns, focused on a circa 1795 gilded mirror above a pier table purchased by President James Monroe in 1817. The mirror and table were to the west of the Blue Room entrance, and a portrait of President Gerald Ford hung to the right of the mirror. The artist did not want anything to distract from the furniture; consequently, he made the portrait barely visible through the columns and added hurricane lamps and poinsettias.

Hallmark reproduced 125,000 of the cards with the sentiment: "The President and Mrs. Reagan extend to you warm wishes that your holidays and the coming year will be filled with happiness and peace." For the staff, 7,000 gift prints were prepared. T.W. Jones received no remuneration for his labor, but he said, "just the honor of being asked is payment enough." Besides being able to keep his original paintings, Jones met some wonderful people while working with the White House. "The staff was more than gracious and very thoughtful of my every need," he recalled. "It was an experience my wife and I will never forget."

On December 15, President Reagan spoke for the last time at the light-

With warmest wishes for the holidays.
The President and Mrs. Reagan

1988

Thomas William Jones painted *The North Entry at Christmas* for the Reagans' last official Christmas card and gift print. HALLMARK CARDS

ing of the National Christmas Tree at the Pageant of Peace ceremony. From the South Balcony of the White House he addressed the crowd of 12,000 on the Ellipse and extended his final official holiday wishes to the nation. In his speech, he discussed the freedoms Americans often take for granted.

Celebrating Christmas for the last time with the White House staff was bittersweet. "I've always thought of the Presidency as an institution of which Presidents are granted only temporary custody; now my custody was coming to an end and the hardest part was having to say good-bye to those who had helped me carry out my responsibilities and had always been there to help us in difficult personal times," Reagan remarked. Over time, this core of people had become family. It was difficult to express appreciation for the sacrifices they had made on behalf of the First Family. Yet at the same time, the Reagans were looking forward to moving back to California. For a few days over Christmas they were going to live in their new home.

Reflecting on his going home, President Reagan said, "During the eight years we lived in the White House, it became a real *home* because Nancy worked to make it that way. I never stopped missing California; I've often said that a Californian (even one transplanted from the Midwest like me) who has to live someplace else lives in a perpetual state of homesickness. California, I like to say, isn't a place, it's a way of life."

In a Christmas message released by his press secretary on December 19, the President wrote: "As we come home with gladness to family and friends this Christmas, let us also remember our neighbors who cannot go home themselves. Our compassion and concern this Christmas and all year long will mean much to the hospitalized, the homeless, the convalescent, the orphaned—and will surely lead us on our way to the joy and peace of Bethlehem and the Christ Child Who bids us come. For it is only in finding and living the eternal meaning of the Nativity that we can be truly happy, truly at peace, truly home."

Ronald Reagan was a man who unashamedly lived his faith. In his farewell address to the nation on January 11, 1989, he read a quote that his mother had written in her Bible: "You can be too big for God to use, but you can never be too small." His mother, who lived by faith and who died with Alzheimer's, would have been proud of her son. His wife of more than 40 years acknowledged: "He has a very deep faith that comes through in practically every speech he gave." In her *Memoirs*, the First Lady attested to the fact that there is no secret to Ronald Reagan. "He is exactly the man he appears to be," she said. "The Ronald Reagan you see in public is the same Ronald Reagan I live with."

With best wishes for all the joy and peace of Christmas.

The President and Mrs. Bush
1989

CHAPTER XII

THE BUSHES
The First Family of "Firsts"

ver since "Poppy" Bush met Barbara Pierce at a Christmas party in December 1941, they have celebrated life together. After 44 years of marriage, raising five children, losing a sixth to leukemia and moving 29 times, George and Barbara Bush relocated, with much fanfare, to 1600 Pennsylvania Avenue. They especially enjoyed celebrating Christmas at the White House with family and friends and the thousands of visitors who came each year to enjoy the beautiful Christmas sights and sounds with them. In so doing, this First Family established four "firsts" in the cards they selected and sent: the first holiday card done by a White House staff artist; the first card to showcase the Oval Office; the first card to reveal the family quarters at Christmas, and the first card depicting activities on the White House lawn during the lighting of the National Christmas Tree.

1989: First Card by a White House Staffer

To capture the mood of the festive White House for their official Christmas card, Mrs. Bush was encouraged to choose an insider, one who had celebrated many Christmases in the mansion. Director of graphics William Gemmell had, over the years, drawn various images for White House invitations and programs but had never been asked to draw the Presidential Christmas card. Mrs. Bush thought it "would be fun to have someone who had worked so long in the White House and who loved it so much to paint our card."

Facing page: The Bushes' first Christmas gift print. HALLMARK CARDS

Coming on the heels of the Reagan Christmas card series by accomplished American painters, Gemmell felt a lot of pressure. "I was scared to death," he said, "but you do the best you can." Previously he had done the Truman Balcony in black and white, from which he now designed two variations. Using the mixed media of watercolor and acrylic, he sought in both to capture the warmth of the Christmas tree in the Blue Room as viewed through the windows from the South Lawn. Exterior Christmas decorations punctuated the familiar scene, but also incorporated was the Bushes' exclusive, personal entrance into the house, the door leading into the Diplomatic Reception Room. "When the deadline came at the end of May," Gemmell said, "I just had to hand it in and walk away." The title, *Celebrating Christmas at the President's House*, was Mrs. Gemmell's contribution.

Mrs. Bush showed both of Gemmell's paintings of the South Portico to Hallmark representatives. She told them the President liked the version with more snow, while she preferred the one with less snow. To break the tie, Hallmark was asked to take both and reduce them to the appropriate size and pick one. Hallmark's Jeannette Lee, by now a retired consultant, said, "We did the one with more snow because he [the President] told us to." Mrs. Bush was thrilled nonetheless. "Bill did a wonderful job. We loved it, because that's the way you think of the White House."

Hallmark reproduced 150,000 of these official Christmas cards for the First Family in 1989. The inside greeting read: "The President and Mrs. Bush extend their warmest wishes that Christmas and the New Year will hold much happiness and peace for you and those you love." The same image was used for 7,500 gift prints. The executive staff and Cabinet members also received a personalized copy of two books: *The Inaugural Addresses, 1789-1989* and *The American Presidents* (The American Bicentennial Presidential Inaugural Edition).

A Story Book Theme

Not only was Mrs. Bush pleased with their Christmas greetings but also with the holiday decorations of the Executive Mansion. In her *Memoirs*, she wrote: "Planning had begun from almost the minute we moved in.... We settled on a Story Book theme, which seemed appropriate to my interest in reading. Down in the bowels of the first floor the flower shop worked all year under the direction of chief floral designer Nancy Clarke. Often when I would drop by I would see figures appearing that looked like Aladdin with smoke coming out of his magic lamp, Babar and Miss Rumphius, a favorite of mine by author Barbara Cooney." Other characters were Mary Poppins, the Mad Hatter, the Tin Man, the Little Lame Prince, Pinocchio, and the Pokey Little Puppy. Books, tied with red bows, became gifts under the tree.

"Bad weather gave us one of the very nicest experiences we had in George's four years as President—watching the Christmas decorations go up," remarked Mrs. Bush. The 18-foot Fraser fir from Spartansburg, Pennsylvania, was decorated in the Blue Room with literary characters that emphasized the importance of reading to children. White House elves also decorated the family tree in the Yellow Oval Room. It was covered with tiny white lights, decorations the family had gathered over the years and edible gingerbread cookie decorations made by the Bushes' beloved housekeeper, Paula Rendon. Of all the perks that come with living in the White House, "one of the greatest is to come home to find your Christmas tree all decorated," said a delighted Mrs. Bush.

Returning home one Saturday evening, the Bushes walked in on the staff and volunteers engaged in a "snowball fight" following the application of artificial snow to the 17 trees in the front entrance. The First Lady was quick to add that she and the President "didn't partake in the activity. The whole house was full of snow. We wouldn't have missed this weekend for anything." As a special treat, President and Mrs. Bush invited the volunteers upstairs to see their family tree and the magnificent 50-piece needlepoint creche that members of St. Martin's Church in Houston had made for them.

Many parties were held in the upcoming days. Among them was the innovation of "eclectic" receptions that became a tradition of the Bush Administration. Staff members mingled with Cabinet members, the Supreme Court, the Secret Service, the press and friends of the First Family. The Bushes entertained the household staff at a special party so they could get to know the spouses and children of those who worked so hard to maintain the house and make them happy.

Another activity that delighted the First Lady was attending a party for tiny tots at northwest D.C.'s Central Union Mission, a shelter for the homeless and needy. After giving out Chrtistmas bags, the First Lady was to read the Christmas story from the Gospel of Luke. Looking over her very young audience, she quickly switched from storyreader to storyteller, giving it her own personal touch, reported the *Washington Post*. "This is a good story," she began. "So good it lasted almost 2,000 years. Who knows the name of the baby?" "What did the shepherds see in the sky? A star? That's right! Where did they go?" she asked. "Bethlehem," a tiny voice answered. "You've heard this story before, haven't you?" she said.

Amidst the celebration of Christmas, the President faced unbelievable changes on foreign fronts. On December 20, he sent troops into Panama to protect the thousands of American families living there during the ouster of dictator Manuel Noriega. Romania's Communist president, Nicolae Ceausescu, had fled his country, only later to be captured and executed.

From the Soviet Union, President Mikhail Gorbachev announced the collapse of Communism in Eastern Europe.

"The Hammer and the Chisel"

There was reason to celebrate when George Bush came to the end of his first year as President. In his speech at the lighting of the National Christmas Tree, he said:

This is the Christmas that we've awaited for 50 years. And across Europe, East and West, 1989 is ending, bright with the prospect of a far better Christmastime than Europe has ever known–a far better future than the world dared to imagine. And 50 winters have come and gone since darkness closed over Europe in 1939–50 years. But last month ... the wall in Berlin came tumbling down ... And today–there's a new sound at the wall. New sound rings out–not the hammer and sickle but the hammer and the chisel. The glad sound you hear is not only the bells of Christmas but also the bells of freedom.

1990: Oval Office in the Spotlight

It was the President's idea to feature the Oval Office on the holiday card. Built in 1909 for President Taft and opened up to look out over the Rose Garden by President Roosevelt in 1934, the office had been decorated by each new President according to his own personal taste.

New York interior designer Mark Hampton had worked previously with the Bushes on the renovation and decoration of their official residence. In the never-ending task of maintaining the Executive Mansion, Mrs. Bush brought in Hampton to redecorate the President's office and freshen up a few rooms. Hampton told *Town & Country* that the Chief Executive was "very vocal about what he likes. President Bush wanted a new rug–blue with a gold seal. I recovered some chairs for his office, too; they were made for the White House in 1818 and had been in and out of storage over the years." Hampton installed curtains in a shade of blue the President preferred and changed the sofas to a more traditional style. When done, the designer presented the President with a watercolor of the room, which also included the traditional Christmas tree–decorated with Paula's cookies.

For their second official card and gift, President and Mrs. Bush asked Hampton to create a more formal rendering of the Oval Office. The "Sunday painter," as he described himself, sent the Bushes a preliminary sketch. The First Lady said, "He sent the most *marvelous* painting for us to approve and there in the middle was Millie! George felt, and I did too, that when you send greetings to Kings and Queens, you don't need the dog in the picture. So he

The Bushes commissioned Mark Hampton to create a watercolor of the Oval Office for their 1990 gift print. The Presidential card "veteran" had previously done a painting of the Green Room for the Reagans' 1983 official Christmas card and gift print.
HALLMARK CARDS

With our warmest wishes for a blessed Christmas and a peaceful new year.
The President and Mrs. Bush
1990

painted another, and I have both of his sketches—for the official card and the unofficial card." Said Hampton: "It was a great thrill and an honor, especially to someone who has been doing watercolors for 50 years."

Hallmark made 153,000 copies of *The Oval Office, The White House* for the Bushes' official 1990 greeting card and also printed 7,000 gift folders. The President gave members of the Cabinet and executive staff personalized copies of *The Americans: The Democratic Experience* from Daniel Boorstin's trilogy.

The 18 1/2-foot Fraser fir in the Blue Room was laden with ornaments in keeping with the year's Nutcracker theme. On a press tour of the 47 Christmas trees and holiday decorations, Mrs. Bush pointed out some of the 45 porcelain dancers from Tchaikovsky's ballet, 50 pairs of ballet slippers and the hundreds of velvet balls and glass ornaments dating back to the Eisenhower Administration. Then, with a twinkle in her eye, she took the press—and her staff—totally by surprise by inviting the reporters for a quick peek at the family's quarters. As described in the *Washington Post*, the only stipulation was that they had to be up and out in 15 minutes, before the arrival of the President's luncheon guests.

UPI correspondent Helen Thomas called the tour a "first" in her many years of White House reporting. ABC correspondent Ann Compton, who had never been beyond the public floors, witnessed a homey suite of rooms filled with stuffed animals, holiday mementos, the 1989 needlepoint creche and many oversized Christmas stockings for the Bush grandchildren. Centered in the window overlooking the Truman Balcony was a 16-foot Fraser fir loaded with family ornaments.

Threat of Persian Gulf War

Christmas 1990 was a time of uncertainty. The line in the sand had been drawn. With American troops already dispatched to the Persian Gulf, the whole world watched and waited. Hovering on the brink of war, President George Bush kept alive the spirit of peace and goodwill. At the lighting of the National Christmas Tree on December 13, he called on all Americans to make their particular contributions as lights in a dark world:

> We're determined that our nation will become a constellation of hope made up of thousands of separate Points of Light, people helping those in need across our land. People like the more than 100 representatives of daily Points of Light here tonight.... And following the lead of these Points of Light, let all of us echo that beautiful carol, "O, Little Town of Bethlehem" and like that long-ago star, let us shine in all "dark streets" and to all people in the "deep and dreamless sleep" of loneliness and despair.

For 300,000 American servicemen and women, Christmas in the desert was without lights, tinsel and trees, Christmas carols and church programs; without family and friends, spouses and spirits. Soldiers stationed in the sand of Saudi Arabia faced a possible attack from Iraq. On duty in an Islamic country where only secular songs are permitted, where non-Islamic religious services are forbidden, where bareheaded women are culturally offensive and alcohol is illegal, they found little reason to be jolly. Therefore, many found solace in the President's Christmas message broadcast to American troops on Christmas Day.

> We're in the Gulf because the world must not reward aggression, because our vital interests are at stake, and because of the brutality and danger of Saddam Hussein. We're there backed by 12 United Nations resolutions and the forces of 25 other countries.... Today at the White House and all across America, candles burn in remembrance of you and all our troops across the country and around the world. There is no way Americans can forget the contribution you are making to world peace and to our country. Whenever we see Old Glory snapping in the breeze, we think of you. Whenever we hear

the inspirational words of "The Star-Spangled Banner," we think of you. And whenever we enjoy the boundless opportunities of a free country, we think of you....

1991: A First View of Family Quarters

War arrived and then the peace. Kuwait was liberated. In March President and Mrs. Bush visited the freed nation as guests of the Kuwaiti government. "The gratitude toward the United States was overwhelming," said the First Lady. Slowly but surely the troops began to return home.

When it came time to plan the 1991 Christmas card, Mrs. Bush remembered her friend Kamil Kubik, an artist who had been a victim of oppression in his native Czechoslovakia, who had escaped Communism in 1948 and ended up in New York in 1962. It was there in his art gallery on Madison Avenue that Barbara Bush, wife of the then Ambassador to the United Nations, found him and his work. In 1991 she invited him to the White House to create the image of a family Christmas. Set up in the Yellow Oval Room on the second floor with photographs from previous Christmases, the impressionistic artist painted for two days. He remembers it as an "incredible experience to be in that elegant room, surrounded by magnificent American paintings."

Kamil Kubik depicted the Bushes as "First a Family" that loved to be surrounded by their "grands." With all the clan assembled, Christmas morning was a time of great excitement and much commotion. In *The Family Tree, Upstairs at the White House*, the artist portrayed a scene of the opened presents and the toys scattered around the fami-

With our warmest wishes for all the joys of Christmas and peace in the new year.

The President and Mrs. Bush
1991

The Family Tree, Upstairs at the White House, by Kamil Kubik, was the art for the Bushes' 1991 gift print.

HALLMARK CARDS

ly's living area. It was the first time the private quarters had been featured on an official Christmas card. Mrs. Bush reported that she really "loved that card!"

Hallmark reproduced 160,000 of Kubik's pastel for the Presidential card. For the White House staff and others there were 5,000 gift prints made. A subsequent Daniel Boorstin book, *The Americans: The National Experience,* was given to the President's top staff.

Inspired by Mrs. Bush's enjoyment of the art, a Needlepoint Christmas was the theme for decorations at the White House in 1991. The Blue Room's 18 1/2-foot Noble fir was laden with 1,200 needlepoint ornaments based on 106 patterns, mostly by the talented Nancy Clarke, who organized the entire project. Under the tree, an electric train ran through an 82-piece, turn-of-the-century, snow-covered needlepoint village. Along the west wall was a display of Noah's Ark, made of wood, featuring 44 pairs of three-dimensional needlepoint animals plus Noah's family. In the south window rested the needlepoint creche given to the Bushes in 1989, which had spawned the theme. Referring to the 150,000 hours of work logged by 600 volunteers since the project's inception in March of 1990, Mrs. Bush said: "We never dreamed it would be this beautiful. I believe this was our prettiest Christmas of all."

Hostages Back Home

Christmas 1991 was very special. Five newly freed Americans were standing on the platform with the President at the lighting of the National Christmas Tree on December 12. They had spent the previous Christmas chained and blindfolded as hostages in Lebanon. This Christmas the President was welcoming them home as heroes. He said:

This is a very special night.... And on behalf of our loving country I say, finally, to Terry Anderson, to Tom Sutherland, Joseph Cicippio and Alann Steen and Jesse Turner, and the others not here: Welcome home.... And when Terry and Tom and Joseph and Alann and Jesse light our Nation's tree tonight, that act will be a reminder of what they and their companions, living and gone, have already done to light our Nation's soul. God bless these five men, this wonderful country...

When Terry Anderson, who had been held the longest—2,455 days—flipped the switch to light the tree, nothing happened! The President tried; again nothing happened. Despite having been tested five times by park engineers, the switch malfunctioned. The 38-foot blue spruce remained in darkness 28 seconds longer than planned. Then, in patriotic red, white and blue, the lights burst forth for the 12,000 people attending. While the engineers

Terry Anderson (center) flips the switch to light the 1991 National Christmas Tree while President Bush and Alann Steen wait through a momentary electrical malfunction. Anderson, Steen and three other Americans were enjoying their first Christmas at home after being held hostage in Lebanon for a varying number of years. GEORGE BUSH PRESIDENTIAL MATERIALS PROJECT

were mortified, the hostages were just glad to be home.

Kamil Kubik was there, on the Ellipse, his easel set up to record this historic evening on canvas. He viewed the panorama of tiers of red, white and blue lights on the National Tree, multicolored flags on each of the state trees, and white snow on the boughs of the tree on the South Lawn. The artist seized the opportunity to create a picture of a warmly lit Presidential home contrasted against an indigo sky. He later said, "I didn't do it with any idea in mind, I just liked the scene and activity at Christmas."

1992: *The National Christmas Tree on Canvas*

The Bushes were thrilled with Kubik's impression of the National Christmas Tree and asked to use it for their official card—the first time the tree was the subject of a White House card. Even though the artist had previously met and painted for four American Presidents, he described the chance to have his work used in this way as "an incredible honor." Having just become an American citizen in 1992, the immigrant from Czechoslovakia said, "During World War II, I escaped from the Communists and found refuge in the American army. Without America, I don't think the civilized world would be today. The President, as Commander-in-Chief ... is the Guardian Angel. For me to be able to do something for the President, I would drop everything at any time."

Hallmark had incorporated 8,500 reproductions of the Kubik painting into a commemorative folder. The greeting card company also reproduced 185,000 official Christmas cards for the First Family with the same image. Once again the executive staff and Cabinet received a Daniel Boorstin book, this time the last in the trilogy, *The Americans: The Colonial Experience*.

Wishing you all the blessings of Christmas and happiness in the new year.
The President and Mrs. Bush
1992

The 1992 Christmas gift print. *The National Christmas Tree* by Kamil Kubik.
HALLMARK CARDS

Champion Cherry Picker Rider

For 12 consecutive years, as the Vice President's wife and then as First Lady, Barbara Bush had been the one to ride to the top of the National Christmas Tree and hang the star. She first did the honors in 1981 when Nancy Reagan couldn't make it. On her last cherry picker ride, the First Lady kidded, "I'm going to be in the *Guinness Book of Records*. No one else will ever be able to say that, partially because I was greedy and wouldn't let Marilyn [Quayle] do it—not that she asked! But I had my mind made up that that was going to be *my* treat." For her enthusiastic support of the Pageant of Peace, James Ridenour, director of the National Park Service, presented her with a special Park Service citation. Mrs. Bush had become as much of a tradition as the star itself.

The election of November 1992 brought a bittersweet ending to the Bush Administration. When Mrs. Bush conducted her tour of White House decorations for the press, the official Christmas card and gift print were on display. In keeping with the theme of Gift Givers, 86 dolls had been dressed, by Nancy Clarke's floral shop elves, in authentic costumes of gift givers as they had evolved through the centuries from the Magi to Santa Claus. Unlike 1990, when Mrs. Bush had generously given reporters a rare peek at the family's tree, in 1992 the press appeared more interested in Somalia than Santas, more curious about the President's spirits than the First Lady's remarks. Not interested in holding a press conference, Mrs. Bush wished them a Merry Christmas, according to the *Washington Post* account, and left the room.

"To the Children"

The President's remarks at the lighting of the National Christmas Tree on December 10 were short and to the point. Despite the dismal rain, about 7,000 people came out to wish him well. He said:

> ... *Barbara and I want to dedicate this Christmas tree to the children of America, for they are more than our future; they are our present. And they remind us that we must love one another in order to achieve peace. We must love one another. Our prayers are with them and the ones they cherish.... May I simply say, let us think of the children of Somalia, too, the children everywhere who live in fear and want. Our prayers are with them, and may their families be safe and the sporadic fighting over there end soon.*

George and Barbara Bush celebrated Christmas in the White House one last time. Each reception and party took on greater meaning. Their children and grandchildren came for one last visit. Over the four years the White House had become their home. They had enjoyed the "snowball fights" in the entry hall, listening to the carolers, talking to the visitors and watching in their pajamas the guests who had come to dance. "As someone blessed with the extraordinary privilege of living here," the First Lady remarked in an article in *American Home,* "it was a bit surprising that this house so quickly became our home ... the White House must be many things to many people: repository of much of our history, seat of government, public museum and, of course, private residence. This wonderful place fills each of these roles magnificently."

THE WHITE HOUSE, *The Blue Room, 1995*

CHAPTER XIII

THE CLINTONS
A Contemporary Christmas

Going shopping at the malls, walking around and watching people always was a big part of Christmas for Bill Clinton, Hillary Rodham Clinton and their daughter, Chelsea—but one tradition not easily carried out as a First Family of the land. Though the Clintons were all "pretty crazy ... about celebrating Christmas," according to the First Lady, the new President's ambitious agenda for the country absorbed most of their attention. They were not prepared for the reality of having to have plans fully under way by May for the official Christmas card, decorating the White House, scheduling entertainment, staging holiday receptions and ordering gifts. Head usher Gary Walters informed Mrs. Clinton of the procedure. "Being the type who's relieved if my tree is up and decorated by Christmas Eve, I was shocked to hear this," she was quoted in the *Washington Times*. Myriads of decisions and responsibilities fell upon her office. Even though planning for mistletoe and holly began during cherry blossom time, the task of choosing the design for the official Christmas card was to present an unexpected challenge for the new administration.

1993: Finally, It's a Photograph

Mrs. Clinton originally wanted to portray the exterior of the White House on the first Clinton Christmas card, said Anne McCoy, deputy social secretary. In June a White House staff artist was asked to do a painting of the South Portico. After it had been completed, as fate would have it, Hallmark

The Fantasy Blue Room of Thomas McKnight was the art for the 1995 official Presidential Christmas card. AMERICAN GREETINGS consultant Jeannette Lee was at the White House to offer her service and expertise on producing the upcoming Presidential Christmas card. Having worked on them for 35 years, she pointed out that the artwork bore a striking resemblance to the 1989 Bush official card, thus saving the new administration from a potentially disastrous political embarrassment.

In August, with the design unsettled, Mrs. Clinton's social office commissioned Washington illustrator Susan Davis to submit a prototype for the card. She chose to paint the Truman Balcony. While the social office staff was initially pleased, the artist was asked to add Socks or a snowman, or both, to make the painting more personal. Of the several choices she offered, none seemed to capture the essence Mrs. Clinton wanted. Davis was then asked to paint the North Portico, and she produced a night scene of the White House in the snow. "I thought it was very peaceful, very gentle and beautiful," declared the artist. "It had a sweet feeling and represented the youthfulness and hope of the family in the White House." Davis was told that "Mrs. Clinton loved it."

With the First Lady having posed for photographs in *Vogue*, however, the First Family decided they would instead use a photograph. Finally, on Veterans Day, New York photographer Neal Slavin took several shots, including a casual one of the North Portico with trees decorated with Christmas folk art. Deciding to use a more stately setting, the State Dining Room became the backdrop for the photograph. The florist shop decorated the mantel and brought in a tree laden with American crafts ornaments. A feeling of warmth emanated from the fire in the fireplace, from the amber glow of the sconces on the wall and from the artfully positioned bright photographer's lights. The Clintons, posing under a pensive portrait of Abraham Lincoln, had finally found the design for their first official Christmas card.

Neel Lattimore, deputy press secretary for Mrs. Clinton, explained to the *Washington Post*, "We started getting ready for Christmas last summer and a lot of things had a lot of incarnations." Although the Clintons' official Christmas card had undergone a metamorphosis like none other, Mrs. Clinton was pleased with the final product. "We love this room and we love the portrait of Lincoln," she said. "Most people who get this card will never get to come to the State Dining Room." Also, while Hallmark had produced at least one Presidential Christmas card for every administration since Eisenhower's, the President's staff chose to engage American Greetings to reproduce the official 1993 Christmas card.

John Barker, American Greetings manager of investor relations, said, "We have a history of working with Democratic administrations." That, along with the fact that Milton Wolfe was a longtime member of the American Greetings' board as well as a friend of President Clinton, may have figured

The 1993 Clinton Christmas card.
AMERICAN GREETINGS

The White House, State Dining Room, 1993

into the administration's choice for a card company.

Chris Riddle, creative director at American Greetings, called on a number of the tricks of his trade to enhance the degree of warmth and the inclusiveness Mrs. Clinton had requested. "We worked very closely with the White House and with Neal Slavin, shipping things daily by jet to get approval. We wanted to make sure the skin tones stayed healthy and that we kept every detail in the Lincoln portrait. It was exciting for us," he recalled. The cards bore a blind embossed Presidential Seal on the inside with an ecumenical message: "Our family wishes you and yours a joyful holiday season and a new year blessed with health, happiness and peace." Eventually, 250,000 cards were produced along with 10,000 keepsake gift prints bearing the same image.

The American Greetings plant in Corbin, Kentucky, handled the initial printing of the artwork on the cards; workers at the Kentucky Bardstown plant embossed the Presidential Seal. In Arkansas, workers at the Osceola plant supplied 300,000 "basic but elegant" envelopes to the President's Christmas package. Paid for by the Democratic National Committee, the cards were printed on recycled paper; the back carried the logos of American Greetings and the teamsters union.

Tight security measures at the Kentucky plants assured the secrecy the White House required, including individual hand inspection, counting and locking up cards at the end of every work session. In an effort to deliver the season's greetings to the Executive Mansion by the first week in December, the cards were printed over Thanksgiving weekend. Having the White House as a customer meant more pressure for plant workers, but most of them probably would have agreed with American Greetings chairman Morry Weiss. "It's been a pleasure to work with the White House in the creation of the first Christmas card of the Clinton Administration," he said. "We are honored to have lent our creative expertise to the Clintons in communicating their holiday greetings." Whatever honor had gone to the volunteers who in previous years had prepared First Family cards for mailing ended, however, as the Democratic National Committee hired a bulk mailer to address, stuff and seal the envelopes. With time of the essence, technology was the solution.

American Crafts Ornaments

Amidst what was described as a "tour de force of American creativity" that enhanced the Clinton White House, the First Lady declared, in the Cleveland *Plain Dealer*, "In looking for a theme that would tie together what we cared about and the kind of fun we wanted to have at Christmas, it seemed to us that highlighting American crafts would be a way to really show what is best about America and also have a beautiful Christmas filled with lots of the symbols of the season." Her staff solicited 70 of the nation's top craft artists to contribute their best work for the White House's permanent display. Hundreds of other artists were asked to design ornaments, primarily angels and musical instruments, to decorate the 22 Christmas trees. In describing the ornaments, the First Lady said, "Some are quite elegant and rather magnificent. Some are funky and down to earth. They run the whole gamut. I like them all." The decorations also included a quilted tree skirt made of 57 patches representing each of the states and territories.

To Anne Gowen of the *Washington Times*, "It was a little disconcerting to see folk art in the very formal White House rooms, a blue gift bag-shaped glass below the portrait of Nancy Reagan, for example, or an assortment of wood balls under the portrait of John F. Kennedy." Defending the Year of the Craft theme, social secretary Ann Stock said, "They might not seem to fit into what seems very traditional, but they really do." Other visitors liked the contrast. One commented, "It certainly puts a different spin on the 18th century White House." Chief White House floral designer Nancy Clarke, who planned the transformation with Stock, called the look "contemporary," saying, "It's a cheerier, happier look for the White House. It's a younger look" for a young First Family.

For Christmas, members of the White House staff received a commemorative gift print of the photographic portrait of the Clintons taken in the State Dining Room. The President also gave leather bookmarks in various colors. Each carried the Presidential Seal, the President's signature, and the words "The White House, 1993." The gift was enclosed in a paper envelope bearing a message from the Chief Executive.

The Clintons' contemporary Christmas was also reflected at the Pageant of Peace ceremony on December 9, with a fiber-optically illuminated sphere perched on the living Colorado blue spruce that had served as the National Christmas Tree since 1978. A shivering crowd of about 9,000 listened to the President, who called on Americans "to bring more peace to the streets, the homes and hearts of our own people, and especially our children."

Presidential Pandemonium

A big part of a Clinton Christmas is going to the malls to shop. Mrs. Clinton is a year-round shopper who admits, "I squirrel things away that people would like." Before assuming the Presidency, Mr. Clinton would go out on Christmas Eve and shop for about six hours with friends, all of whom were trying to figure out what to buy their wives for Christmas. When he expressed concern about how, as President, he would accomplish his shopping, the First Lady told him: "We're going to do it. I don't quite know how yet, but we are." When the Clintons finally took time off for last-minute Christmas shopping in a Georgetown mall, their short visit caused pandemonium and brought surprised shoppers to the balconies. Consequently, the President spent only 30 minutes in only one store, but did manage to fill two shopping bags with gifts selected by all the family. "It still was a lot of fun, so we'll probably figure out ways for us to shop," said Mrs. Clinton as she jokingly hinted at a disguise. "Groucho Marx glasses or something? We'll have to work on that," she told *USA Today's* Katy Kelly.

Admitted Ann Stock, the Clinton staff learned a lot that first year about how to prepare for Christmas at the White House. At a logistical debriefing in January, Mrs. Clinton and her staff evaluated what worked and what needed refining. One thing was sure—their approach for the second year would be very different from the first one.

1994: Enchanted Red Room

After personally being a part of the first Clinton Christmas card, the First Lady decided that with the second Presidential card she wanted "to highlight the house and the feeling that the house has during Christmas, which really is magical," according to *USA Today*. Mrs. Clinton was partial to the popular, contemporary Thomas F. McKnight, a romantic figurative artist known in the art world for his boldly colorful silkscreens. Before coming to Washington, the Clintons had acquired a serigraph print of McKnight's *Constitution*, which was used as the official image for the historic document's Bicentennial. It was included in "our idiosyncratic little collection of stuff that we have accumulated over the years," said Mrs. Clinton. McKnight's print hangs in the White House solarium, which serves as the Clintons' living room. According to *Greenwich Time*, the First Lady said to her press secretary, Lisa Caputo: "We just love Thomas McKnight. We'd love to have him do our Christmas card."

McKnight met the Clintons at a reception in the White House in October 1993. Ann Stock showed him around the State Rooms and commissioned him to paint the 1994 official Christmas card. The artist returned to the White House during Christmas of 1993 and took lots of photographs

THE WHITE HOUSE, THE RED ROOM, 1994

*Our family wishes you and yours a joyful holiday season
and a new year blessed with health, happiness, and peace*

Bill Clinton   Hillary Rodham Clinton

McKnight's Red Room was the art for the 1994 gift print. AMERICAN GREETINGS

from which to paint. Back in his studio in Palm Beach, visions of Christmas did not come naturally, as he admitted to the *Palm Beach Daily News*: "You're not exactly inspired to do Christmas scenes in Florida." Eventually, though, he painted fantasy interiors of both the Red Room and Blue Room on canvas in casein, a milk protein/water-based pigment that produces a velvety matte finish. In March he sent transparencies of his images to the White House to await approval. Because the Blue Room was on the agenda to be renovated, the Clintons chose McKnight's sensuous silkscreen of the Red Room decked out in Clintonian Christmas finery. The First Lady, exclaimed Ann Stock, was "immediately drawn to it because of its warmth. This was exactly as he painted it. She required no changes to be made. She loved it!"

Inspired by Henri Matisse's *Red Studio*, McKnight had given the Red Room an enchanted, almost humorous look, a marked departure from the traditionally formal Red Room scene of the Kennedy and Reagan Christmas cards. In keeping with his recognizable style, the artist brought the Washington and Jefferson monuments in full view of one looking out a Red Room window. His light source was a dreamy moon, the icon of his work. Wrote McKnight in his *Voyage to Paradise*: "I attempt to evoke with color, form and imagination the essence of a place or thing without so much regard for historical accuracy."

Consequently, McKnight removed 19th century paintings from the walls of the Red Room and added personal images that were not a part of the room. Above the door, he portrayed himself and his wife's dog, Shadow, gazing over the rolling hills of Middletown, where he had attended Wesleyan University in the 1960's. "The view is actually from a classroom window on the Wesleyan campus," he told the *Litchfield County Times*. Above the fireplace he rendered a fanciful picture of the White House. Traditionally, there had never been a Christmas tree in the Red Room until the artist superimposed one along with other images that were sentimental to the First Family. On the mantel, McKnight hung three stockings designed with American flags; under the gracefully decorated tree he placed a new saxophone for the President and a sled for Chelsea; under the chair he caught the Clinton cat napping; on the table he placed a tea set for the tea-loving Mrs. Clinton and books in keeping with the family's avid reading habits.

While some suggest that McKnight's inspiration easily could have come from the children's book *Good Night Moon* by Margaret Brown, the artist had never seen the work before doing the painting. "I must have read *Good Night Moon* 10,000 times," admitted the First Lady, who, for *USA Today*, described the card as "magical."

American Greetings, according to chairman Morry Weiss, produced 250,000 Presidential holiday cards and 15,000 gift prints. Again, the Democratic National Committee paid for printing the Presidential cards on recycled paper and for mailing them out. The envelopes, made at the American Greetings plant in Osceola, Arkansas, were addressed by computer, stuffed by machine and stamped by meter. For the first time, those who didn't make the mailing list could view a color graphic of the card by computer at the Internet home page http://www.whitehouse.gov.

The Twelve Days of Christmas

At about the same time the White House Christmas card was being unveiled, the Blue Room tree, an 18-foot Missouri-grown Colorado blue spruce, arrived from Clinton County. The theme of the decorations was the Twelve Days of Christmas, which, according to Mrs. Clinton, is one of the family's favorite carols. "It's one that traditionally for our family we sing and act out—which is something we will not do in public—for the benefit of everyone's sensibility.... This will be a wonderful Christmas, although a little bittersweet, because my father won't be here and my husband's mother won't be here either."

On December 7, with springlike temperatures, more than 9,000 people gathered for the lighting of the National Christmas Tree. Scott Bowles of the *Washington Post* wrote: "The event is quintessential Washington: White House Staff members and Secret Service officers elbow to elbow; traffic snarls that turn the mall into a parking lot; stand still lines (everyone attending has to pass through metal detectors and submit bags for police searches); and better views from homes across the country than at the scene. But ... it is one of the few Washington spectacles that draws out the local crowd." President Clinton called the National Christmas Tree "a symbol of the enduring values in our lives."

The Clintons enjoyed their second White House Christmas with friends, helping those in need and going to church—all the traditions important to the President and his family. Mrs. Clinton added: "I would love for the Christmas season to enter into the heart of every American and for the Spirit of Christmas and the Christmas story to be a part of how we treat one another and feel about ourselves. And really the root of the Christmas story is love and hope, and that to me is the greatest gift that anyone can give."

1995: *Fantasy Blue Room*

With the defeat of the administration's health care bill, the First Lady diverted her energy from reform to the renovation of the Blue Room, a project made public in February of 1995. As far back as 1990 the Committee for the Preservation of the White House had concluded that the Blue Room had become unpresidentially frayed and recommended that it be renovated. In 1994, the oval room's carpet, which had been woven in Peking around 1850 for a French palace, was pronounced beyond repair. The First Lady observed that the entire room had become "a little bit tired" since its restoration in 1972. Following a long period of research and planning, work on the room began as soon as the 1994 Christmas tree was removed. Mrs. Clinton determined that the color would be a stronger blue than it had been in 23 years.

The new Blue Room was showcased on the Clintons' Christmas card in 1995. The First Family requested that Thomas McKnight again provide an artistic image for their official card. Despite the honor such an assignment held, the artist had mixed feelings about a repeat performance. "It takes a lot of work to get it right. It has to be fairly accurate. A lot of my work is fantasy and it comes right out of my head," he told the *Palm Beach Daily News*. The previous year, to give the Clintons a choice of either the Red Room or the Blue Room for their holiday card, McKnight had painted a more formal Blue

Room scene that wasn't used. This second time, the artist did a more cozy one.

Comfortable in the fanciful setting was the First Cat, Socks, snuggling under a blanket below a Christmas tree decorated with miniature American flags. Socks' apparent White House guest was Mrs. McKnight's dog, Shadow, who had also appeared in a painting in the 1994 rendering of the Red Room. The curious painting between the windows was a substitute for the portrait of President James Madison that normally hangs in the room. The artist does not duplicate existing paintings but instead creates new ones. In this case, he painted the view of his neighbor's backyard in Litchfield, Connecticut. "It's my own fantasy," claimed McKnight. The backyard scene even included the historic Sheldon's Tavern where George Washington was said to have stayed. "I put this image in the painting because I love New England, and Litchfield is a beautiful old New England town. What could be more reflective of America?" queried the artist in the *Litchfield County Times*. He also admitted that he truncated the distance between the fireplace and the window in order to get both of the windows in the rendering. The Blue Room actually has three windows overlooking the Washington Monument, which he skewed to highlight a dreamy trademark full moon.

American Greetings' Chris Riddle said, "It was very important to Mrs. Clinton that everything in the Blue Room be exact in color and design. On our trip to Washington, D.C., we toured the Blue Room with the artist, and received actual samples of the drapery from the office archives to compare with our color proofs." Quality control continued at the American Greetings plant in Corbin, Kentucky. "Everyone works their hardest to make sure it's the best it can be," said third-shift press operator Eddie Hubbard in *Expressions*. In the same publication, Maureen Stratton, director of marketing/public relations and trade relations for American Greetings, said: "We are contributing to a historical event. Presidential Christmas cards become part of our nation's archives. This makes American Greetings part of our country's official history."

American Greetings reproduced 300,000 official cards and 15,000 gift prints for the President and First Lady. McKnight's full-color image was "tipped on" to the front of an off-white folder with a natural deckle edge. The card was enhanced by a gold hot-stamped border and a blind embossed Presidential Seal.

"The Night Before Christmas"

McKnight's original painting of the Blue Room was displayed in the Blue Room along with an 18 1/2-foot Fraser fir from Ashe County, North Carolina. The official theme for the Clintons' third White House Christmas was "The Night Before Christmas." Said Ann Stock, "The selection was a personal one. The President has read the Clement Moore poem to his daughter every Christmas since she was born." Awaiting the Clintons upon their return from a five-day European trip were 32 Christmas trees, all decorated with hand-crafted ornaments, and a gingerbread house fashioned after the First Lady's childhood home.

Meeting the press at the annual unveiling of the White House Christmas decorations, Mrs. Clinton was preoccupied by the President's decision to send American troops into Bosnia on a peacekeeping mission. Having just met with the wives of officers and enlisted men stationed in Germany, she revealed plans to ask Americans to write letters to single soldiers and to the families of the troops bound for the Balkans. Standing behind her husband's decision, Mrs. Clinton said, in the *Washington Times*, "It's easier in some ways to stay mired in the past and live with a heritage of hatred; it takes courage to break the chain and go that extra mile for peace.... I think the United States has played a major role in taking those risks."

Speaking at the lighting of the National Christmas Tree on December 6, President Clinton asked the American people to join him "to be peacemakers. For just as many nations around the world and so many children around the world cry for peace, so do we need peace here at home in our toughest neighborhoods, where there are children, so many children who deserve to have their childhood and their future free and peaceful."

On Christmas Eve, President and Mrs. Clinton invited to the White House members of seven families of servicemen and women serving in the Armed Forces. In their presence the President taped a message to American troops everywhere. He said: "There is too much at stake in Bosnia today for our nation to sit on the sidelines, and that's why we've turned to you, our men and women in uniform. You provide us with the power to meet threats to our security. You have the strength to bring hope and stability to people exhausted by war. We know, and the people of Bosnia know, that you will get the job done and that you will do it right...."

The First Family spent a quiet Christmas at the White House in 1995. The President and Chelsea did get out to do some last-minute shopping at the Georgetown Park mall the day before Christmas, but there was no indication

The 1995 National Christmas Tree.

Poised before the 1995 tree, the Clintons are the latest First Family to celebrate the holidays at the White House. BOB NEELY/THE WHITE HOUSE

as to what kinds of gifts the family exchanged. A spokesperson indicated that they "really want to keep it kind of a private Christmas." The *Washington Times*, however, carried a Christmas Day photograph of the President reading "The Night Before Christmas" to Metropolitan Area children he and Mrs. Clinton had invited to the White House. The *Times* also released the President's Christmas message that called for "a solemn commitment to the children of our communities, our nation, and the world. Let us," he said, "pledge to love and nurture them and promise to give them strong values and a chance to make the most of their God-given talents. Let us resolve that they will grow up in a world that is free and at peace."

1996: The People's Choice

The planning for the 1996 Clinton Christmas will probably be supervised from the campaign trail. When asked about her participation in the Presidential election, the First Lady replied, "I will be very involved and active. All of us who care about the quality of life for ourselves and our children will be involved in it."

Regardless of who the people choose in November, the election will not greatly alter Christmas at the White House. It has been observed that neither wars, death, international crises, energy shortages nor depression have extinguished the nation's spirit of Christmas. Every year, come December, the long months of careful planning are revealed. Once again the halls and trees in the Executive Mansion are bedecked in yuletide finery.

From the Clinton White House has come this statement: "The holidays are a season for traditions and an opportunity to give thanks for the blessings we share as families, as friends, and as a nation. Christmas is, and always has been, a special time for our family, and particularly so as we celebrate the traditional White House festivities. May the spirit of love and hope that is the Christmas story find a place in your heart throughout the year."

The tradition continues. Over the years, the President and the First Lady have extended to everyone across the nation and around the world Season's Greetings from the White House.

SELECTED TREE-LIGHTING SPEECHES
OF THE PRESIDENTS

1928
Calvin Coolidge

Speaking at Sherman Square: In token of the good-will and happiness of the holiday season and as an expression of the best wishes of the people of the United States toward a Community Christmas Tree, in behalf of the city of Washington, I now turn on the current which will illuminate this tree.

1931
Herbert Hoover

Speaking at Sherman Square: Mr. Vice President, the people of Washington and of our whole country wide: This is the season and this is the occasion when the whole Nation unites in good cheer and good wishes. We dedicate it particularly to our children, and we give devotion to the faith from which it is inspired.

It gives me great pleasure to join in this ceremony of the lighting of this tree, which is indeed symbolic of that in every household in our country. I ardently wish to every home a Merry Christmas and a Happy New Year.

1933
Franklin D. Roosevelt

Speaking at Sherman Square: We in the Nation's capital are gathered around this symbolic tree celebrating the coming of Christmas. In spirit we join with millions of others, men and women and children, throughout our own land and in other countries and continents, in happy reverent observance of the spirit of Christmas.

For me and my family it is, I am sure, the happiest of Christmases. To the many thousands of you who have thought of me and have sent me greetings (and I hope all of you are hearing my voice), I want to tell you how profoundly grateful I am. If it were within my power so to do I would personally thank each and every one of you in every part of the land for your remembrances of me, but there are so many thousands of you that that happy task is impossible. But even more significant is the deep conviction that this year marks a greater national understanding of the significance in our modern life of the teachings of Him whose birth we are celebrating. To more and more of us the words "thou shalt love thy neighbor as thyself" have taken on a meaning that is showing itself and proving itself in our purposes and daily lives. May the practice of that high ideal grow in us all in the year to come, and so I give you and send you, one and all, old and young, a merry Christmas and a truly happy New Year. And so for now and for always, "God bless us every one."

1936
Franklin D. Roosevelt

Speaking at Lafayette Square: I have been reading the *Christmas Carol* to my family, in accordance with our old custom. On this eve of Christmas I want to quote to you the pledge of old Scrooge when, after many vicissitudes, he had come to understand in his heart the great lesson and the great opportunity of Christmastide.

"I will honor Christmas in my heart and try to keep it all the year. I will live in the Past, the Present and the Future. The Spirits of all Three shall strive within me. I will not shut out the lessons that they teach."

And at the end of the story is this glorious passage:

Scrooge was better than his word. He did it all and infinitely more; and to Tiny Tim, who did not die, he was a second father. He became as good a friend, as good a master and as good a man as the good old city knew, or any other good old city, town or borough in the good old world. Some people laughed to see the alteration in him, but he let them laugh and little heeded them; for he was wise enough to know that nothing ever happened on this globe for good, at which some people did not have their fill of laughter in the outset. His own heart laughed; and that was good enough for him.

The teaching of the Sermon on the Mount is as adequate to the needs of men and of Nations today as when it was first proclaimed among the hills above the Sea of Galilee. In such measure as its spirit is accepted men and nations may lay claim to be seekers after peace on earth.

We of the Western Hemisphere have this year rendered special tribute to the spirit of Christmas, for we have pledged anew our faith in the arbitrament of reason and the practice of friendship. To that faith we bear witness tonight. May that faith make us happy today and tomorrow and through all the coming year.

1938
Franklin D. Roosevelt

Speaking at Lafayette Square: Tonight is Christmas Eve. We are gathered again around our Community Tree here in Lafayette Park, across the street from the White House. Darkness has fallen over the Capital but all about us shine a myriad of brilliant lights. All our hearts, warmed by the eternal fire of Christmas, rejoice, because new life, new hope, new happiness are in them.

In this setting I wish my fellow countrymen everywhere a merry Christmas with peace, content and friendly cheer to all. I wish also to thank the thousands who have remembered me and my family this Christmas with individual greetings. We shall always treasure these friendly messages.

At this time let us hope that the boon of peace which we in this country and in the whole Western Hemisphere enjoy under the providence of God may likewise be vouchsafed to all nations and all peoples. We desire peace. We shall work for peace. We covet neither the lands nor the possessions of any other nation or people.

We of the western world, who have borne witness by works as well as words to our devotion to the cause of peace ought to take heart tonight from the atmosphere of hope and promise in which representatives of twenty-one free republics are now assembled in the Pan-American Conference at Lima, Peru.

I consider it a happy circumstance that these deliberations will be successfully concluded soon after the birthday of the Prince of Peace. It is indeed a holy season in which to work for good will among men. We derive new strength, new courage for our work from the spirit of Christmas.

We do not expect a new Heaven and a new Earth overnight, but in our own land, and other lands—wherever men of good will listen to our appeal, we shall work as best we can with the instruments at hand to banish hatred, greed and covetousness from the heart of mankind.

And so the pledge I have so often given to my own countrymen I renew before the whole world on this glad Christmas Eve, that I shall do whatever lies within my power to hasten the day foretold by Isaiah, when men "shall beat their swords into ploughshares and their spears into pruning hooks; nation shall not lift up sword against nation, neither shall they learn war any more."

1939
Franklin D. Roosevelt

Speaking at the Ellipse: My neighbors of Washington and my neighbors in homes in every part of the nation:

The old year draws to a close. It began with dread of evil things to come and it ends with the horror of another war adding its toll of anguish to a world already bowed under the burden of suffering laid upon it by man's inhumanity to man. But, thank God for the interlude of Christmas.

This night is a night of joy and hope and happiness and promise of better things to come. And so in the happiness of this Eve of the most blessed day in the year I give to all my countrymen the old, old greeting—"Merry Christmas—Happy Christmas!"

A Christmas rite for me is always to re-read that immortal little story by Charles Dickens, <i>A Christmas Carol.<p> Reading between the lines and thinking as I always do of Bob Cratchit's humble home as a counterpart of millions of our own American homes, the story takes on a stirring significance for me.

Old Scrooge found that Christmas wasn't a humbug. He took unto himself the spirit of neighborliness. But today neighborliness no longer can be confined to one's own little neighborhood. Life has become much too complex for that. In our country neighborliness had gradually spread its boundaries—from home to town, to county, to State—and now at last to the whole nation.

For instance, who a generation ago would have thought that a week from tomorrow—January 1, 1940—tens of thousands of elderly men and women in every State and every county and every city of the nation will begin to receive checks every month for old age retirement insurance—and not only that but also insurance benefits for the wife, the widow, the orphan children and even dependent parents?

Who would have thought, a generation ago, that people who lost their jobs would, for an appreciable period, receive unemployment insurance and that the needy, the blind and the crippled children are receiving some measure of protection which will reach down to the millions of Bob Cratchits, the Marthas and the Tiny Tims of our own little four-room houses, in every part of the nation.

In these days of strife and sadness in many other lands, let us in this nation and in the other nations which still live at peace, forbear to give thanks not only for our good fortune in our peace. Let us rather pray that we may be given strength to live for others, to live more closely to the words of the Sermon on the Mount, and to pray that peoples in the nations which are at war may also read, learn and inwardly digest these deathless words. May their import reach into the hearts of all men and of all nations. And so I offer them as my–Christmas message:

> Blessed are the poor in spirit: for theirs is the Kingdom of
> Heaven.
> Blessed are they that mourn: for they shall be comforted.
> Blessed are the meek; for they shall inherit the earth.
> Blessed are they which do hunger and thirst after
> righteousness: for they shall be filled.
> Blessed are the merciful: for they shall obtain mercy.
> Blessed are the pure in heart: for they shall see God.
> Blessed are the peacemakers: for they shall be called the
> children of God.
> Blessed are they which are persecuted for righteousness' sake:
> for theirs is the Kingdom of Heaven.

1941
Franklin D. Roosevelt
Speaking from the South Portico of the White House
With British Prime Minister Winston Churchill as guest

The President:

There are many men and women in America–sincere and faithful men and women–who ask themselves this Christmas: How can we light our trees? How can we give our gifts? How can we meet and worship with love and with uplifted hearts in a world at war, a world of fighting and suffering and death?

How can we pause, even for a day, even for Christmas Day, in our urgent labor of arming a decent humanity against the enemies which beset it?

How can we put the world aside, as men and women put the world aside in peaceful years, to rejoice in the birth of Christ?

These are natural–inevitable–questions in every part of the world which is resisting the evil thing.

Even as we ask those questions, we know the answer. There is another preparation demanded of this Nation beyond and beside the preparation of weapons and materials of war. There is demanded also of us the preparation of our hearts; the arming of our hearts. And when we make ready our hearts for the labor and the suffering and the ultimate victory which lie ahead, then we observe Christmas Day–with all of its memories and all of its meanings–as we should.

Looking into the days to come, I have set aside a Day of Prayer, and in that Proclamation I have said:

"The year 1941 has brought upon our Nation a war of aggression by powers dominated by arrogant rulers whose selfish purpose is to destroy free institutions. They would thereby take from the freedom-loving people of the earth the hard-won liberties gained over many centuries.

"The new year of 1942 calls for the courage and the resolution of old and young to help to win a world struggle in order that we may preserve all we hold dear.

"We are confident in our devotion to country, in our love of freedom, in our inheritance of courage. But our strength, as the strength of all men everywhere, is of greater avail as God upholds us.

"Therefore, I ... do hereby appoint the first day of the year 1942 as a day of prayer, of asking forgiveness for our shortcomings of the past, of consecration to the tasks of the present, of asking God's help in days to come.

"We need His guidance that this people may be humble in spirit but strong in the conviction of the right; steadfast to endure sacrifice, and brave to achieve a victory of liberty and peace."

Our strongest weapon in this war is that conviction of the dignity and brotherhood of man which Christmas Day signifies–more than any other day or any other symbol.

Against enemies who preach the principles of hate and practice them, we set our faith in human love and in God's care for us and all everywhere.

It is in that spirit, and with particular thoughtfulness of those, our sons and brothers, who serve in our armed forces on land and sea, near and far–those who serve for us and endure for us–that we light our Christmas candles now across the continent from one coast to the other on this Christmas Eve.

We have joined with many other Nations and peoples in a very great cause. Millions of them have been engaged in the task of defending good with their life-blood for months and years.

One of their great leaders stands beside me. He and his people in many parts of the world are having their Christmas trees with their little children around them, just as we do here. He and his people have pointed the way in courage and in sacrifice for the sake of little children everywhere.

And so I am asking my associate, my old and good friend, to say a word to the people of America, old and young, tonight–Winston Churchill, Prime Minister of Great Britain.

The Prime Minister:

Fellow workers in the cause of freedom.

I have the honor to add a pendant to the necklace of that Christmas goodwill and kindness with which my illustrious friend the President has encircled the homes and families of the United States by the message of Christmas Eve which he has just delivered.

I spend this anniversary and festival far from my country, far from my family, and yet I cannot truthfully say that I feel far from home. Whether it be the ties of blood on my mother's side, or the friendships I have developed here over many years of active life, or the commanding sentiment of comradeship in the common cause of great peoples who speak the same language, who kneel at the same altars, and who to a very large extent pursue the same ideals–whichever it may be—or all of them together—I cannot feel myself a stranger here in the center of the summit of these United States. I feel a sense of unity and fraternal association which through all your kindness convinces me that I have a right to sit at your fireside and share your Christmas joys.

Fellow workers, fellow soldiers in the cause, this is a strange Christmas Eve. Almost the whole world is locked in deadly struggle. Armed with the most terrible weapons which science can devise, the nations advance upon each other.

Ill would it be for us this Christmastide if we were not sure that no greed for the lands or wealth of any other people, no vulgar ambition, no morbid lust for material gain at the expense of others had led us to the field. Ill would be for us, if that were so.

Here in the midst of war, raging and roaring over all the lands and seas, creeping nearer to our hearts and homes—here, amid all these tumults, we have tonight the peace of the spirit in each cottage home and in every generous heart.

Therefore we may cast aside, for this night at least, the cares and dangers which beset us, and make for the children an evening of happiness in a world of storm.

Here then for one night only, each home throughout the English-speaking world should be a brightly lighted island of happiness and peace. Let the children have their night of fun and laughter—let the gifts of Father Christmas delight their play. Let us grownups share to the full in their unstained pleasures before we turn again to the stern tasks and formidable years that lie before us, resolved that by our sacrifice and daring these same children shall not be robbed of their inheritance or denied their right to live in a free and peaceful world.

And so in God's mercy, a happy Christmas to you all.

1945
Harry S. Truman

Speaking from the South Lawn of the White House: This is the Christmas that a war-weary world has prayed for through long and awful years. With peace come joy and gladness. The gloom of the war years fades as once more we light the National Community Christmas Tree. We meet in the spirit of the first Christmas, when the midnight choir sang the hymn of joy: "Glory to God in the highest, and on earth peace, good will toward men."

Let us not forget that the coming of the Savior brought a time of long peace to the Roman World. It is, therefore, fitting for us to remember that the spirit of Christmas is the spirit of peace, of love, of charity to all men. From the manger of Bethlehem came a new appeal to the minds and hearts of men: "A new commandment I give unto you, that ye love one another."

In love, which is the very essence of the message of the Prince of Peace, the world would find a solution for all its ills. I do not believe there is one problem in this country or in the world today which could not be settled if approached through the teaching of the Sermon on the Mount. The

poet's dream, the lesson of priest and patriarch and the prophet's vision of a new heaven and a new earth, all are summed up in the message delivered in the Judean hills beside the Sea of Galilee. Would that the world would accept that message in this time of its greatest need!

This is a solemn hour. In the stillness of the Eve of the Nativity when the hopes of mankind hang on the peace that was offered to the world nineteen centuries ago, it is but natural, while we survey our destiny, that we give thought also to our past—to some of the things which have gone into the making of our Nation.

You will remember that Saint Paul, the Apostle of the Gentiles, and his companions, suffering shipwreck, "cast four anchors out of the stern and wished for the day." Happily for us, whenever the American Ship of State has been storm-tossed we have always had an anchor to the windward.

We are met [meeting] on the South Lawn of the White House. The setting is a reminder of Saint Paul's four anchors. To one side is the massive pile of the Washington Monument—fit symbol of our first anchor. On the opposite end of Potomac Park is the memorial to another of the anchors which we see when we look astern of the Ship of State—Abraham Lincoln, who preserved the Union that Washington wrought.

Between them is the memorial to Thomas Jefferson, the anchor of democracy. On the other side of the White House, in bronze, rides Andrew Jackson—fourth of our anchors—the pedestal of his monument bearing his immortal words: "Our Federal Union—it must be preserved."

It is well in this solemn hour that we bow to Washington, Jefferson, Jackson, and Lincoln as we face our destiny with its hopes and fears—its burdens and responsibilities. Out of the past we shall gather wisdom and inspiration to chart our future course.

With our enemies vanquished we must gird ourselves for the work that lies ahead. Peace has its victories no less hard won than success at arms. We must not fail or falter. We must strive without ceasing to make real the prophecy of Isaiah: "They shall beat their swords into plowshares and their spears into pruning hooks: nation shall not lift up sword against nation, neither shall they learn war any more."

In this day, whether it be far or near, the Kingdoms of this world shall become indeed the Kingdom of God and He will reign forever and ever, Lord of Lords and King of kings. With that message I wish my countrymen a Merry Christmas and joyous days in the New Year.

1947
Harry S. Truman

Speaking from the South Lawn of the White House: We are met on the south lawn of the White House. Above the barren treetops rises the towering shaft of the Washington Monument. The scene is peaceful and tranquil. The shadows deepen and the Holy Night falls gently over the National Capital as we gather around our Christmas tree.

Down the ages from the first Christmas through all the years of nineteen centuries, mankind in its weary pilgrimage through a changing world has been cheered and strengthened by the message of Christmas.

The angels sang for joy at the first Christmas in faraway Bethlehem. Their song has echoed through the corridors of time and will continue to sustain the heart of man through eternity.

Let us not forget that the first Christmas was a homeless one. A humble man and woman had gone up from Galilee out of the City of Nazareth to Bethlehem. There is a sense of desolation in St. Luke's brief chronicle of Mary "brought forth her firstborn son, wrapped Him in swaddling clothes, and laid Him in a manger; because there was no room for them in the inn."

For many of our brethren in Europe and Asia this too will be a homeless Christmas. There can be little happiness for those who will keep another Christmas in poverty and exile and in separation from their loved ones. As we prepare to celebrate our Christmas this year in a land of plenty, we would be heartless indeed if we were indifferent to the plight of less fortunate peoples overseas.

We must not forget that our Revolutionary fathers also knew a Christmas of suffering and desolation. Washington wrote from Valley Forge two days before Christmas in 1777: "We have this day no less that 2,873 men in camp unfit for duty because they are barefooted and otherwise naked."

We can be thankful that our people have risen today, as did our forefathers in Washington's time, to our obligation and our opportunity.

At this point in the world's history, the words of St. Paul have greater significance than ever before. He said:

"And now abideth faith, hope, charity these three; but the greatest of these is charity."

We believe this. We accept it as a basic principle of our lives. The great heart of the American people has been moved to compassion by the needs of those in other lands who are cold and hungry.

We have supplied a part of their needs and we shall do more. In this, we are maintaining the American tradition.

In extending aid to our less fortunate brothers we are developing in their hearts the return of "hope." Because of our efforts, the people of other lands see the advent of a new day in which they can lead lives free from the harrowing fear of starvation and want.

With the return of hope to these peoples will come renewed faith—faith in the dignity of the individual and the brotherhood of man.

The world grows old but the spirit of Christmas is ever young.

Happily for all mankind, the spirit of Christmas survives travail and suffering because it fills us with hope of better things to come. Let us then put our trust in the unerring Star which guided the Wise Men to the Manger of Bethlehem. Let us hearken again to the Angel Choir singing

"Glory to God in the highest and on earth peace, good will toward men."

With hope for the future and with faith in God, I wish all my countrymen a very Merry Christmas.

1951
Harry S. Truman

Speaking from his home in Independence, Missouri: Christmas is the great home festival. It is the day in all the year which turns our thoughts toward home.

And so I am spending Christmas in my old home in Independence with my family and friends. As the Christmas tree is lighted on the White House grounds in Washington, I am glad to send this greeting to all of my countrymen.

Tonight we think of the birth of a Little Child in the City of David nineteen and a half centuries ago. In that humble birth God gave his message of love to the world. At this Christmas time the world is distracted by doubt and despair, torn by anger, envy and ill will. But our lesson should still be that same message of love, symbolized by the birth of the Redeemer of the World in a manger "because there was no room for them in the inn."

Our hearts are saddened on this Christmas Eve by the suffering and the sacrifice of our brave men and women in Korea. We miss our boys and girls who are out there. They are protecting us, and all free men, from aggression. They are trying to prevent another world war. We honor them for the great job they are doing. We pray to the Prince of Peace for their success and safety.

As we think of Korea, we should also think of another Christmas, 10 years ago, in 1941. That was just after Pearl Harbor, and the whole world was at war. Then almost every country. almost every home, was overshadowed by fear and sorrow.

The world is still in danger tonight, but a great change has come about. A new spirit has been born, and has grown up in the world, although perhaps we do not fully realize it. The struggle we are making today has a new and hopeful meaning.

Ten years ago total war was no longer a threat but a tragic reality. In those grim days, our Nation was straining all its efforts in a war of survival. It was not peace—not the prevention of war—but the stark reality of total war itself that filled our minds and overwhelmed our hearts and souls at Christmas 1941.

Tonight we have a different goal, and a higher hope. Despite difficulties, the free nations of the world have drawn together solidly for a great purpose; not solely to defend themselves; not merely to win a bloody war if it should come; but for the purpose of creating a real peace—a peace that shall be a positive reality and not an empty hope; a just and lasting peace.

When we look toward the battlefields of Korea, we see a conflict like no other in history. There the forces of the United Nations are fighting—not for territory, not for plunder, not to rule the lives of captive people. In Korea the free nations are proving, by deeds, that man is free and must remain free, that aggression must end, that nations must obey the law.

We still have a long struggle ahead of us before we can reach our goal of peace. In the words of the Bible, the day is not yet here when the bow shall be broken, and the lance cut off, and the chariot burned. But we have faith that that day will come.

We will be strong so long as we keep that faith—the faith that can move mountains, the faith which, as St. Paul says, is the substance of things hoped for, the evidence of things not seen.

Let us ask God to bless our efforts and redeem our faults. Let us resolve to follow his commandments—to carry the gospel to the poor; heal the brokenhearted; preach deliverance to the captive; give freedom to the slave. Let us try to do all things in that spirit of brotherly love that was revealed to mankind at Bethlehem on the first Christmas day.

The victory we seek is the victory of peace. That victory was promised to us long ago, in the words of the angel choir that sang over Bethlehem: "Glory to God in the highest, and on earth peace, good will toward men."

To all my countrymen: Merry Christmas.

1952
Harry S. Truman

Speaking from the White House Lawn: As we light the National Christmas tree tonight, here on the White House lawn—as all of us light our own Christmas trees in our own homes—we remember another night long ago. Then a Child was born in a stable. A star hovered over, drawing wise men from afar. Shepherds, in a field, heard angels singing: "Glory to God in the highest, and on earth peace, good will toward men." That was the first Christmas and it was God's greatest gift to us.

This is a wonderful story. Year after year it brings peace and tranquillity to troubled hearts in a troubled world. And tonight the earth seems hushed, as we turn the old, old story of how "God so loved the world, that He gave His only begotten Son, that whosoever believeth in Him should not perish, but have everlasting life."

Tonight, our hearts turn first of all to our brave men and women in Korea. They are fighting and suffering and even dying that we may preserve the chance of peace in the world. The struggle there has been long and bitter. But it has a hopeful meaning.

It has a hopeful meaning because it is the common struggle of many free nations which have joined together to seek a just and lasting peace. We know, all of us, that this is the only way we can bring about peace in the conditions of our time on this earth. Whether we shall succeed depends upon our patience and fortitude. We still have a long road ahead of us before we reach our goal. We must remain steadfast.

And as we go about our business of trying to achieve peace in the world, let us remember always to try to act and live in the spirit of the Prince of Peace. He bore in His heart no hate and no malice—nothing but love for all mankind. We should try as nearly as we can to follow His example.

Our efforts to establish law and order in the world are not directed against any nation or any people. We seek only a universal peace, where all nations shall be free and all peoples shall enjoy their inalienable human rights. We believe that all men are truly the children of God.

As we worship at this Christmastide, let us worship in this spirit. As we pray for our loved ones far from home—as we pray for our men and women in Korea, and all our service men and women wherever they are—let us also pray for our enemies. Let us pray that the spirit of God shall enter their lives and prevail in their lands. Let us pray for a fulfillment of the brotherhood of man.

Through Jesus Christ the world will yet be a better and a fairer place. This faith sustains us today as it has sustained mankind for centuries past. This is why the Christmas story, with the bright stars shining and the angels singing, moves us to wonder and stirs our hearts to praise.

Now, my fellow countrymen, I wish for all of you a Christmas filled with the joy of the Holy Spirit, and many years of future happiness with the peace of God reigning upon this earth.

1953
Dwight D. Eisenhower

Speaking from inside the White House: This evening's ceremony, here at the White House, is one of many thousands in America's traditional celebration of the birth, almost 2,000 years ago, of the Prince of Peace.

For us, this Christmas is truly a season of good will—and our first peaceful one since 1949. Our national and individual blessings are manifold. Our hopes are bright even though the world still stands divided in two antagonistic parts.

More precisely than in any other way, prayer places freedom and communism in opposition, one to the other. The Communist can find no reserve of strength in prayer because his doctrine of materialism and statism denies the dignity of man and consequently the existence of God. But in America, George Washington long ago rejected exclusive dependence upon mere materialistic values. In the bitter and critical winter at Valley Forge, when the cause of liberty was so near defeat, his recourse was sincere and earnest prayer. From it he received new hope and new strength of purpose out of which grew the freedom in which we celebrate this Christmas season.

As religious faith is the foundation of free government, so is prayer an indispensable part of that faith.

Tonight, richly endowed in the good things of the earth, in the fellowship of our neighbors and the love of our families, would it not be fitting for each of us to speak in prayer to the Father of all men and women on this earth, of whatever nation, and of every race and creed—to ask that He help us—and teach us—strengthen us—and receive our thanks.

Should we not pray that He help us? Help us to remember that the founders of this our country came first to these shores in search of freedom—freedom of man to walk in dignity; to live without fear; beyond the yoke of tyranny; ever to progress. Help us to cherish freedom for each of us and for all nations.

Might we not pray that He teach us? Teach us to shun the counsel of defeat and of despair of self-pride and self-deceit. Teach us and teach our leaders, to seek to understand the problems and the needs of all our people. Teach us how those problems may reach solution in wisdom and how best those needs may be met. But teach us, also, that where there may be special problems, there can be no special rights; and though there may be special needs, there can be no special privileges. Teach us to require of all those who seek to lead us, these things: integrity of purpose; the upright mind, selfless sacrifice, and the courage of the just. Teach us trust and hope and self-dependence. Teach us the security of faith.

And may we pray that He strengthen us. Strengthen us in understanding ourselves and others—in our homes, in our country, and in our world. Strengthen our concern for brotherhood. Strengthen our conviction that whatever we, as Americans, would bring to pass in the world must first come to pass in the heart of America. Strengthen our efforts to forge abroad those links of friendship which must one day encircle the world, if its people are to survive and live in peace.

Lastly, should we not pray that He receive our thanks? For certainly we are grateful for all the good we find about us; for the opportunity given us to use our strength and our faith to meet the problems of this hour. And on this Christmas Eve, all hearts in America are filled with special thanks to God that the blood of those we love no longer spills on battlefields abroad. May He receive the thanks of each of us for this, His greatest bounty and our supplication that peace on earth may live with us, always.

1956
Dwight D. Eisenhower

Speaking at the Pageant of Peace on the Ellipse: In this Nation's capital city we are joined tonight with millions in all our forty-eight States, and, indeed, throughout the world, in the happiness and in the hope that Christmas brings.

Not that everyone is filled with happiness and hope in this season of rejoicing. Far from it. There is weariness—there is suffering for multitudes. There is hunger as well as happiness, slavery as well as freedom in the world tonight. But in the myriads of Christmas candles we see the vision of a better world for all people.

In the light of Christmas, the dark curtains of the world are drawn aside for the moment. We see more clearly our neighbors next door; and our neighbors in other nations. We see ourselves and the responsibilities that belong to us. Inspired by the story of Christmas we seek to give of our happiness and abundance to others less fortunate. Even now the American people, on the farm and in the city, rallying through the Red Cross and other voluntary agencies to

meet the needs of our neighbors in Hungary, are true to the spirit of Christmas.

Even more important, there are particularly manifested during this season those spiritual qualities of freedom and honor and neighborliness and good will—great virtues that make all peoples one. Through them, and faith in them, we see how men can live together in peace; for one glorious moment we sense progress toward that aspiration of every religious faith—"Peace on earth, good will to men."

These are hallowed words; through ages they have heartened and moved mankind, even though their message of peace is far too often drowned by the strident voices of the fearful or the arrogant, who fill our minds with doubt and pessimism. They blur our vision with clouds of hate.

But the spirit of Christmas returns, yet again, to enable us to gain understanding of each other; to help each other; to obey the elemental precepts of justice; to practice good will toward all men of every tongue and color and creed; to remember that we are all identical in our aspirations for a peaceful, a decent, a rewarding life.

In the warm glow of the Christmas tree, it is easy to say these things, but when the trees come down and the lights are put away—as they always are—then we have a true testing of the spirit. That testing will be answered, throughout the year ahead, by the success each of us experiences in keeping alive the inspiration and exaltation of this moment.

We must proceed by faith, knowing the light of Christmas is eternal, though we cannot always see it.

We must believe that the truth of Christmas is constant; that men can live together in peace as Lincoln said, "with charity for all, with firmness in the right."

In this spirit, I now turn on the lights of the National Christmas Tree. [The lights are turned on.]

By the light of Christmas charity and Christmas truth, we enter the New Year with gratitude and strength. In this spirit, let us make sure that 1957 will add a memorable chapter to the story of mankind.

Now, on behalf of Mrs. Eisenhower and myself, may I wish for all of you in this audience—throughout our nation—throughout the world truly, Merry Christmas. And may the Father of us all bless all who dwell upon the earth.

Thank you very much.

1960
Dwight D. Eisenhower

Speaking at the Pageant of Peace on the Ellipse: Through the Ages men have felt the uplift of the spirit of Christmas. We commemorate the birth of the Christ Child by the giving of gifts, by joining in carols of celebration, by giving expression to our gratitude for the great things that His coming has brought about in the world. Such words as faith and hope and charity and compassion come naturally and gladly to our lips at this wondrous time of the year.

And Christmas inspires in us feelings even deeper than those of rejoicing. It impels us to test the sincerity of our own dedication to the ideals so beautifully expressed in the

Christian ethic. We are led to self examination.

We are grateful for all the material comforts with which we have been blessed. We take great pride in our country's pre-eminent position in the family of nations. Yet as we look into the mirror of conscience, we see blots and blemishes that mar the picture of a nation of people who devoutly believe that they were created in the image of their Maker.

Too often we discern an apathy toward violations of law and standards of public and private integrity. When, through bitter prejudice and because of differences in skin pigmentation, individuals cannot enjoy equality of political and economic opportunity, we see another of these imperfections, one that is equally plain to those living beyond our borders. Whenever there is denied the right of anyone, because he dares to live by the moral code, to earn for himself and his family a living, this failure, too, is a blot on the brightness of America's image.

But one of America's imperishable virtues is her pride in the national ideals proclaimed at her birth. When danger to them threatens, America will fight for her spiritual heritage to the expenditure of the last atom of her material wealth; she will put justice above life itself. America will never cease in her striving to remove the blemishes on her own reflection.

Though we boast that ours is a government of laws, completeness in this work cannot be achieved by laws alone, necessary though these be. Law, to be truly effective, must command the respect and earnest support of public opinion, both generally and locally. And each of us helps form public opinion.

Before us, then, is a task that each must himself define and himself perform. Good it is that Christmas helps to make us aware of our imperfections. Better it is that we rededicate ourselves to the work of their eradication.

A year ago last night I returned from a trip that took me to the other side of the world, to eleven nations of wide variations in race, color, religion, and outlook. That homecoming had added meaning for me because I came back at this time of year, when we are unfailingly reminded that, under God, we are all brothers in one world.

In this season next year a new President will address you as I address you now. Each succeeding Christmas will, we pray, see ever greater striving by each of us to rekindle in our hearts and minds zeal for America's progress in fulfilling her own high purposes. In doing so, our veneration of Christmas and its meaning will be better understood throughout the world and we shall be true to ourselves, to our Nation, and to the Man whose birth, 2,000 years ago, we now celebrate.

And now, I ask Mrs. Eisenhower to join me. It is our privilege to turn on the lights of our National Christmas Tree.

1962
John F. Kennedy

Speaking at the Pageant of Peace on the Ellipse: With the lighting of this tree, which is an old ceremony in Washington and one which has been among the most important responsibilities of a good many Presidents of the United States, we initiate, in a formal way, the Christmas Season.

We mark the festival of Christmas which is the most sacred and hopeful day in our civilization. For nearly 2,000 years the message of Christmas, the message of peace and good will towards all men, has been the guiding star of our endeavors. This morning I had a meeting at the White House which included some of our representatives from far-off countries in Africa and Asia. They were returning to their posts for the Christmas holidays. Talking with them afterwards, I was struck by the fact that in the far-off continents Moslems, Hindus, Buddhists, as well as Christians, pause from their labors on the 25th day of December to celebrate the birthday of the Prince of Peace. There could be no more striking proof that Christmas is truly the universal holiday of all men. It is the day when all of us dedicate our thoughts to others; when all are reminded that mercy and compassion are the enduring virtues; when all show, by small deeds and large and by acts, that it is more blessed to give than to receive.

It is the day when we remind ourselves that man can and must live in peace with his neighbors and that it is the peacemakers who are truly blessed. In this year of 1962 we greet each other at Christmas with some special sense of the blessings of peace. This has been a year of peril when the peace has been sorely threatened. But it has been a year when peril was faced and when reason ruled. As a result, we may talk at this Christmas, just a little bit more confidently of peace on earth, good will to men. As a result, the hopes of the American people are perhaps a little higher. We have much yet to do. We still need to ask that God bless everyone. But yet I think we can enter this season of good will with more than usual joy in our hearts.

And I think all of us extend a special word of gratitude and appreciation to those who serve the United States abroad; to the one million men in uniform who will celebrate this Christmas away from their homes; to those hundreds of young men and women and some older men and women who serve in far-off countries in our Peace Corps; to the members of the Foreign Service; to those who work in the various information services, A.I.D. agencies, and others who work for us abroad who will celebrate this December 25th thousands of miles from us at sea, on land, and in the air, but with us. It is to them that we offer the best of Christmases and to all of you I send my very best wishes for a blessed and happy Christmas and a peaceful and prosperous New Year. Thank you.

This [indicating the electric switch] was first pressed by President Coolidge in 1923 and succeedingly by President Hoover, Vice President Curtis, by President Franklin Roosevelt on many occasions, by President Harry Truman, by President Eisenhower, by Vice President Johnson. I am delighted to be in that illustrious company and we therefore light the tree.

1963
Lyndon B. Johnson

Speaking at the Pageant of Peace on the Ellipse: Tonight we come to the end of the season of great national sorrow, and the beginning of the season of great eternal joy. We mourn our great President, John F. Kennedy, but he would have us go on. While our spirits cannot be light, our hearts need not be heavy.

We were taught by Him whose birth we commemorate that after death there is life. We can believe, and we do believe, that from the death of our national leader will come a rebirth of the finest qualities of our national life.

On this same occasion 30 years ago, at the close of another troubled year in our Nation's history, a great President, Franklin D. Roosevelt, said to his countrymen, "To more and more of us the words 'Thou shalt love thy neighbor as thyself' have taken on a meaning that is showing itself and proving itself in our purposes and in our daily lives. I believe that this is no less true for all of us in all of our regions of our land today.

There is a turning away from things which are false and things which are small, and things which are shallow. There is a turning toward those things which are true, those things which are profound, and those things which are eternal. We can, we do, live tonight in a new hope and new confidence and new faith in ourselves and in what we can do together through the future.

Our need for such faith was never greater, for we are heirs of a great trust. In these last 200 years we have guided the building of our Nation and our society by those principles and precepts brought to earth nearly 2,000 years ago on that first Christmas.

We have our faults and we have our failings, as any mortal society must. But when sorrow befell us, we learned anew how great is the trust and how close is the kinship that mankind feels for us, and most of all, that we feel for each other. We must remember, and we must never forget, that the hopes and the fears of all the years rest with us, as with no other people in all history. We shall keep that trust working, as always we have worked, for peace on earth and good will among men.

On this occasion one year ago, our beloved President John F. Kennedy reminded us that Christmas is the day when all of us dedicate our thoughts to others, when we are all reminded that mercy and compassion are the really enduring virtues, when all of us show, by small deeds and by large, that it is more blessed to give than to receive.

So in that spirit tonight, let me express to you as your President the one wish that I have as we gather here. It is a wish that we not lose the closeness and the sense of sharing, and the spirit of mercy and compassion which these last few days have brought for us all.

Between tonight and Christmas Eve, let each American family, whatever their station, whatever their religion, whatever their race or their region—let each American family devote time to sharing with others something of themselves; yes, something of their very own. Let us, if we can do no more, lend a hand and share an hour, and say a prayer—and find some way with which to make this Christmas a prouder memory for what we gave instead of what we receive.

And now here, as we have done so many years, we turn on in your Capital City, the lights of our National Christmas Tree, and we say that we hope that the world will not narrow into a neighborhood before it has broadened into a brotherhood.

1965
Lyndon B. Johnson

Speaking at the Pageant of Peace on the Ellipse:
Guest: British Prime Minister Harold Wilson

Once again it is Christmas. Once again that time has come when the heart of man opens to the holiness of life. Once again we tell the ancient story of a baby, born into poverty and persecution, whose destiny it was to lift the iron burden of despair from his fellow men.

In the 20 centuries that have transpired since the sacred moment of His birth, mankind has never been wholly free of the scourge of war and the ravages of disease, illiteracy, and hunger. Yet the star of Bethlehem burns in our hearts on this December evening with a warmth that is not diminished by the years or discouraged by our failures. It reminds us that our first and most compelling task is peace.

As in other Christmas seasons in the past, our celebration this year is tempered by the absence of brave men from their homes and from their loved ones. We would not have it so. We have not sought the combat in which they are engaged. We have hungered for not one foot of another's territory, nor for the life of a single adversary. Our sons patrol the hills of Vietnam at this hour because we have learned that though men cry "Peace, peace," there is no peace to be gained ever by yielding to aggression. That lesson has been learned by a hundred generations. The guarantors of peace on earth have been those prepared to make sacrifices in its behalf.

On this platform with me this evening is the very distinguished and very great Prime Minister of Great Britain. He speaks for a people who have made such sacrifices in behalf of peace. On the battlefield and at the conference table, his countrymen have fought and have labored to create a just peace among the nations.

The distinguished Prime Minister, Harold Wilson, and I have spoken of this task this afternoon. We have spoken not only of the security of mankind, but of the countless opportunities for cooperation that are the true works of peace.

He has told me that his Government will renew the quest for peace as cochairman of the Geneva Conference. I have told him that any new way he can find to peace will have a ready response from the United States.

We know too that peace is not merely the absence of war. It is that climate in which man may be liberated from the hopelessness that imprisons his spirit.

In this strong and prosperous land, there are many that are still trapped in that prison where hope seems but a dream. We shall never rest until that dream becomes a reality.

But hope cannot be our province alone. For we shall never know peace in a world where a minority prospers and the vast majority is condemned to starvation and ignorance. This evening, inspired once more by Him who brought comfort and courage to the oppressed, we offer our hand to those who seek a new life for their people.

Above all things, we dedicate ourselves to the search for a just settlement of disputes between nations. We declare once more our desire to discuss an honorable peace in Vietnam. We know that nothing is to be gained by a further delay in talking. Our poet Emerson once said that "the god of victory is one-handed—but peace gives victory to both sides."

So in the name of a people who seek peace for their brothers on this earth—"that we may be the children of our Father which is in heaven; for He maketh His sun to rise on the evil and on the good, and sendeth rain on the just and on the unjust"—I turn on the lights of this tree, and pray that the Spirit that we revere this evening may illuminate the heart of every man on earth.

1967
Lyndon B. Johnson

Speaking at the Pageant of Peace on the Ellipse: Yesterday, in the great State of California, a team of scientists announced that they had come closer than men had ever come before to creating life in a laboratory.

Yesterday, and today, men sat at missile sites and airfields throughout the world. They wore different uniforms and they spoke different languages. But they all controlled the power to destroy a human being, a human life, on an unprecedented scale.

Today a child was born in an American hospital. His chances of living a long life, of being educated, of being gainfully employed, of enjoying the amenities of a good life, and of passing even wider opportunities on to his children, are greater than they have been for any child, born at any time, in any nation, in recorded history.

Today, a young soldier, in the prime of his life, was killed in the central highlands of Vietnam. A life that might have been spent productively, in the works of peace, has now been swiftly cut off in the waste of war.

These expressions of man in our time—of the power to create life, and the power to destroy life, of the flowering of hope, and the renewal of tragedy—are in some ways very unique. But in other ways they are typical of the human condition in every age.

In a few days we shall all celebrate the birth of His Holiness on earth. We shall recreate in our minds, once more, the ancient coming of that Spirit who remains alive for millions in our time. We shall acknowledge the Kingdom of a Child in a world of men.

That Child—we should remember— grew into manhood Himself, preached and moved men in many walks of life, and died in agony.

But his death—so that Christian faith tells us—was not the end. For Him, and for millions of men and women ever since, it marked a time of triumph—when the spirit of life triumphed over death.

So—if this Christmas season in a time of war is to have real meaning to us, it must celebrate more that the birth of a Baby. It must celebrate the birth of a Spirit who endured scorn and hardship and the tragedy of an unjust death—and who yet speaks to us, across 20 centuries, of the promise of life.

Half a million American families will celebrate His birth this year without a beloved son or husband near them.

Half a million brave American men—who love their country and are willing to die for their land—will be celebrating Christmas in a strange land, surrounded by the weapons of war.

A part of every American heart will be with them.

What sustains us—as we turn on the lights of this tree, and of millions of trees in millions of American homes—is the belief that the spirit of life will triumph over death. It is the conviction that peace will come, and will permit us to give our lives completely to building, instead of giving our lives to destroying.

It is the faith that says the creation of new hope for man, through scientific discovery, is finally much more important than great destructive power—that also came from science.

It is the hope that says a life of peace and promise is more likely for man than a life of war and misery.

This is the message of the holy season. May it—in an hour of trial—fill us with its deep, abiding joy. Thank you and good evening.

1970
Richard M. Nixon

Speaking at the Pageant of Peace on the Ellipse: I know we want to express our very grateful appreciation to the Mormon Choir and to the Friends University Symphonic Choir for their participation and particularly under the rather adverse weather conditions which I know are very hard for those of you in the audience.

As I was preparing my Christmas message to the Nation, it occurred to me that when we light the National Christmas tree, we do so not only as a Nation but really as a family, a family of more that 200 million members. This week and next week millions of trees all over America will be lighted just as we light this tree today. And all over America families will be gathering together.

At Christmas I think we all think of things like Currier and Ives prints, of snow and Santa Claus, of love and laughter and homecoming. For this is part of the spirit of Christmas. It speaks to something deep and eternal in the human spirit, a yearning for hope, a celebration of life, a wish to put aside all the care and the discord that press in upon us so much of the rest of the year, a wish to let 'the better angels of our nature' sing a little and to sing along with them. The spirit of Christmas is joyous, because it is the spirit of peace–a spirit of loving, of giving, of caring, and letting the light of life shine through.

I received a Christmas card the other day–and thousands of Christmas cards come to the President of the United States and his family–but this one particularly I remember from a lady in California. She wrote something on it. Let me read what she wrote:

"During this Christmas season and throughout the new year, all Americans would like to have peace in the world, peace in our homes, and especially peace in our hearts"– peace in the world, peace in our homes and peace in our hearts.

In the Christmas season, we do find peace in our hearts. We find it because this is a time for celebrating the simple things and the personal things, the things that mean so much to us in human terms. We celebrate the love that unites a family and the little acts of kindness, the touch of a hand, the words of comfort, the extra care that a mother takes as she bakes a Christmas pie.

And we think of the poor and the needy and the lonely, and we think of them not as problems, but as people with problems, and we try to help. And in the act of giving we discover once again how good it feels to give. We find peace in our hearts that way.

As families gather together and those who have been away come home, we discover once again the joys of sharing. We remember the past Christmases. We remember the little incidents of our childhood and how important the little things can be, the mending of a broken toy, the happiness of a grandfather at the sight of his grandchild's smile, and, together again, we find peace in our families.

And then in this larger family, this national family that we call America, of which all of us are a part, we find ourselves drawn together. We find that in the spirit of Christmas, in the spirit of peace, we can put aside what divides us and rediscover what really unites us–the concern for one another, the love of liberty and justice, the knowledge that we are a great Nation because we are a great and diverse people.

We are a national family of many different outlooks and many different hopes and many different problems. But what holds us together is that we respect one another, that we care about one another so that we draw strength from our differences as we address our problems.

Just the other evening when I opened the White House Conference on Children, I recalled something that Edmund Burke once said. What patriotism really means is love of country. And Burke reminded us that for us to love our country, our country must be lovely.

I want young Americans to learn to love America, not because it is the richest country in the world, and it is, and not because it is the strongest country in the world or merely because you happen to have been born here, but I want young Americans and all Americans to love America because this is a good country, and because we can, in our

making it better, and because it therefore is truly a lovely country.

This, I think, is the spirit of the American family, knowing that there is much to be done, striving together to do it, and knowing that at heart, in the human sense of heart, this is a lovely country. In this spirit, we can find peace in our larger family.

And our greatest hope in this Christmas season and in all seasons is, of course, peace in the whole world. We can be grateful in this Christmas season that already we have been able to bring 200,000 men back from Vietnam, more coming home. We can look forward with assurance to an end of that war. And as we look around the world, we see that there are still many other danger spots. And there are also many other threats to the peace of the world.

But because of the progress that we have made over the past two years, as I stand here before you, the American people, in this Christmas season, I believe that I can confidently say that we now have the best chance since the end of World War II to build what we have not had in this whole century, a full generation of peace. As we look forward to that great hope of a generation of peace, we think especially of our children, and at Christmas we think especially of our children.

And as we light this great tree, and as millions of other trees are lighted in homes across the land, we do so in a spirit of peace and love and gathering together. And as the lights go on, we know that these lights will reflect the light in the eyes of millions of children and the light of hope that stirs in millions of hearts, for the true light of Christmas is not the light on the tree. It is the light in the eyes of a child.

And now we come to the big moment we have all been waiting for. We are going to light the tree, and because this is a very big tree, I understand that I am going to have some help to light it. And I am going to go down here in the audience and pick out one of the children to help me press the button to light the tree. I see we have lots of volunteers. Now, we picked this boy out. He is the smallest boy here. But he can do this, I know very well. And his name is Andre.

1973
Richard M. Nixon
Speaking at the Pageant of Peace on the Ellipse
50th Anniversary of Tree-Lighting Ceremony

I think one of the greatest privileges that a President of the United States has is to light the Christmas tree, the Nation's Christmas tree, because it belongs to all the nation, here in the Nation's Capital.

This year, as the Secretary has already indicated, the tree is different. This year Christmas will be different in terms of lights, perhaps, all across America. Instead of having many lights on the tree as you will see over there in a few moments, there will be only one on it, the star at the top, and the other lights you see will simply be the glitter from the ground lights which are around the tree.

And in a way, I suppose one could say with only one light

on the tree, this will be a very dreary Christmas, but we know that isn't true, because the spirit of Christmas is not measured by the number of lights on a tree. The spirit of Christmas is measured by the love that each of us has in his heart for his family, for his friends, for his fellow Americans and for people all over the world. And this year, while we have a problem, a problem the Secretary has alluded to, the problem of energy, I think that what we can all be thankful for is that it is a problem of peace and not a problem of war. That is what Americans can be thankful for.

This year we will drive a little slower. This year the thermostats will be a little lower. This year every American perhaps will sacrifice a little, but no one will suffer. But we will do it for a great goal, the goal, first of seeing to it that in a year when our energy supplies are not as high as we need, we can prepare for the future, and also a year in which America will make a great stride forward toward a new, great goal, and that is, by the year 1980 this Nation, which will celebrate its 200th anniversary of independence in 1976–by 1980 will celebrate Project Independence, when we are independent of any other country in the world where our energy supply is concerned. That we can do.

As we consider these problems of peace, I think also we must be thankful, as the Secretary has already indicated, for the fact that this is the first Christmas in 12 years that a President has stood here at a time when America was at peace with every nation in the world. It is the first Christmas in eight years when no American prisoner of war is away from home at Christmas. And to all of these young people, and particularly to our very distinguished young people who participated in this program, it is also a Christmas for the first time in 20 years when no young American is being drafted for the armed services. That is what peace means to America.

It would be well, of course, for us to stand simply on that achievement, but we know that there will always be threats to the peace of the world, and that is where we come in, and where each American comes in, looking to the future. Because as we look at the chances not just of getting peace, which we have now achieved, but of keeping peace, which we have not been able to do for a full generation, for a century, then what happens in America will decide it, whether America has the strength not just of its arms but more, of its spirit to provide the leadership that the world needs to keep the trouble spots in the world from blowing up into war and to build that permanent structure of peace that we all want.

It is that to which we dedicate ourselves as we light the Nation's Christmas tree tonight. Let the year 1974 be one in which we make great progress toward the goal of a lasting peace, peace not only for America but for all nations, peace between peoples who have different forms of government, but who nevertheless can be friends.

A moment ago when the flowers were presented to Mrs. Nixon by Tyna, I remembered an occasion in 1959 when a little girl presented flowers to her in the Ural Mountains in Russia. We were driving through the mountains, and a group of schoolchildren stopped the cavalcade for a few moments and they presented flowers to Mrs. Nixon. And when they did so in this year 1959, when the cold war was still going on, they shouted out "Friendship, friendship" in English. When we got back into the car, our guide, Mr. Zhukov, said to me that the first word that a Russian child who learns English and studies English in a Russian school learns is the word "Friendship." That is the first English word the Russian child learns.

Now I do not mean to suggest by that that because a Russian child is taught, when he first studies English, the word "friendship" that it is inevitable that the Russian people and the American people are not going to have differences as far as their governments are concerned, but I do know this: We have had the great privilege, Mrs. Nixon and I, of traveling to most of the nations of the world, to the nations of Africa, to the nations of Asia, to China, to Russia, and I can tell you that the people of the world want peace, the people of the world want friendship, and every American, I know, wants his country and his Government to take the lead in building a world of peace.

As this Christmas season begins, let us just remember we do have some problems which we will overcome, but they are the problems of peace. And we also have a great challenge, the challenge of helping to build a structure of peace that all the 3 billion people in this world can enjoy. What a wonderful achievement that can be.

There are times, of course, when we tire of the challenge. There are times when we would not like to accept that position of leadership, but let us remember that unless America, at this time in history, accepts the responsibility to lead for peace, we may not have it in the world.

I think we can meet the challenge. I am sure we will. And on this particular day, in this year 1973, as we look at the beginning of the year 1974, let us so conduct ourselves as a nation in our leadership toward peace that in the years to come, people, not only in America but all over the world, will look back at what we have done, will look back and say, "God bless America."

1976
Gerald R. Ford

Speaking at the Pageant of Peace on the Ellipse: As our Bicentennial Year comes to a close, it is especially appropriate to gather once more around the traditional symbol of family ties and friendly reunions, our Nation's Christmas tree. In doing so, we combine our year-long celebration of historical events with a personal rededication to timeless values.

The message of Christmas has not changed over the course of 20 centuries. Peace on Earth, good will toward men–that message is as inspiring today as it was when it was first proclaimed to the shepherds near Bethlehem. It was first proclaimed, as we all know, then.

In 1976 America has been blessed with peace and a significant restoration of domestic harmony. But true peace is more than an absence of battle. It is also the absence of prejudice and the triumph of understanding. Brotherhood among all peoples must be the solid cornerstone of lasting peace. It has been a sustaining force for our Nation, and it remains a guiding light for our future.

The celebration of the birth of Jesus is observed on every continent. The customs and traditions are not always the same, but feelings that are generated between friends and family members are equally strong and equally warm.

In a few moments I will turn the switch that lights up our national Christmas tree. As beautiful as that tree is, it will be only a symbol if its light is not matched by the glow of love in our hearts. It is my personal prayer on this Christmas of 1976 that the tree which I light tonight is only the beginning, that each of you will also light a flame of love—love that is reflected in the eyes of all our brothers and sisters across the Nation, and around the world.

Now, Betty joins me in wishing you all a very, very Merry Christmas and a Happy New Year. Thank you and God bless you.

1977
Jimmy Carter

Speaking at the Pageant of Peace on the Ellipse: This is a time of year when we try to forget our worries and our tribulations, our arguments and our differences, our doubts and fears about the future, and look on the positive side of life.

We try to search for confidence and for security. We try to reach out our hands to our friends, those whom we see every day and those whom we tend to forget during the rest of the year.

Christmas is also a time of tradition. This is a time to look back, to see the fine things of life that, because they are so good and decent, have been preserved.

This evening, we have a ceremony that will commemorate one of those commitments. For more than 50 years, since Calvin Coolidge lived in the White House, every single President has been over to join in the lighting of the National Christmas Tree. This also commemorates a continuity of beliefs—belief in one another, belief in our Nation, belief in principles like honesty and justice and freedom, and our religious beliefs, above all.

Ours is a nation of peace, and I thank God that our Nation is at peace. We not only preserve a peaceful life for those who live in the United States, but one of the major commitments of our leaders before me and now is to try to institute an opportunity for peaceful existence for others. In regions that might be torn with war, we try to bring friendship, and in regions of the world that are torn by disputes, we try to bring understanding.

We've seen two great leaders in recent weeks, the President of Egypt, the Prime Minister of Israel, lead in a dramatic way and, indeed, inspire a world with courage. And it is strange, isn't it, that it requires courage to search for peace under some circumstances. Well, our Nation has been a bulwark where those who want peace can turn, and the

staunchness of our commitment has been and can be an inspiration to others.

A few months ago, I designated December 15, today, as a day of prayer. And I hope that all of you in this great audience and all who watch and listen on television and radio, will make a special promise to yourselves during this holiday season to pray for guidance in our lives, purposes, guidance for wisdom and commitment and honesty of public officials and other leaders, guidance that we can see our Nation realize its great potential and the vision that formed it 200 years ago, and guidance that we will fulfill our deepest moral and religious commitments.

We look back on our own personal lives. Cecil Andrus remembered his family. I remember my own when I was a child and when Christmas was a day that we thought about 365 days a year—looking forward with anticipation, trying to measure up with standards, looking around our shoulders to see who was watching our performance. And sometimes I know that when we look back, we tend to put a rosy attitude or picture of what actually occurred. My favorite poet is Dylan Thomas, and he wrote "A Child's Christmas in Wales," and he tried to point out the confusion that sometimes exists in the mind of an adult about childhood, when he said he couldn't remember whether it snowed six days and six nights when he was 12 or snowed 12 days and 12 nights when he was six. But it didn't really matter, because the memory was precious even though it was slightly confused.

We've never seen it snow in Plains on Christmas, but we're going back to Plains next week to be with our friends, to be with our families, to be with those who have loved us throughout a lifetime and those whom we still love, for Christmas is a time of celebration, of festivity, of enjoyment, of pleasure, of self-gratification, even. And there is no incompatibility between memories, religious beliefs, tradition, peace, and going back home and being happy. They all kind of go together.

Our Nation is not one of solemn faces and sad demeanors, but our Nation is one of hope and vision and even happiness. And Christmas is a time to remind us that even when we do suffer and are disappointed in the United States and live even a dismal life, compared to our own immediate neighbors, compared to most of the rest of the world, we indeed have a joyous life and a wonderful life. God has blessed us in this country.

Well, in closing, let me say that Christmas has a special meaning for those of us who are Christians, those of us who believe in Christ, those of us who know almost 2,000 years ago, the Son of Peace was born to give us a vision of perfection, a vision of humility, a vision of unselfishness, a vision of compassion, a vision of love.

Those are exactly the same words that describe our theme this year. The theme is "The American Family." And I hope that we'll make every effort during this Christmas season not only to bring our immediate family together but to look at the family of all humankind, so that we not any longer cherish a commitment toward animosity or the retention of enemies but that we forgive one another and indeed, form a worldwide family where every human being on Earth is our brother or our sister.

Thank you for letting me come and meet with you and to remind each of you that Christmas is a time for recommitment of each life to the finest ideals that we can possibly envision.

Thank you very much.

1978
Jimmy Carter

Speaking at the Pageant of Peace on the Ellipse: As you well know the theme of this year's Pageant of Peace is unity. There is much to divide us in this world. And sometimes we concentrate too much of our attention on those divisions among us. But Christmas is a good time to recall how much unites us as people and also as nations. We are united in our belief in human dignity, in our conviction that the most likely way to find truth is to silence people's voices and to try to make them deny what they really believe.

Our country is entering a period of healing and of hope. We are joining together as a people again, realizing the strength of a common purpose. We are blessed with warm fires and warm memories and the voices of children singing of joy in the night. I think that God in His great wisdom knew that we needed these things to help us face the cold and sometimes lonely times. We need the joy of children's voices to remind us that the only things that we can truly give each other are the only things that we truly need—an ear to listen, a heart to care, a word of encouragement, and a hand to help.

At Christmas, we have not only this year's special moments but the rich store of all Christmases past to remember and to use.

When I was growing up, President Franklin Roosevelt was lighting the Nation's Christmas tree. During the difficult years of the Depression, and later during the Second World War, too many of our own Nation's Christmases have been shadowed by war. We are fortunate as we light this Christmas tree tonight that our Nation and most of the nations of the world are not at war.

This is always a matter of concern, the threat of violence in many corners of the globe. But this Christmas is a time of relative calm and also a time of great hope. Two ancient enemies are on the threshold of an agreement that could bring peace to the Middle East. It is my earnest prayer that the day will soon come when all children in the Middle East can play in the sunshine without fear, when their young men and women can turn their energies and talents away from war and death, to making the deserts fruitful and to building, instead of preparing to destroy.

The Prophet Isaiah, who wrote about ancient wars between Israel and her neighbors, tells us that the work of righteousness is peace. The United States has tried this year to help other nations find peace. We have succeeded in sev-

eral troubled areas in getting people to talk to each other and to work out their differences without resorting to violence and to war.

I hope that the time has passed when people excuse the pain and destruction and death and see war in itself as a demonstration of national heroism. This generation, our generation has seen too much of war's desolation. We've seen what it can do spiritually, as well as physically, to a people. War is no longer the brave sound of parades and drums and trumpets. We've seen it as it is, the loss of the young in the full flower of their promise, the death of families and entire communities, and the threat of nuclear devastation for the world.

I think the world is more ready than ever before to understand the thrust of Ralph Waldo Emerson's words that peace is victory for both sides. I believe that nations may be ready now to accept the possibility that those whom they have called enemies might live undisturbed on Earth and that we might at last learn to call even enemies brothers and sisters.

Perhaps at last the same fervor and commitment and sense of high purpose with which we once sought victory in war can now be devoted to our search for peace. And then we will truly be able to say in our hearts, for the fulfillment of the ancient promise of peace on Earth, good will toward men.

The evergreen tree that we use at Christmas is a symbol of eternal life, and also of the perpetual renewal of life. As I light our Nation's Christmas tree, and whenever you see a glowing tree this Christmas, I hope that you will see it as a rekindling of our faith and hope and our dedication to the cause of unity and a great nation's influence throughout the world for peace on Earth.

Thank you very much. And now we'll proceed to wish all the world a happy Christmas by lighting the Christmas tree together.

1979
Jimmy Carter

Speaking at the Pageant of Peace on the Ellipse: Christmas means a lot of things. It means love. It means warmth. It means friendship. It means family. It means joy. It means light. But everyone this Christmas will not be experiencing those deep feelings. At this moment there are 50 Americans who don't have freedom, who don't have joy, and who don't have warmth, who don't have their families with them. And there are 50 American families in this Nation who also will not experience all the joys and the light and the happiness of Christmas.

I think it would be appropriate for all those in this audience and for all those listening to my voice or watching on television to pause just a few seconds in a silent prayer that American hostages will come home safe and come home soon—if you'd please join me just for a moment. [Pause for silent prayer.] Thank you very much.

Nineteen seventy-nine has not been a bad year. Many

good things have happened to us individually and have also happened to our Nation. Not far from here, on the north side of the White House, we saw a remarkable ceremony, headed by a Jew, the leader of Israel, a Moslem, the President of Egypt, and myself, a Christian, the President of our country, signing a treaty of peace. This peace treaty was a historic development, and it was compatible with the commitment that we feel so deeply in the religious season now upon us.

Our Nation also opened up its arms of understanding, diplomatic relationships, and friendship—our Nation, the strongest on Earth, and China, the most populous nation on Earth. The establishment of new friendships is part of the Christmas season.

I went to Vienna and met with President Brezhnev. And he and I signed the SALT II treaty, which will help to limit and to reduce the spread of nuclear weapons, to bring about a better understanding between our two great countries, and to search for the kind of reduction of armaments that will lead, I think, to the realization of the true spirit of Christmas.

This fall we had a visit from a great spiritual leader, Pope John Paul II, who traveled throughout our country and who spoke in a quiet voice of understanding, of compassion, of love, of commitment, of morality, of ethics, of the unchanging things that are part of the spirit of Christmas. And I remember one thing in particular that he said on the White House lawn. He said, "Do not be afraid. Do not be afraid." And as you know that's the same message that the angels brought to the shepherds near Bethlehem the night that our Savior was born: "Fear not. Be not afraid." Many of the problems in our world derive from fear, from a lack of confidence in ourselves and, particularly, a lack of confidence in what we can do with God.

We hope we'll soon see peace in Zimbabwe-Rhodesia, a nation that has suffered much in the last few years. But we've also seen some needs for additional effort.

This is the Year of the Child, but it's possibly true that in Cambodia, or Kampuchea, the children will have suffered more in 1979 than in any other year in our lifetime—children so weak, so starved, that they don't even have the strength to cry. We've seen Vietnam refugees put to sea with very little hope of ever reaching land again. And our country has reached out its arms to help those starving children and those refugees adrift.

We've seen divisions among people because of religious beliefs. The recent events in Iran are an unfortunate example of that misguided application of belief in God. But I know that all Americans feel very deeply that the relationships between ourselves and the Moslem believers in the world of Islam is one of respect and care and brotherhood and good will and love.

So, we do have disappointments; we do have suffering; we do have divisions; we often have war. But in the midst of pain, we can still remember what Christmas is—a time of joy, a time of light, a time of warmth, a time of families, and a time of peace.

In our great country we have an awful lot for which we can be thankful: the birth of our Savior, the initiation of religious holidays tomorrow night for the Jews of America, and a realization that in our Nation we do have freedom to worship or not worship as we please. So let's remember our blessings, yes, but let's also remember the need for us to be more fervent in our belief in God and especially in sharing of our blessings with others.

Thank you very much. Merry Christmas to you all.

1982
Ronald Reagan

Speaking from the Rose Garden of the White House: My fellow Americans, the Christmas and Hanukkah decorations are up around the country, and in a moment we'll be lighting the National Christmas Tree here in the Nation's Capital.

In this holiday season, we celebrate the birthday of one who, for almost 2,000 years, has been a greater influence on humankind than all the rulers, all the scholars, all the armies, and all the navies that ever marched or sailed, all put together. He brought to the world, the simple message of peace on Earth, good will to all mankind.

Some celebrate the day as marking the birth of a great and good man, a wise teacher and prophet, and they do so sincerely. But for many of us it's also a holy day, the birthday of the Prince of Peace, a day when "God so loved the world that He sent us His only begotten Son" to assure forgiveness of our sins.

The Yuletide season is characterized in our country by the giving of gifts, a spirit of charity, and yes, good will, more so than at any other time of the year. Already traditional programs are underway, drives to collect food and clothing for those who are in need. The U. S. Marine Reserves have a toy collection drive to make sure that old St. Nicholas—Santa Claus—has enough to go around. And this is matched in countless American communities by firemen, policemen, churches, religious groups and service clubs.

Let me give you one specially moving example of what the Christmas spirit can do. I told this the other night. In Bridgeport, Connecticut, the Police Athletic League for years has maintained a kind of Christmas Center. It consists of a ranch type house, a manger and all the other things associated with Christmas. And during the holiday season it's manned by a Santa Claus, elves, and helpers. Thousands of children visit it every year, and thousands of toys are given to them.

This year, on Tuesday, December 7th, it was destroyed by fire set by a suspected arsonist. The mayor of Bridgeport called an emergency meeting. He asked for constructionists, carpenters, electricians, all the skills that are needed to help rebuild such a place. The answer to his call was instantaneous. More than 250 volunteers worked in shifts around the clock.

On Sunday, December 12th, five days later, at about 1:30 p.m. I phoned the mayor. He was officiating at the reopening of that Christmas Center to the cheers of hundreds and hundreds of citizens of Bridgeport. It had been rebuilt in only 4 days between the fire and the opening ceremony.

A recent initiative of Postmaster General William Bolger's will make it easier for all of us to do our part. He has instructed post offices across the country to display lists of the Christmas food, clothing and toy drives in their local areas, a guide to holiday giving open to all Americans.

This holiday season, as we work our way out of a recession, too many still find themselves without jobs, forced to cut back on things that they once thought of as their normal pattern of living. They aren't statistics; they're people. They're our neighbors, friends, and yes, family, and they make up that group that right now we call the unemployed. Their number's greater than it has been for some time past. Still, for every unemployed individual there are nine of us who do have jobs, and with that ratio of 1 out of 10 in mind, I'd like to make a suggestion. How about those of us who are employed making sure that those who aren't will nevertheless have a merry Christmas. This is something that needs doing at the community level—neighbor helping neighbor.

The people we're talking about may be members of your church, brothers and sisters in your local union, or that family across the street or down the block in your neighborhood. Surely between the nine of us, we can find a way to make Christmas merry for that one who temporarily can use our help. But remember, time is growing short, and Christmas is almost here, which brings us back to lighting the National Christmas Tree. This beloved tradition, which began nearly 60 years ago, has a special symbolism for our people. It's as if, when we light this tree, we light something within ourselves as well. And during the Christmas season I think most Americans do feel a greater sense of family, friendship, giving, and joy. And there's a special joy in our children at this time of year. I've heard from many of them recently. I wish Nancy and I could personally thank all you children who've written in, but I want you to know how good your cards, letters and artwork make us feel.

Now, while Christmas is a time for children, it's also a time to think of those who are less fortunate than we are, and let us also remember the constant vigil of the families of our missing in action. As we light this Christmas tree, may it lift hope in the hearts of those who are lonely and needy.

In Ephesians we read that "Each of us has been given his gift, his portion of Christ's bounty." Well, let us share our bounty this Christmas season. Let us offer not only our hearts and prayers but a generous hand to those who need our help. And as we light this tree, let us brighten the lives of those here at home and around the world whose Christmas may not be as glowing and as cheerful as ours.

So, to all of you, God bless you and keep you during this cherished holiday season. And now let's turn on the National Christmas Tree.

And there it is. It's lighted.

1983
Ronald Reagan

Speaking from inside the White House: In just a moment we'll be lighting our National Christmas Tree, continuing a wonderful tradition that was started by President Coolidge 60 years ago. I know there's a special feeling that we share when we push the button lighting up that tree. It's as if each one of those twinkling lights sends a new spirit of love, hope, and joy through the heart of America. And of course, the brightest light of all is the Star of Peace, expressing our hopes and prayers for peace in our families, our communities, our nation, and the world.

On behalf of our fellow citizens, Nancy and I would like to thank all of you on the Ellipse who have given America such a beautiful Christmas present, the 1983 Pageant of Peace.

Christmas is a time for giving, and as we reach out to family and friends, I hope we'll also open our hearts to those who are lonely and in need, citizens less fortunate than ourselves, brave soldiers working to preserve peace from the tip of Alaska to the shores of Lebanon, to the DMZ in Korea, families maintaining a constant vigil for their missing in action, and millions forbidden the freedom to worship a God who so loved the world that He gave us the birth of the Christ Child so that we might learn to love each other. I know they would welcome your expressions of love and support.

Many stories have been written about Christmas. Charles Dickens' "Carol" is probably the most famous. Well, I'd like to read some lines from a favorite of mine called "One Solitary Life," which describes for me the meaning of Christmas. It's the story of a man born of Jewish parents who grew up in an obscure village working in a carpenter shop until he was 30 and then for three years as a preacher. And, as the story says, he never wrote a book, he never went to college, he never traveled 200 miles from the place where he was born. He never did one of the things that usually accompany greatness.

While still a young man, the tide of popular opinion turned against him. His friends ran away. One of them denied him. He was turned over to his enemies. He went through the mockery of a trial. He was nailed on a cross between two thieves. While he was dying, his executioners gambled for the only piece of property that he had on Earth. When he was dead he was taken down and laid in a borrowed grave.

Nineteen wide centuries have come and gone. And today He's the centerpiece of much of the human race. All the armies that ever marched, all the navies that were ever built, and all the parliaments that ever sat, and all the kings that ever reigned, put together, have not affected life of man upon Earth as powerfully as this One Solitary Life.

I have always believed that the message of Jesus is one of hope and joy. I know there are those who recognize Christmas Day as the birthday of a great and good man, a wise teacher who gave us principles to live by. And then there are others of us who believe that he was the Son of God, that he was divine. If we live our lives for truth, for love, and for God, we never need be afraid. God will be with us and He will be part of something much larger, much more powerful and enduring than any force here on Earth.

Now tonight I have a very special person here with me to spread our Christmas joy. Her name is Amy Benham, and she comes all the way from Westport, Washington. Amy recently wrote the leaders of a public-spirited project named "Make a Wish" and said, "The Christmas tree that lights up for our country must be seen all the way to heaven. I would wish so much to help the President turn on those Christmas lights."

Well, Amy, the nicest Christmas present I could receive is helping make your wish come true. When you press the button over here—we're going over there—the whole world will know that Amy Benham lit up the skies, sending America's love, hope, and joy all the way to heaven and making the angels sing.

And now, you and I will walk over so you can light the tree. And then after that's done we'll all join in singing one of our favorite Christmas carols, "Joy to the World." So, let's go over here.

1985
Ronald Reagan

Speaking from the White House: My fellow Americans, thank you for joining Nancy and me on this festive evening. The menorah stands lighted in Lafayette Park, for this is also the time of Hanukkah, and this season is rich in the meaning of our Judeo-Christian tradition. In a moment we'll be lighting the National Christmas Tree, carrying forward what is now a 62-year tradition first begun by Calvin Coolidge.

Tonight we're drawn in warmth to one another as we reflect upon the deeply holy meaning of the miracle we shall soon celebrate. We know that Mary and Joseph reached the stable in Bethlehem sometime after sunset. We do not know the exact moment the Christ Child was born, only what we would have seen if we'd been standing there as we stand here now; Suddenly, a star from heaven shining with brilliant beauty across the skies, a star pointing toward eternity in the night, like a great ring of pure and endless light, and then all was calm, and all was bright. Such was the beginning of one solitary life that would shake the world as never before or since. When we speak of Jesus and of His life, we speak of a man revered as a prophet and teacher by people of all religions, and Christians speak of someone greater—a man who was and is divine. He brought forth a power that is infinite and a promise that is eternal, a power greater than all mankind's military might, for His power is Godly love, love that can lift our hearts and soothe our sorrows and heal our wounds and drive away our fears. He promised there will never be a long night that does not end. He promised to deliver us from dark torment and tragedy into the warming sunlight of human happiness, and beyond that, into paradise. He's never been a halfway giver; His generosity is pure and perfect and sure.

This, then expresses the true meaning of Christmas. If each of us could give but a fraction to one another of what He gave to the whole human family, how many hearts could heal, how much sorrow and pain could be driven away? There's still time for joy and gladness to touch a sad and lonely soul, still time to feed a hungry child, to wrap a present for a kind old man feeling forlorn and afraid, and to reach out to an abandoned mother raising children on her own. There's still time to remember our Armed Forces, to express our profound gratitude to those keeping watch on faraway frontiers of freedom, and to redouble our energies to account for our MIA's. They are not and never will be forgotten. And there's still time to remember the deepest truth of all: that there can be no prisons, no walls, no boundaries separating the members of God's family.

Let us reach out tonight to every person who is persecuted; let us embrace and comfort, support and love them. Let us come together as one family under the fatherhood of God, binding ourselves in a communion of hearts, for tonight and tomorrow and for all time. May we give thanks for an America abundantly blessed, for a nation united, free, and at peace. May we carry forward the happiness of the Christmas spirit as the guiding star of our endeavors 365 days a year. And as we light this magnificent tree, may all the youthful hope and joy of America light up the heavens and make the angels sing.

Merry Christmas, and God bless you all. And now we're going to light the tree.

1988
Ronald Reagan

Speaking from the South Balcony of the White House: Merry Christmas, Joe [Riley, Chairman of the Pageant of Peace} and a very Merry Christmas to all. Nancy and I are together with you in celebration and reflection—celebration of the great miracle nearly 2,000 years ago that brought the Christ child to us and reflection on the great gifts He has bestowed upon us.

Christmas casts its glow upon us, as it does every year. And it reminds us that we need not feel lonely because we are loved, loved with the greatest love there has ever been or ever will be. In the bustle and rush of daily life, we sometimes forget how very much we have and how much we have to thank God for providing—for things as beautiful as a winter snow or babies who will be seeing their first Christmas, seeing the wonder of its beauty in their eyes. And yes, from the poorest among us to the most fortunate, we are all blessed.

Christmas reminds us, as well, that He taught us all we need to know about caring for our fellow man and to take responsibility for the very condition of the world. Thus we must reflect: We must ever reflect upon the love we have for others and the joy we take in giving of ourselves to those who are less fortunate. From those who must depend on charity to see that their children receive a Christmas present to the tragic victims of famine and earthquake worldwide, we know what it is we must do and how ennobling an experience it is to have done it.

We Americans live with bounties that those who lived at the time of the Christ child's birth could never have imagined. The bounties are material, yes, but chiefly they are spiritual. Those who would worship the birth of our Lord may do so in the church of their choosing. Those among us who do not so celebrate the birth are free to share with us in this, our time of joy. In this day, when our freedom to worship is most precious, let us redouble our efforts to bring this and other greatest freedoms to all peoples of the Earth.

May we give thanks for a free America, an America united in the wonder of a season that includes not only Christmas but Hanukkah as well. And as we light this glorious tree, may Nancy and I offer a final wish to all Americans: that every Christmas that follows will be as full of joy as we have these past years to work in your service. May God bless you all. And now Nancy will help me light the tree. And again, a very Merry Christmas!

1989
George Bush

Speaking at the Pageant of Peace on the Ellipse: Well, my special thanks to Santa Claus—that Santa mold will never be the same again. [Laughter] But to Loretta and—first Willard Scott, and then to Loretta and Peggy, Tommy Tune, Marilyn McCoo and Billy Davis, the great Air Force band and this marvelous team from Roanoke.

This is the Christmas that we've awaited for 50 years. And across Europe, East and West, 1989 is ending, bright with the prospect of a far better Christmastime than Europe has ever known—a far better future than the world dared to imagine. And 50 winters have come and gone since darkness closed over Europe in 1939—50 years. But last month, as Lech Walesa was coming to the White House, the wall in Berlin came tumbling down.

And another winter descended across Europe. Spring returned to Prague—an unconquerable people, unquenchable dreams. And today—there's a new sound at the wall. New sound rings out—not the hammer and sickle but the hammer and the chisel. The glad sound you hear is not only the bells of Christmas but also the bells of freedom. And in this new season of hope, the triumph looms. It's just like the joy of Christmas: not a triumph for one particular country or one particular religion but a triumph for all humankind. The holidays are—as we've seen here tonight—a time of laughter and children and counting our blessings, a time when songs fill the air and hope fills our hearts for peace on earth, good will to men.

And we've worked hard this year, all of us, all of you, to help build a better America, help someone else, help make this a kinder and gentler nation. But there remains a world of need all around us. In this holiday season, reach out to someone right where you live. Because from now on in America, "There's no room at the inn," that's simply not an acceptable answer.

From now on in America, any definition of a successful life must include serving others. For Christmas is measured not by what's beneath your tree but by what's inside your heart. And so this year, the spirit of the holidays is at long last matched by the spirit of the time. And it's the beginning of a new decade at the ending of an old century. And whatever your dream, whatever star you're following, the future is bright with possibility.

So, Barbara and I want to wish all of you a very Merry Christmas. And now, with simultaneous tree lightings from coast to coast, in Charleston and Santa Cruz, let's show our Thousand Points of Light—let's turn on the National Christmas Tree.

1990
George Bush

Speaking at the Pageant of Peace on the Ellipse: Thank you very much. Thank you, Joe Riley. And thank you, Jane Powell and Willard Scott and Ricky Van Shelton and Ruth Brown and the Army Band, the magnificent University of Wyoming Chorale and our members of the clergy, the California Raisins and, of course, Santa Claus. And may I give a special welcome to the American hostages just home from Kuwait and Iraq, who are with us here tonight. And my thanks to Secretary Lujan and the Department of the Interior, and a special thanks to the National Coal Association for this year's holiday gift: the 57 beautiful State and territorial trees lining our Pathway of Peace. It's a wonderful 1990's tale of careful stewardship and rebirth, for these trees were grown on mined land that has been reclaimed.

This Christmas tree lighting is always a very special moment. People talk of the magic of the season. Well, what is more magical than the way light dispels the darkness? And I've read that white light is actually made up of all the colors of the rainbow. So, that's what we see in the glow of this tree—red and blue and yellow bulbs mixing together to become something new—one light that represents both unity and diversity. And that's how I like to look at America: all of us, all different, all working together, giving the best of ourselves to make this country the strong, beautiful land that it is.

You know, there are so many emotions that we share tonight. We feel joy thinking of how freedom has at last illuminated the dark corners of Eastern Europe—and democracy coming to most of our own hemisphere. We feel pride thinking of our young men and women standing strong in the harsh, distant deserts and on the waters of the Persian Gulf—and for their courage is the true eternal flames which will never be extinguished. And we think of their parents and their loved ones here at home who miss them very much. And we join them all in praying for the safe return of their soldier or their airman or their marine or their sailor. And let us also add a prayer for those Americans—for many years, but still held hostage against their will in the Middle East.

And here tonight we also feel determination that the bright warmth of this holiday season will stay with us all year and that we will be guided by our inner North Star, making family unity and community service and national pride the center of our lives. We're determined that our nation will become a constellation of hope made up of thousands of separate Points of Light, people helping those in need across our land. People like the more than 100 representatives of daily Points of Light here tonight—individuals like W.W. Johnson, and volunteers for groups like the Higher Achievement Program and the D.C. Central Kitchen and Mary's House. And following the lead of these Points of Light, let all of us echo that beautiful carol, "O, Little Town of Bethlehem" and like that long-ago star, let us shine in all "dark streets" and to all people in the "deep and dreamless sleep" of loneliness and despair.

For nearly 70 years Presidents have taken part in this tradition: flipping a switch to send thousands of lights sparkling into the chill night sky. As we gather here, we're doing what generations before us have done: watching our national Christmas tree become a brilliant symbol of hope, of peace, and of compassion for all the world. And so, let us pledge together that we will keep forever bright this shining legacy we celebrate here tonight. God bless the United States of America, and happy holidays to everybody. Merry Christmas! And now I will light the tree.

1991
George Bush

Speaking at the Pageant of Peace on the Ellipse: Well, thank you, Joe [Riley]. Please be seated, all of you, and it's good to see the Secretary of the Interior, so many other special guests here. And of course, a warm thank you to Marilyn Horne; this marvelous Tucson Boys Chorus; the Navy Band; Joe Williams; our favorites, the Gatlin Brothers over here; and all the performers who brought the Christmas spirit to Washington tonight.

And thanks to Santa. His big night is coming up. And we don't have to ask this particular Santa, Willard Scott, what the weather's going to be like on Christmas Eve. He's predicting it. And he is right every once in awhile.

This is a very special night. And I look over my shoulder here at the very special guests, the brave men who are with us here tonight. And on behalf of our loving country I say, finally, to Terry Anderson, to Tom Sutherland, Joseph Cicippio and Alann Steen and Jesse Turner, and the others not here: Welcome home.

Welcome home, to this, the most generous and proud and free Nation on the face of the Earth. It is more than just appropriate, it is almost miraculous that we can celebrate with these five the lighting of our Nation's Christmas Tree. The idea is so moving because these men have come out of darkness into the bright light of liberty. And as you hear these remarkable men talk, you realize they were never lost in that darkness of sorrow, anguish and despair. Even at the worst moments, they were guided by a stubborn spark that cruelty could not extinguish, the spark of human spirit.

Their precious gift to us is to rekindle our Nation's belief in the light of faith and our belief in ourselves. And when Terry and Tom and Joseph and Alann and Jesse light our

Nation's tree tonight, that act will be a reminder of what they and their companions living and gone, have already done to light our Nation's soul.

There have been special guests at these ceremonies before. Even Winston Churchill helped to light the tree during World War II, but this Nation has never been honored by the presence of men whose spirit meant more to all of us. Your fortitude, your humor, and generosity tell us the true meaning of this season. And at this time of year especially, these men remind us that the glitz and glamour of material things don't matter. The courage, the faith and the love of these men, that they embody, are all we need to recognize what's really important.

The way they've returned to their families and to us proves they live by the challenge of that beautiful prayer of St. Francis: "Grant that I may not so much seek to be consoled as to console; to be understood as to understand; to be loved as to love. Where there is despair, let us sow hope; where there is hatred, love; and where there is darkness, ever light."

When history remembers Christmas 1991, let it remember that tonight we gathered with men who show us that this is a season of spirit, not a celebration of plenty.

Let history remember that tonight we stood with these heroes and asked for God's blessing on this world. And finally, in the words of the carol we'll sing in a few minutes, let history remember that at Christmas 1991, this Nation united to give thanks to God and to ask God for peace on earth, good will to all. God bless these five men, this wonderful country, and now I'd like to ask them to join me as we light the Nation's Christmas Tree.

1994
William J. Clinton

Speaking at the Pageant of Peace on the Ellipse: Thank you John Betchkal [chairman of the Pageant of Peace], Mrs. Betchkal, Reverend Leon [pastor, St. John's Episcopal Church]. I want to thank especially our wonderful entertainment tonight: Willard Scott, who would make anybody believe in Santa Claus; Trisha Yearwood, it's wonderful to see you again; Richard Leech, you are terrific. If I had a voice like you, I would have stayed out of politics [laughter]. And I want to say a word of thanks and congratulations to the magnificent Aretha Franklin, who was recently honored at the Kennedy Center Honors. We are glad to see all of you here tonight. Thank you. We congratulate the Cathedral Choir of Men and Boys for the wonderful job they did.

Let me say that Hillary and Chelsea and I are delighted to be back here for our second Pageant of Peace. I don't know how many of you were here last year, but it was a lot colder. And I still feel in the Christmas spirit and more comfortable doing so. I'm glad to be here tonight, and I appreciate this wonderful weather.

This year we have a lot to be grateful for. This is the first Christmas since the beginning of the cold war when our parents can tuck all of their children into bed on Christmas Eve knowing that there are no Russian missiles with nuclear warheads pointed at them.

In holy Bethlehem and throughout the Middle East, ancient enemies are taking giant steps toward peace and reconciliation. Peace is making progress in Northern Ireland, in South Africa, in Haiti, and Eastern and Central Europe, where people are making courageous steps to escape the shackles that have bound them.

Here at home, I appreciate what Willard Scott said about prosperity coming back. And we do have the strongest economy we've had in many years, but let us never forget that many of our people are living in poverty and others are working hard in insecurity, and that as we celebrate the birth of Jesus Christ, the Prince of Peace, let us not forget His lesson that one day we will be asked whether we lived out his love in ways that treated all of our brothers and sisters as we would have treated Him, even the least of them. He taught us all to seek peace and to treat all people with love.

In this holiday season as we gather our families and often go back to the places where we grew up, this is a time to rededicate ourselves to the things which matter most, to our responsibilities, to our families, our communities, and our country.

With all of our challenges in this holiday season, we can take great comfort in knowing that when we come together and seek God's help, we can come meet any challenge, At this holiday season, also my fellow Americans, let us extend our special gratitude and prayers for the men and women of our Armed Forces who protect the peace and stand sentry for our freedom. Many of them are very, very far from their families and friends; they must be close to our hearts.

Finally let me say, this wonderful evergreen Christmas tree, the "Tannenbaum" about which Aretha Franklin sang, is a symbol of the enduring values of our lives. As we light it, let it rekindle in our hearts faith and hope and love for one another. And now I wish God's blessings on you all this special season, and I'd like to ask Hillary and Chelsea to join me as we light the Christmas tree.

1995
William J. Clinton

Speaking at the Pageant of Peace on the Ellipse: Thank you so much. To John Betchkal, the Pageant of Peace chairman; Reverend John Tavlarides. To the Sherando High School Choir, congratulations. You guys were great tonight. To Brendan and Bridget Walsh, the Washington Ballet; to Denise Graves and Jack Jones and Kathy Lee Gifford, and the Navy Band; and of course, to Santa Claus. I would come here every year just to see Santa Claus.

We gather to begin our nation's celebration of the Christmas season with the lighting of this magnificent tree—a symbol, as evergreens have always been, of the infinite capacity of nature and people to renew themselves. We give gifts and we count our blessings.

My fellow Americans, I have just returned from a very moving trip to Europe—to England and to Northern Ireland and the Republic of Ireland; to Germany to see our troops, and to Spain. And I can tell you that among the things that I feel most grateful for at this Christmastime is the way people around the world look at our America. They see a nation graced by peace and prosperity; a land of freedom and fairness. And even though it imposes extra burdens on us, they trust us to work with them to share the blessings of peace.

This is my second Christmas tree lighting of the season, for just a few days ago I was in Belfast with the people of Northern Ireland, Protestant and Catholic alike, searching, yearning, longing for peace—celebrating their second Christmas of peace. I'm proud that I was introduced there by two children—a little Catholic girl named Catherine Hamill, and a young Protestant boy named David Sterrett, who joined hands and told the world of their hopes of the future; a future in which the only barriers they face are the limits of their dreams. That is the future we should want for our children and for all the children of the world.

I am pleased that Catherine Hamill, who touched the whole world with the story of suffering and her family's losses in Northern Ireland, and her family are here with us tonight to celebrate this lighting of the Christmas tree. And I'd like to ask her to stand up right down here and ask all of you to give her a fine hand. She has come all the way from Northern Ireland.

Remember at this Christmastime we celebrate the birth of a homeless child, whose only shelter was the straw of a manger, but who grew to become the Prince of Peace. The Prince of Peace said, "Blessed are the peacemakers." Let us bless the peacemakers at this Christmastime from the Middle East to Northern Ireland to our own troops in Bosnia. Let us pray especially for our peacemakers, those who will go to Bosnia and those who are soon to come home from Haiti.

And let us resolve, my fellow Americans, to be peacemakers. For just as many nations around the world and so many children around the world cry for peace, so do we need peace here at home in our toughest neighborhoods, where there are children, so many children who deserve to have their childhood and their future free and peaceful.

And let us remember from the example of the Prince of Peace how even the humblest of us can do [with] the acts of goodness and reconciliation extraordinary things. And as we light this wonderful Christmas tree, let us all remember that together a million small lights add up to make a great blaze of glory—not for ourselves, but for our families, our nation and the world, and for the future of our children.

Merry Christmas, and blessed are the peacemakers.

SOURCES

THE COOLIDGES

"Calvin Coolidge Says," syndicated newspaper column, Dec. 24, 1930.

Coolidge, Calvin. *The Autobiography of Calvin Coolidge.* Plymouth, Vermont: The Calvin Coolidge Memorial Foundation, 1989.

Coolidge, John. Interview with author. Plymouth Notch, Vermont, June 13, 1994.

Coolidge, Mrs. Calvin. "What Christmas Means to Me,"*Delineator Digest*, Dec. 1929.

Hoover, Irwin Hood. *Forty-Two Years in the White House.* Boston: Houghton Mifflin Company, 1934.

Library of Congress, Manuscript Division. Fish, H.J., letter to Sanders, E., Oct. 26, 1925; Moody, P., letter to President, Dec. 12, 1923; Sanders, E., telegram to Leach, Hon. George, Dec. 15, 1925.

National Archives. Records of the White House Files, 1900-35, Record Group 130: Hardy, L.W., letters to Slemp, C.B., Nov. 30, 1923, and Dec. 4, 1923; Hardy, L.W., letter to President, Dec. 20, 1923; Slemp, C.B., letter to Hardy, L.W., Dec. 21, 1923.

New York Herald Tribune, July 9, 1927.

New York Times, Dec. 25, 1924; Dec. 25, 1926; Dec. 25, 1928.

Parks, Lillian Rogers, in collaboration with Frances Spatz Leighton. *My Thirty Years Backstairs at the White House.* New York: Fleet Publishing Company, 1961.

Ross, Ishbel. *Grace Coolidge and Her Era.* New York: Dodd, Mead and Company, 1962.

Washington Herald, Dec. 23, 1923; Dec. 26, 1928.

Washington Post, Dec. 25, 1923; Dec. 25, 1924; Jan. 2, 1925; Dec. 25, 1925; Dec. 25, 1926; Dec. 24, 1928.

Washington Star Dec. 12, 1923; Dec. 24, 1924; Dec. 25, 1924; Dec. 24, 1925; Dec. 25, 1926; Dec. 27, 1927; Dec. 25, 1928.

Williams, W.K. "The Presidents and Their Christmas Trees," *American Forests,* Dec. 1965.

THE HOOVERS

Amyx, Raleigh DeGeer. Interview with author. Warrenton, Virginia, March 1993.

Genn, Lillian G. "Herbert Hoover-Hero," *NPTA Journal,* Sept./Oct. 1979.

Herbert Hoover Library, West Branch, Iowa: Ruth Fesler File. Christmas 1929 card list and etching; photographs used as Christmas 1929 gifts; Christmas 1930 gift list and summary; Christmas 1931 gift inventory; Lipman, Ruth Fesler, transcribed interview with Mr. Henle.

Long, Ava, interview. *Ladies Home Journal,* Dec. 1935.

New York Times, Dec. 25, 1929; Jan. 2, 1930; Dec. 25, 1930; Dec. 24, 1930; Dec. 25, 1931.

Parks, Lillian Rogers, in collaboration with Frances Spatz Leighton. *My Thirty Years Backstairs at the White House.* New York: Fleet Publishing Company, 1961.

Public Papers of the Presidents of the United States: Herbert Hoover, 1929-33, 4 vols. Washington: GPO, 1974-77. Dec. 24, 1931.

"Twas the Night Before Christmas." *American Heritage,* Vol. 22, No. 1, 1970.

Washington Post, Dec. 17, 1929; Dec. 25, 1929; July 3, 1975.

Washington Star, Dec. 25, 1930.

THE ROOSEVELTS

Elsey, George. Interview with author by telephone, 1994.

Franklin D. Roosevelt Library. FDR Papers File 512: Early, S., letter to Eadie, H., Oct. 25, 1934; McIntyre, M.H., letter to Eadie, H., Oct. 8, 1934. President's Personal File 1051: Early, S., letter to Fisher, S., Oct. 21, 1937; Fisher, S., letter to Roosevelt, J., Oct. 19, 1937; Lowd, D., letter dated Jan. 2, 1934; President of Board of Commissioners, D.C., letter to President, Dec. 7, 1943. President's Secretary's File: Belmont Advertising, letter to Tully, G., Sept. 3, 1943; Christmas 1943; Cook, Nancy, letter to LeHand, M., July 30, 1937; D-Day Prayer of FDR; FDR memo to Tully, G., Oct. 18, 1943; Latta, M.C., memo to Summerlin; Scheider, M., letter to Marshall, A.E., at Brewood's, Sept. 7, 1937, 60.1, Box 575. Bills of Sale: The Forge: To President, Nov. 29, 1939, for letter holders; to Scheider, M., Dec. 15, 1937; to Mrs. Roosevelt, Dec. 5, 1938; to President, Dec. 17, 1938. Others: LeHand, M.A., letter to Cartier, Nov. 30, 1940, Dec. 6, 1940; LeHand, M., letter to Cook, N., Aug. 3, 1937; LeHand, M.A., letter to Fitch, F.A., Mark Cross Co., Nov. 30, 1940; Dec. 18, 1941; LeHand, M.A., letter to Hammacher Schlemmer Nov. 30, 1940, Jan. 6, 1941. Val-Kill Folder 2: Wright, Emily, "Eleanor Roosevelt and Val-Kill Industries 1925-1938," manuscript, Oct. 1978, Vertical File.

Nesbitt, Henrietta, *White House Diary.* New York: Doubleday & Co., 1948.

New York Times, Dec. 24, 1933; Dec. 25, 1935; Dec. 25, 1936; Dec. 7, 1937; Dec. 23, 1937; Dec. 25, 1938; Dec. 25, 1939; Dec. 25, 1940; Dec. 24, 1941; Dec. 25, 1941; Jan. 2, 1942; Nov. 27, 1942; Dec. 25, 1942; Dec. 14, 1943; Dec. 23, 1943; Dec. 25, 1943; June 7, 1944; Dec. 25, 1944.

Public Papers and Addresses of FDR. New York: Random House. 1937-38.

Roosevelt, Eleanor, *Christmas 1940.* New York: St. Martin's Press.

———. *Eleanor Roosevelt's Christmas Book.* New York: Dodd, Mead & Company, 1963.

———. *On My Own.* New York: Harper & Brothers Publishers.

———, "The Right to Give," *Home Companion,* Dec. 1934.

———.*This I Remember.* Westport, Connecticut: Greenwood Press Publishers, 1949.

Roosevelt, James, and Shalett, Sidney, *Affectionately FDR, A Son's Story of a Lonely Man.* New York: Harcourt Brace & Co. 1959.

Washington Herald, Dec 31, 1933.

Washington Post, Dec. 25, 1934; Jan. 13,

1940; Dec. 25, 1940; Dec. 25, 1941; Dec. 25, 1942; Dec. 25, 1943.

Washington Star, Dec. 23, 1933; Dec. 25, 1933; Dec. 25, 1935; Dec. 25, 1936; Dec. 25, 1937; Dec. 25, 1941; Dec. 22, 1943.

THE TRUMANS

"Family Man, Truman Loved," *Arkansas Gazette*, Dec. 25, 1979.

Fields, Alonzo. *My Twenty-One Years in the White House*. New York: Coward-McCann, Inc. 1961.

Harry S. Truman Library. The President, letter to Deviny, J., of GPO, Jan. 5, 1951. Memorandum re: The President and Mrs. Truman's Christmas Gifts and cards. Oct. 18, 1947; memorandum re: President's Christmas Gift 1947, Eben, M.; Eben, M., memorandum for Barrows, Dec. 11, 1947; Eben, M., memorandum for Conway, Jan. 5, 1951; memorandum for Connelly, Nov. 6, 1951; Connelley, M.J., memorandum for M. Eben, PSF: Gifts and Greetings. Museum File Medals and Medallions: Bronze Casting of Presidential Seal, 1949.

New York Times, Dec. 24, 1945.

National Archives. R.M. Nixon Files: Fact Sheet on Harry S. Truman, Dec. 27, 1972.

Parks, Lillian Rogers, in collaboration with Frances Spatz Leighton. *My Thirty Years Backstairs at the White House*. New York: Fleet Publishing Company, 1961.

Public Papers of the Presidents of the United States: Harry S. Truman, 1945-53.

Truman, Harry, letter to Mama and Mary, May 8, 1945. The Seeley Collection.

Truman, Margaret. *Bess W. Truman*. New York: MacMillan Publishing Co., 1986.

———, "Dreaming of a White House Christmas," *Family Weekly*, Dec. 12, 1980.

Washington Post, Dec. 25, 1945; Dec. 25, 1952.

Washington Star, Dec. 22, 1945; Dec. 15, 1946; Dec. 25, 1951.

West, J.B., with Mary Lynn Kotz. *Upstairs at the White House*. New York: Coward, McCann and Geoghegan, Inc., 1973.

THE EISENHOWERS

Dwight D. Eisenhower Library. President's Personal File, Boxes 8, 11-18: Correspondence between Hall,

J.C., and the President: Dec. 3, 1953; Jan. 23, 1954; July 29, 1954; Dec. 6, 1954; Nov. 7, 1955; Dec. 10, 1955. President's letter to Brownell, H., Dec. 22, 1954; President's letter to Glew, D.H., Jr., Jan. 27, 1959; Rayburn, S., letter to the President, Jan. 4, 1960; McCaffree, Mary Jane, Papers, Boxes 1-4: McCaffree, M.J., letter to Hall, J.C., Oct. 27, 1954; Lee, J., letter to McCaffree, M.J., Oct. 21, 1958; Other Papers, Stewart, L., memorandum to Hall, J.C., Jan. 11, 1955; Hall, J.C., letter to Stephens, T.E., Feb. 18, 1954.

Dwight D. Eisenhower Museum, Abilene, Kansas.

Hall, J.C. *When You Care Enough*. Hallmark: Kansas City, Missouri, 1992.

Hallmark Archives, Kansas City, Missouri: Ardrenhold, Hans. Interview with Sharman Robertson; E 2E.7, A Request from the White House; *Ike's Art,* Wide World Photo.

Philadelphia Inquirer, Dec. 22, 1959.

Public Papers of the Presidents of the United States: Dwight D. Eisenhower, 1953-61.

Washington Post, Dec. 19, 1955.

Washington Star, Dec. 24, 1953; Dec. 11, 1958; Dec. 24, 1960.

West, J.B., with Mary Lynn Kotz. *Upstairs at the White House*. New York: Coward, McCann and Geoghegan, Inc., 1973.

THE KENNEDYS

Amyx, Raleigh DeGeer. Interview with author. Warrenton, Virginia, April 30, 1995.

Armentrout, Russell. Interview with author. July 1994.

Bethlehem Globe, Dec. 13, 1962.

"Bucks County Artist, Ed Lehman," Doylestown *Daily Intelligence*, 1990.

John F. Kennedy Library, President's Office File, Box 129, Folder: Christmas List.

White House Social File, Box 120, Folder: Christmas Card List 1960: Baldrige, L., memorandum to O'Donnell, K., Nov. 16, 1961; Mrs. Kennedy letter to Hall, J.C., Dec. 7, 1962. Tuckerman, N., memorandum to White House staff, Dec. 1963.

White House Central File, Box 351, H07 Invitations; Box 350, Hopkins, W.J., memorandum to O'Donnell, K., Nov. 30, 1961.

Hallmark Archives: Baldrige, L., letter to Hall, J.C., Dec. 13, 1961; Lee, J., letter

to Clifton, T., Nov. 14, 1963; Lee, J., memorandum about President's Christmas Cards for 1970; Lee, J., telegram to Turnure, P., Nov. 22, 1963; Stewart, L. memorandum to Cutler, C., Nov. 1, 1963; Turnure, P., letter to Lee, J., Aug. 23, 1963, Sept. 20, 1963.

Kansas City Star, Sept. 11, 1963; Nov. 16, 1982.

Lee, Jeannette. Interview with author. Hallmark Archives, Kansas City, Missouri, July 27, 1993.

Lehman, Edward. Interview with author. Quakertown, Pennsylvania, Sept. 3, 1993.

———. personal files: Mrs. Kennedy letter to Lehman E., July 27, 1962; Turnure, P., letter to Lehman, E., Dec. 10, 1962; Feb. 12, 1963; Jan. 14, 1964.

Life, Sept. 1, 1961.

Look, Dec. 1963.

Newsweek, Feb. 26, 1962.

New York Times, Sept. 12, 1963.

Perbasie News Herald, Edward Lehman clipping.

Philadelphia Bulletin, Feb. 9, 1962.

Public Papers of the Presidents of the United States: John F. Kennedy, 1961-63.

Scouten, Rex. Interview with author. The White House, Nov. 3, 1993.

Stoughton, Cecil. Interview with author. Merritt Island, Florida, July 18, 1993.

Time, Feb. 23, 1962.

Washington Post, Nov. 22, 1960; Dec. 14, 1961; Dec. 21, 1961; Dec. 13, 1962.

Washington Star, Dec. 14, 1961; Dec. 24, 1961.

West, J.B., with Mary Lynn Kotz. *Upstairs at the White House*. New York: Coward, McCann and Geoghegan, Inc., 1973.

"The White House Christmas Tree Past and Present," *American Christmas Tree Journal*, Nov. 1981.

THE JOHNSONS

Abell, Bess. Interview with author. Potomac, Maryland, July 13, 1993.

American Greetings: Press Release, Presidential Greeting Cards: An Overview, Sept. 14, 1981; Pakish, E., letter to Abell, B., Feb. 15, 1965; memoranda to Stone, H, Nov. 15, 1966, Dec. 28, 1967, Jan. 3, 1969.

Cleveland *Plain Dealer*, Oct. 11, 1964.

Hallmark Archives: Presidential Christmas Cards Recap, Dave LeMoyne; Lee, J., memorandum to Fox, S., Dec. 17, 1963.

Johnson, Lady Bird., *A White House Diary*.

New York: Holt, Rinehart and
Winston, 1970.
Johnson, Mrs. Lyndon, "Christmas
Memories From the White House,"
McCalls, Dec. 1968.
Laessig, Robert. Interview with author.
Cleveland, Ohio, October 21, 1993.
Lyndon B. Johnson Library, White House
Central File, H07, #21: Christmas
Card List, Dec. 16, 1993; Duke, A.B.,
memorandum to the President, Nov.
27, 1963. Clifton, memorandum to
Abell, B., May 19, 1964; Sinclair, I.,
memorandum to Jenkins, W., Dec. 16,
1963.
White House Social File: Abell, B., let-
ter to Stone, H., May 23, 1967;
Johnson, Lady Bird, letter to Laessig,
R., Dec. 28, 1965; Nathan, R., letter to
Abell, B., May 8, 1964; Photographs
and description of LBJ Christmas
stocking; Poage, W.R., letter to
President and Mrs. Johnson, Dec. 31,
1963; Stone, H., to Abell, B., June 4,
1965, Oct. 21, 1965, June 6, 1968.
New York Times, Dec. 16, 1966; Dec. 24,
1967.
Pakish, Ed. Interview with author.
American Greetings, Cleveland, Ohio,
Oct. 21, 1993.
*Public Papers of the Presidents of the United
States: Lyndon B. Johnson*, 1963-69.
Robb, Lynda Bird Johnson. Interview with
author. June 22, 1995.
Smith, Marie. *The President's Lady*. New
York: Random House, New York,
1964.
Washington Post, Dec. 23, 1963; Dec. 24,
1963; Dec. 10, 1966; Dec. 19, 1966;
Dec. 16, 1967.
West, J.B., with Mary Lynn Kotz. *Upstairs
at the White House*. New York: Coward,
McCann and Geoghegan, Inc., 1973.
The White House Gardens and Grounds,
White House Historical Association.
The White House. Press Release, Dec. 22,
1967.
Williams, W.K., "The Presidents and Their
Christmas Trees," *American Forests*,
Dec. 1965.

THE NIXONS

Allen, Douglas and Allen, Douglas, Jr.
N.C. Wyeth. New York: Bonanza
Books, 1972.
"Christmas at the White House, With
Julie Nixon Eisenhower and Charles
Kuralt," CBS TV special, Dec. 25,
1969.

Conger, Clement E. Interview with
author, the White House, Nov. 4,
1993.
Hallmark Archives. "Presidential
Christmas Card Fact Sheet, 1990,"
news release; "President Nixon's
Christmas Cards Are Unique Design,"
press release, Dec. 11, 1970; Guyton,
S., memorandum to Fox, S., 1971.
"Mrs. Nixon's White House Restoration,"
unpublished summary from Helen
Smith files.
National Archives. White House Central
File, H012: Friedersdorf, M.L., letter to
Kuykendall, D., Nov. 30, 1973;
McGuire, K., letter to Woods, R.M.,
Dec. 30, 1970; the President's letter to
Hall, J., Dec. 19, 1969; Stewart, S., let-
ter to the President, Dec. 21, 1973;
Winchester, L., memorandum to
Hullin, T., Nov. 6, 1972; Winchester,
L., memorandum to Mrs. Nixon,
"Christmas Gift List, 1972"; Office of
Staff Director: 1970 Christmas Display
of White House Christmas Cards.
New York Times, Dec. 15, 1971.
Nixon, Mrs. Richard, "Christmas at the
White House," *House and Garden*, Dec.
1971.
Nixon, Richard. *In the Arena*. New York:
Pocket Books of Simon & Schuster,
1990.
"The Nixon Touch in the White House,"
U.S. News and World Report, Dec. 28,
1970.
"Pat Nixon Made a Quiet Contribution,"
Providence Sunday Journal, June 27,
1993.
*Public Papers of the Presidents of the United
States: Richard M. Nixon*, 1969-1973.
Smith, Helen. Interview with author,
Washington, D.C., July 14, 1993.
Washington Post, Dec. 16, 1969; Dec. 17,
1969; Nov. 26, 1970; Dec. 17, 1971;
Dec. 17, 1972; Dec. 16, 1972; Dec. 14,
1973; Dec. 15, 1973.
Washington Star, Dec. 16, 1969.

THE FORDS

"Christmas at the New Winter White
House," *Globe Democrat Sunday
Magazine*, Dec. 8, 1974.
Conger, Clement E. Interview with
author, Washington, D.C., Nov. 4,
1993.
———. *A Nation's Pride: Art in the White
House*. Washington, D.C.: White
House Historical Association, 1992.
Ford, Betty. Interview with author by tele-

phone. February 15, 1996.
———. *The Times of My Life*. New York:
Harper & Row Publishers, 1978.
Gerald R. Ford Library. National Park
Service, news release, Dec. 18, 1975;
Office of the Press Secretary memo-
randum to Mrs. Ford, Dec. 15, 1975;
news release to Mrs. Ford Dec. 9,
1976.
Weidenfeld Files Boxes 35, 36: 1974
Christmas Card List; "Christmas
1975."
Hallmark Archives. "Presidential
Christmas Card Fact Sheet, 1990,"
news release.
Nesle, A.R., letter to Conger, C.E., August
24, 1972. Unpublished; printed with
permission of A.R. Nesle.
*Public Papers of the Presidents of the United
States: Gerald R. Ford*, 1973-75.
U.S. News and World Report, Dec. 30,
1974.
Washington Star, Dec. 19, 1975.
Washington Post, Dec. 14, 1974; Dec. 15,
1974; Dec. 18, 1974.
Weidenfeld, Sheila. *First Lady's Lady*.

THE CARTERS

Administration of Jimmy Carter, 1977-81.
Remarks on the Lighting of the
National Christmas Tree.
American Greetings Overview.
Antique Monthly, Jan. 15, 1979.
Carter, Rosalynn. Interview with author
by telephone, Nov. 9, 1995.
Conger, Clement E. Interview with
author, Washington, D.C., Nov. 4,
1993.
Gamarekian, Barbara, "The Carter
Favorites," *The New York Times
Magazine*, Jan. 29, 1978.
Jimmy Carter Library. White House
Central File HO16-1: Carter, H., mem-
orandum to Weddington, S., re:
Christmas cards, Sep. 6, 1979;
Poston, G., memorandum to Jordan,
H., Aug. 23, 1977; "Press Preview of
Christmas Decorations," memoran-
dum from Poston, G., to Mrs. Carter,
Dec. 15, 1980; "Summary of
Christmas Card Project, 1978,
Recommendations for 1979," memo-
randum from Simpson, J., to Carter,
H., Mar. 2, 1979; Torricelli memoran-
dum to Berman, M., re: Use of appro-
priated funds for Christmas greeting
cards. June 18, 1979.
National Park Service, news release, Nov.
1, 1977.

SOURCES

New York Times, Dec. 17, 1982.
U.S. News and World Report, Dec. 25, 1978; Dec. 24, 1979.
Washington Post, Dec. 6, 1977; Dec. 14, 1977; Dec. 23, 1977; Dec. 14, 1979; Dec. 21, 1980; Dec. 21, 1980; Dec. 25, 1985.
Washington Star, Dec. 13, 1978.

THE REAGANS

Administration of Ronald Reagan, 1981–89. Remarks on the Lighting of the National Christmas Tree.
Bailey, Patricia, "Thomas William Jones," *USArt*, Jan./Feb. 1990.
Cauble, Diane, "From a Quiet Place, *Focus/Santa Fe*, Jan.-Feb.-Mar 1994.
"Christmas Wish Comes True for Little Amy Benham," National Park Service news release, Dec. 15, 1983.
Hampton, Mark. Interview with author by telephone, Oct. 8, 1993.
Jones, Thomas William. Interview with author, Snohomish, Washington. Oct. 10, 1993.
Journal American, Dec. 5, 1986.
Los Angeles Times, Dec. 19, 1983.
Philadelphia Inquirer. Dec. 25, 1982.
Reagan, Nancy. Interview with author by telephone. Oct. 11, 1995.
———, "Christmas Memories," *Washington Home*, Dec. 16, 1982.
———. *My Turn, The Memoirs of Nancy Reagan*, New York: Random House, 1989.
Reagan, Ronald. *An American Life*. New York: Simon and Schuster, 1990.
Ronald Reagan Library. Office of the Press Secretary, Message by the President, "Christmas 1984." Dec. 21, 1984, "Christmas, 1988," Dec. 19, 1988; "Text of the Radio Address by the President to the Nation," Dec. 25, 1982; Memorandum: Recommended Telephone Call to Amy Benham, April 13, 1984; Staffing Memorandum, December 11, 1985; "Remarks, Christmas in Washington Concert"; "Christmas in Washington," videotape. White House Social Files: Brandon, M., letter to Roussel, C., Nov. 16, 1981; Shankman, S., Executive Director of Second Genesis, letter to Mrs. Reagan, Dec. 15, 1982; Sheila Tate Files: Weinraub, Judith, "Interview With the First Lady," Dec. 8, 1982 (draft).
Steinmeyer, James. Interview with author by telephone, May 10, 1994.

Wall Street Journal, Nov. 13, 1983.
Washington Post, Dec. 6, 1981; Nov. 30, 1984; Dec. 9, 1986.
Washington Times. Dec. 6, 1983.
Wyeth, Jamie. Interview with author by telephone, Nov. 3, 1995.

THE BUSHES

Administration of George Bush. Remarks on the Lighting of the National Christmas Tree; Message on the Observance of Christmas; Christmas Message to American Troops.
Bush, Barbara. Interview with author by telephone. Nov. 22, 1995.
———. *A Memoir*. New York: Charles Scribner's Sons, 1994.
Gemmell, Bill. Interview with author, Washington, D.C., Dec. 10, 1993.
Hampton, Mark. Written interview for the author, Oct. 8, 1993.
Kubik, Kamil. Interview with author, North Bergen, New Jersey, Sept. 4, 1994.
Linden, Patricia, "I'm glad they elected you President, Darling—but really, that wallpaper in the Office has got to go." *Town & Country*, June 1992.
Lee, Jeannette, and Unverferth, Fayrol. Interview on tape at Hallmark Archives, Kansas City, Missouri, July 27, 1993.
"The People's House of Barbara Bush," *Washington Home*, Jan. 16, 1992.
Press Tour of the White House Christmas Decorations, Dec. 1989.
Town and Country, June 1991.
Washington Post, Dec. 14, 1989; Dec. 11, 1990; Dec. 10, 1991; Dec. 16, 1991; Dec. 2, 1992; Dec. 8, 1992.

THE CLINTONS

American Greetings. *Expressions*, Dec. 1, 1995; "Facts About the 1995 White House Christmas Card," booklet.
Anderson News of Lawrenceburg, Kentucky, Nov. 17, 1993.
Arkansas Times, Dec. 2, 1993.
Chicago Tribune, Nov. 8, 1993.
Cleveland *Plain Dealer*, Nov. 23, 1993; Dec. 7, 1993.
Clinton Family, "A Holiday Message From our Family to Yours," *Parade* Sunday supplement, Dec. 19, 1993.
Clinton, Hillary Rodham, "A White House Christmas," *Washington Times*, Dec. 1995.
———, press preview of White House decorations, taped interview, Dec 6, 1994.

Clinton White House. Christmas statement at author's request, May 28, 1996.
Davis, Susan. Interview with author, by telephone, May 9, 1995.
Detroit News, Dec. 7, 1994.
Greenwich Time, Dec. 1, 1995.
Hartford Courant, Dec. 1995.
Journal Messenger, Jan. 27, 1995.
Kotz, Mary Lynn, "Art in the White House," *ART News*, Sept. 1994.
Lawton Constitution, Dec. 4, 1994.
Lee, Jeannette. Interview with author. Hallmark Archives, Kansas City, Missouri, July 27, 1993.
Litchfield County Times, December 1995.
Lloyd, Nancy, "A White House Christmas," *Family Circle*, Dec. 21, 1993.
McCoy, Anne. Interview with author, by telephone, May 9, 1995.
McKnight, Thomas. Interview with author, by telephone, June 12, 1995, Dec. 13, 1995.
———. *Voyage to Paradise*. San Francisco: Harper, 1993.
New York Times, Dec. 26, 1992; Dec. 7, 1993; Dec. 5, 1995.
Office of the Press Secretary, Remarks by the President at the Pageant of Peace; Remarks by the President in Christmas Eve Message to the Troops in Bosnia, Dec. 24, 1995.
Palm Beach Daily News, Dec. 4, 1994; Dec. 6, 1995.
Philadelphia Daily News, Dec. 7, 1993.
Richmond Times, Dec. 7, 1993.
State Journal of Frankfort, Kentucky, Nov. 18, 1993.
Stock, Ann. Interview with author, Washington, D.C., Jan. 7, 1994, Jan. 10, 1995.
Times Leader of Martins Ferry, Ohio, Dec. 4, 1994.
USA Today, Dec. 7, 1993; Dec. 1, 1994.
Washington Post, Nov. 3, 1993; Nov. 4, 1993; Dec. 7, 1993; Dec. 25, 1993; Dec. 9, 1994. Washington Home Section, Dec. 9, 1993.
Washington Times, Dec. 7, 1993; Dec. 5, 1995; Dec. 25, 1995; Dec. 26, 1995.
Williams, Jeannie, "White House's Best Wishes," *USA Today*, Dec. 7, 1993.

PERMISSIONS

For more information about
The Seeley Collection
Traveling Exhibits and Lectures,
contact:
A Presidential Christmas
P.O. Box 272667
Tampa, FL 33688
E-Mail: MLS42@aol.com